"You [the government] make everything illegal then selectively enforce the law to keep the people in line [and] remove those that are a threat to you. This is classic tyranny building, and we have a classic tyranny being constructed right in front of us."

—John Stossel *Everything Illegal*

From French Cuffs to Handcuffs

A Former CEO's Survival Advice For Executives, Business Owners, and Politicians Facing Federal Prosecution

Michael W. McCoy
Consulting Editor

phoenix BUSINESS PUBLISHING

Published By: Phoenix Business Publishing, USA., Sacramento, CA., Irvine, CA., and Charleston, SC.

Phoenix Business Publishing books may be purchased in bulk for educational and business purposes. For information, please email us at info@phoenixbusinesspublishing.com.

Book Design by: Jeff Braden
Exsiteit Web Design
www.exsiteit.com

DISCLAIMER AND DISCLOSURE NOTICE

This publication contains the opinions, ideas, and personal experiences of its author(s). They are intended to provide helpful and informative material on the subject matters contained and covered herein. They are therefore sold with the understanding that the author(s) and publisher are not engaged in rendering legal advice from the book or from any other product or service obtained from the website. If the reader requires personal assistance or advice, a competent, licensed professional should be consulted.

The author(s) and publisher specifically disclaim any responsibility for any liability, loss, risk, personal or otherwise, which incurred as a consequence, directly or indirectly, of the use and application of any of the contents of this book or from any products sold from the website.

Phoenix Business Publishing
ISBN: 0-615-77523-3
ISBN-13: 978-0-615-77523-4
Printed in the United States of America

CONTENTS

DEDICATION

Today, along with me, my daughters, Michelle and Niqui, are walking with the Lord, serving Him, and raising their children in the nurture, admonition and sovereignty of His unchanging Word.

PRAISE FOR: FROM FRENCH CUFFS TO HANDCUFFS

“Had the experience and wisdom found in this book *From French Cuffs to Handcuffs* been available to me prior to my battle with the government, I would have saved a *minimum* of $250,000 in attorney’s fees. Everyone in business should be armed with this information.”

—Steven Pitchelsky,
former CEO and Chairman of Nationwide Mortgage, Inc.

A truly complete and comprehensive guide to the reality of facing and navigating the federal criminal justice system. Unfortunately for me, reading this book was a march down memory lane. This inspiring work will help those accused and their families survive, use their time in prison to their advantage, and to make a full recovery.

—William “Bill” Zannanti,
MD., Ph.D. and CEO of Zannanti
Surgical Design Group, Inc.

“Praise for Michael McCoy’s powerful contribution of his highly informative book *From French Cuffs To Handcuffs*, which is indeed a ‘road map’ for anyone entering the federal prison system. Virtually every page offers a startling, eye-opening revelation.”

—Herbert A. Bates, Executive, International Banking

“Had I read just half of the book, *From French Cuffs to Handcuffs*, my family and I would have saved $25,000 in unnecessary prison consulting fees, that resulted in absolutely no net benefit to me when I was sentenced to federal prison for filing a false income tax return.”

—Jeremy Levine,
President and General Contractor,
JSL Construction, Inc.

I cannot stress the utmost importance to every executive, business owner and politician in America how valuable and instructive the book *From French Cuffs To Handcuffs* is even if they remotely suspect being a target of a federal probe or a criminal investigation. Trust me, it's better to read this book today than to live it later.

—Gerald R. Sullivan, M.P.A., CPA, and CPC

ACKNOWLEDGEMENTS

When I first entered federal prison in the spring of 1995, I certainly did not think I would write a book about my dreadful experiences. Frankly, who would? But the lessons I have learned, as I was told, were far too valuable to keep to myself. When crafting this book, I was careful not to make it a book about me, per se, for I kept it true to its categorization, that being a "how-to" survival book. This book is a proven record of how one can not only survive federal prison, but thrive while in federal prison—even in the face of a traumatic twenty-five year federal prison sentence. As with so many before me, I came to learn that prison life is someone else's problem. Not mine. I, for one, chose not to live it. Yes, although I was enslaved by it, I knew I had to find a way to triumph over it in lieu of it triumphing over me. Through this book, my hope is to inspire you to do the same.

With that, I cannot say enough about the rare few (and believe me, only a few) positive-minded men who encouraged me to write about this subject. Hence, my journey with this book began with one man, who, after suffering in his own rights, reached out to bless me beyond measure. Seeing the promise in me, my brother in Christ, Jeff Braden, offered to reach out and help me. From this friendship, Jeff became my eyes, ears and legs for the duration of my prison sentence. That was over ten years ago. To this day, Jeff remains as my right hand to all that I have built and continues to build in my quest for a corporate comeback. Mere words fall woefully short when attempting to express my deepest gratitude for Jeff Braden.

As for this specific project, I want to thank my friends, my brothers, and my young protégés, Malik Wade and Robert Love, who pushed me to see my affliction, combined with my wisdom, for what they were: an extraordinary opportunity to help others. They were right. Thanks so much, Malik and Rob.

And over the many years, I have also come to know special, God-sent men who helped me with this book, men who were readers of my earliest drafts—men who also inspired me to press onward and upward. I thus want to give special thanks to Donald Anderson, Dr.

William Zannanti, and my biggest fan and dear friend, Gerald Thomas. Then there's my editing and review team, Gerald Sullivan, Neil C. Aquino, Thomas Law, aka, "Mr. Smoothe", Herbert Bates and Peter Ye. What a manifold blessing all of you were and still are to me. Thank you much. Last, but not least, my publisher, The Phoenix Publishing Group, for giving me a platform from which to launch into the second half of my life with dignity.

My thanks and prayers remain with you all.

"Go, sit in your cell,
and your cell will teach
you everything."
–St. Moses the Ethiopian

WHY WE WROTE THIS BOOK FOR YOU

Are you aware there's been a major tectonic shift in America's jurisprudence—a shift that directly affects you? Now, more than ever, criminal defendants are being forced to accept a plea bargain (for crimes they did not commit) in lieu of exercising their constitutional right to a full and fair trial. Or perhaps you are unaware that Congress has gradually, yet dangerously increased the potential sentence for certain types of non-violent business crimes, such as fraud offenses, to 20 years from five years. Well, if you are a business person in today's America, we're not taking any chances with you losing your freedom due to lack of knowledge. So we felt compelled to write this book that you should know. . .

According to a 2011 study[1], guilty pleas in America have soared as the number of federal criminal defendants has doubled since 1990[2]. In this book, *From French Cuffs to Handcuffs*, our core focus is to bring to the forefront of society's consciousness the staggering reality surrounding America's federal prison system. Our aim is to alert business owners, executives and politicians alike how 1-in-100 citizens are behind bars in America, with no relief in sight.

The stark reality is that a growing number of these citizens are regular people like you, or like your friends, or like your neighbors—citizens who are upwardly mobile and striving for financial independence by taking the risk of starting and expanding their own businesses. This book is not so much about prison statistics, insomuch as it is about the relentless growth in unconstitutional, coercive plea bargaining that has sparked a backlash among lawyers, legal scholars and

---

[1] Source: the Transactional Branch Archive Clearinghouse at Syracuse University, 2011

[2] According to the U.S. Supreme Court's decision in (Missouri v. Frye ____ U.S. _____ 132 S. Ct. 1376, 1387, 182 L Ed. 2 398 2012), "ninety-seven percent of federal convictions are the result of guilty pleas" (citing Department of Justice, Bureau of Statistics, Sourcebook of Criminal Justice Statistics Online, table 5.22.2009 http://www.albany.edu/sourcebook/pdf/t5222010.pdf), further stating in its decision that, "To a large extent. . . horse trading between prosecutor and defense counsel determines who goes to jail and for how long. That is what plea bargaining is."

judges—which has prompted two major decisions recently handed down by our U.S. Supreme Court[3], highlighting how criminal defendants are being coerced into pleading guilty to crimes they did not commit.

Bottom line, this book and our website can help. Both were created to raise awareness, as well as to educate unsuspecting business owners, about the risks of going to federal prison for unintentionally committing a crime while running their businesses. Oftentimes, however, that's not possible. One-in-100 citizens stand convicted of these crimes already, and are destined for federal prison as we speak. If that's you, this book and our interactive website have just become your best friends.

Through this book, we reveal proven prevention and survival methods to those who may have become targets of over-zealous federal prosecutors. We reveal their most powerful weapon known as "plea bargains" which have become the gold star of a prosecutor's resume. Today, prosecutorial careers are built by chalking up scores of criminal convictions at any cost, instead of living up to their oath to protect society, and to uphold the Constitution of the United States.

When I was initially contacted for this consulting assignment, I was, quite honestly, greatly perplexed. Truth be told, I encountered an array of mixed emotions before accepting such an unusual assignment, for I found myself thinking, "To what advantage is there in interviewing and editing the work of a convicted felon who's broken the law and is rightly in prison paying his debt to society?"—that is, until learning who this man was. He's not just any man, but one whom we shall refer to as "Mr. CEO". Mr. CEO was the

---

[3] Sources: Missouri v. Frye ___ U.S. ___ 132 S. Ct. 1376, 182 L Ed. 2 398 (2012), and Latler v. Cooper, post, ___ U.S. ___ 132 S. Ct. 1376, 182 L Ed. 398 (2012))

founder of a $200 million a year industrial finance and investment firm, a man who's currently serving 25 years in federal prison for 77 routine business acts many businesses commit daily without realizing it.

I found myself drawn to Mr. CEO's plight due to his remarkable ability to reinvent himself from inside federal prison. Today, from prison, Mr. CEO is an active consultant to several business owners who find themselves questioning their every move. In other words, what were once benign business activities could now obliterate business owners' families and bury them in prison for years.

According to lawyers and businessmen critics, *From French Cuffs to Handcuffs* has been noted as "intelligence driven by experience" since it was written by a man, who, himself, is a former lawyer and corporate CEO, one who has long been disbarred and disgraced; yet, in spite of his fall, Mr. CEO has managed to transform his setback into a set-up for his major comeback. In like manner, Mr. CEO can do the same for you should you or someone you know face a federal indictment or worse yet, face the threat of time away in federal prison for what was surely thought to be a legal, day-to-day business transaction.

WHY WE BUILT A WEBSITE FOR YOU

Along with this book, our interactive website (aafpamerica.com), provides practical, instructive, and the most accurate information to those seeking a single, comprehensive website and consultancy comprising the intricate workings of America's federal prison system. The information contained in our site will assist anyone who:

- suspect they (or someone they know) could soon be facing a federal criminal indictment

- has been sentenced by the court, but awaiting designation orders to a specific prison camp or FCI

- has been taken into federal custody, be it pre- or post-sentencing, or

- knows a friend or have a family member who has been left behind by a spouse who is presently serving time in a federal prison

In addition, you will discover specific information on each of the 120 federal prison facilities and the 255 federal halfway houses nationwide—information from a prisoner's perspective and a lawyer's perspective regarding:

- being indicted by a federal grand jury for allegedly committing a crime—and what to do

- entering into federal prison or a halfway house for the first time—and how to survive it, and

- exiting prison and re-entering society—and how to be made whole

WHAT MAKES US THE AUTHORITY ON FEDERAL PRISONS?

For academic and judicial purposes, we are your "go-to" authority. How so? Experience. We have served real time at the USP level, the FCI level and the prison-camp level, thus affording our firm the consulting advantage over criminal attorneys or prison consultants, neither of whom have actually experienced life inside all four federal prison security levels. In addition, this book and our comprehensive website are second to none. Our website alone aggregates highlights of Internet research from America's universities and her most respected independent research institutions. We offer the accumulated intellectual output available to law students and professors, pre-trial and probation officers, families of federally-incarcerated inmates, and to taxpayers who foot the bill for America's rapidly growing federal prison system—all in one easily accessible place. We therefore urge you to contact us without delay should a question arise during or following your review of this book. Your questions are crucial. Keep in mind, someone's life and liberty might be at stake—perhaps even yours. Sometimes just one question that draws from our federal-prison experience can be the difference between years of languishing in federal prison or a lifetime of joy and freedom at home with family and friends.

—Michael W. McCoy
Consulting Editor
January 2012

"A 'federal probe' is nothing more than a euphemism for meaning someone's indeed going to federal prison. The time between the announcement of the probe and the issuance of an indictment exists solely to determine the number of co-defendants needed to render the indictment worthwhile. —Author Unknown

In this chapter . . .

When French Cuffs Were In

One Bad Decision

Choosing The Right Attorney

Analyzing Your Indictment

Crisis And Strategic Management

Focus On Your Family

Co-Defendant(s) Gone Wild

Leveraging Your Inner-Circle

Do I Man Up Or Draw Down?

Consider A Plea Agreement When Or If

Consider Going To Trial When Or If

Frequently Asked Questions

CHAPTER ONE

WHO, ME? INDICTED? NO WAY!

When French Cuffs Were In

It was once said that "all you really need to know about a person can be discovered from the uniqueness of their signature."

Indeed my signature is unique to me, just as yours is unique to you. All of us have a signature difference about us, a difference that distinguishes us from all others; be it the way we sign a document, or the type of vehicle we drive, or the home in which we live. Everything is, in essence, a signature difference, unique to each of us.

As business people, we have a certain fashion signature that distinguishes us from others. Along the winding road of personal growth and success, we have been taught the distinguishing significance of power: power colors, power ties, power speech, the power of knowledge—all perfected in us by the wisdom of powerful people in powerful positions. As students of corporate America, we have all read about, and later mastered the techniques that induce others to give us exactly what we want when we want it. We have mastered the art of persuasion through poetic words of expressing who we are and how we want the world to perceive us. I am a benefactor of them all: advanced schooling in law, business, and finance, followed by intense power-training techniques—all designed to make me different. I then paid my dues in the real world of business, and made the necessary sacrifices of starting and building multiple companies—many of which went bust before I finally solved the riddle of success toward building a two-hundred million dollar a year asset-based lending firm. Ironically, above all the things I have ever owned or accomplished, the least and most inconspicuous possession that rose to define my signature difference were my French cuffs.

As a CEO, I wore custom-tailored suits that were never flashy and always business conservative. But it was my blind-embossed French-cuffed shirts and my rare collection of antique cufflinks that became my ultimate signature.

My French cuffs became the epicenter from which many conversations flowed, conversations that later led to some of my most lucrative deals. Before long, my small fashion statement became infectious to friends, family, colleagues, and even to my clients. In time, they began to collect rare or unique cufflinks for me, either as a personal gift or as a gesture of their appreciation for my work.

Soon my name became synonymous with French cuffs, to the extent that my personal clothier even established an antique cufflink collection for his retail store.

I never intended to turn my French-cuff fetish into a signature brand for who I was. It just sort of crept up on me—then stuck. I loved the look and feel of French cuffs, much like my business colleague from Europe preferred the look and feel of his Hermès belts with the gold buckle in the shape of the letter "H". Or my personal banker in New York, who enjoyed the look and feel of his fine Italian shoes with tassels. With me, my French cuffs exceeded a mere fashion statement; instead, they took on a life of their own by ostensibly becoming my brand, my signature difference. Only when my French cuffs were forcibly taken from me did I discover the significance they had in my life.

That happened on June 19, 1995, following the loss of my month long jury trial, when I was committed to the custody of the U.S. Marshal's Service, bound for federal prison. While standing beside my attorney in open court, I was suddenly flanked by two deputy

Marshals who escorted me out of courtroom and into the bowels of the prisoners' holding chamber. Once inside, I observed another deputy marshal, in his early sixties, seated behind a matte-gray metal desk.

He was a large Middle Eastern man in his sixties with low-cropped gray hair, hooded eyes, and a strong nose. As he sat behind his desk, gazing at my approach, he gave me a long head-to-toe once-over before his eyes came to rest on my French cuffs. "Nice cufflinks," he uttered as if in admiration, only to smirk, "From French cuffs . . . to handcuffs." From that comment his fellow deputies chuckled as they removed my suit coat and my cufflinks before directing me inside a holding cell.

Right then it dawned on me how "authentically me" my French cuffs were. "From French cuffs to handcuffs." Those words, so cruel yet so revealing, left an scalding, indelible mark on me, even to this day. That was twenty years ago . . .

When Tragedy Began

It was on August 2, 1991, the exact evening President George H. W. Bush declared war (Desert Storm) on Iraq. As I sat in the capacious opulence of my family room in Anaheim Hills, California, watching the evening's Breaking News, I was struck with a surge of adrenaline that comes when a long-awaited opportunity of great wealth finally presented itself before my very eyes. It is that expectant opportunity with which a visionary CEO positions his company and himself to capture. However, the scope, size, and quickness of this opportunity short circuited my judgement and rationale. It was like casually combing across a beautiful Caribbean beach and stumbling upon a "genie in the bottle" so to speak, the kind that appears without warning. Yet before you realize what is happening, the genie escapes her bottle. And in the blink of an eye, there she is. Sitting right there. Square and center on your lap.

Right then, in the middle of the news broadcast, I snatched up the phone and called the president of our industrial finance subsidiary. At this company, we specialized in government contract financing. But little did any of us know, we had been placed on the Department of Defense's (DOD) list of Lenders for Priority Vendors, which provided the opportunity to finance Priority DOD classified contracts. As I waited for what seemed like an eternity, Fred finally answered, "Hello?"

"Hey, watching the news?" I asked.

"You mean President Bush?" he asked.

"Yep."

Fred replied, "Looks like we hit pay dirt," a term often used in our oil and gas division.

I then ordered, "Call the operations team tonight—all of them. I want every DOD contractor in our portfolio on the phones first thing in the morning. Have them tool up for Uncle Sam. Then offer them the checkbook."

"I'm on it." Fred replied.

We ended the phone call.

At that same time, our securities lawyers were in town for three days, for two reasons: audit our Securities and Exchange (SEC) compliance records and to assist with our new investment offering that would increase our capital position to finance the surge of military and domestic oil-drilling operations.

That afternoon, on August 3, 1991, the chief securities lawyer and I were wrapping up three days of review and compliance before his return to San Francisco. Earlier that day, however, we had a disconcerting exchange concerning investor proceeds that were held in trust from a pre-offering solicitation they knew nothing about. Our pre-offering was in response to the impending conflict in Iraq, from which we projected an immediate need of $65 million in DOD loan requests from our contractors in the span of one week. When Desert Storm hit, it hit twice: once in Iraq, and once in my office. Suddenly the amount of capital we needed doubled. Even more challenging, the time in which to raise it shrank from a week to a day. In other words, an unexpected $140 million increase in Priority Defense Contracts came to us in a single day!

One Bad Decision

To a DOD contractor, a Priority Contract means that everything in its production pipeline stops. Thus, DOD orders are moved to the front of the line, as in last in first out. Failure to comply results in penalties and permanent expulsion from government contracting. To compound matters, that same day, I personally received a call from the DOD senior official who posed an alarming question to me: "Need my office be concerned with your firm's capacity to perform on such short notice?"

To which I replied, "Not at all."

"Because you know," the DOD official warned in no uncertain terms, "you are also Priority. Just covering all the bases."

In retrospect, therein lay the one decision that radically changed my life and my family's life forever. Why? Because I flat out lied to the government, and I lied to myself. No, financially we weren't the least bit prepared. Yet I used the investor proceeds anyway. It was like I was the lone skier perched at the top of an uncharted, dare-devil mountain slope, I looked down at the steep, powdery-white drop. I pondered the topography before taking in a long, deep breath. At that very moment, a still small voice told me not to jump. But my hubris got the best of me, so I jumped nonetheless . . . and so beautiful a jump. Now airborne, and at full throttle into my angle of attack, I suddenly discovered I had jumped into an abyss that was white as snow, but then it gradually morphed into a twenty-five year free fall into a world of raven darkness.

This brings me to you, my reader. On what uncharted dare-devil slope are you standing? Or like me, have you already jumped?

To help you gauge where you might be on this slippery slope toward receiving a federal indictment at this very moment, consider one of the following questions:

> 1. Are you or someone you know acting as a fiduciary over another's money or property, and, in the interim, have exposed this money or property to adverse risks without full disclosure to its owner(s)?
>
> 2. Are you a manager or mid-level executive within an organization that you know—or should have known—is engaged in any fraudulent activities?
>
> 3. Have you or someone you know backdated material documents in your business or government office in order to cover for another's unscrupulous actions?
>
> 4. Is there anyone using your state or federal licenses or permits without official permission?
>
> 5. Or are you in any way knowledgeable of, or a party to, any combination of any of the above?

If you answered "yes" or "probably so" chances are, you've jumped. And how exhilarating a jump it was. At last, you're airborne, with the icy-cool wind pressing against your face. As you lean into your angle of attack, only seconds from touching down, a thought crosses your mind: maybe I shouldn't have jumped either.

All too often, we as executives, business owners, politicians and even mid-level employees of these businesses fall victim to federal prison without realizing it.

Whatever the case may be, your name is already a matter of many records. And in case you are thinking about quitting or changing occupations, or simply turning a blind eye to the situation, know this: by no means are you separated from prior criminal acts should they exist, unless the statute of limitations has run its course. If not, your name, title, signature, and role in those criminal acts are enshrined in the record, be it the record of a civil case in progress, or the record of a federal criminal indictment in progress.

With your entire universe at stake, why not heed my advice and consult a federal criminal lawyer today? Not tomorrow. Today! What do you have to lose other than the cost of this book? Then again, imagine the real, life-changing costs if you discover that I am right, but waited too late—or did nothing to affect the outcome?

Today, thousands of former executives, business owners, mid-level managers and politicians are sitting in federal prison because of their pride, arrogance and denial. Like me, they just could not get their heads around the possibility that we were in a federal prosecutor's crosshairs. So while you are free and able, do not sit in denial by saying, "Who me? Indicted? No way!"—as I so foolishly did. You owe it to your family's future to know exactly where you stand. Now that I have your attention, let's talk about the "right" federal criminal defense attorney before you make that call or pay a dime towards a retainer fee.

Choosing the "Right" Attorney

Allow me, if you will, to preface with this metaphor: You have just been targeted and forcibly drafted into a Cold War. Government commandos (aka: federal prosecutors) are amassing arms and are quietly and secretly circling your camp. They are patient, methodical, and deliberate—oh, and so well-financed. Plus, they have the best of FBI Investigators at their disposal to investigate you.

You, on the other hand, are the lone soldier, plunged into a hostile foreign land while still inside your own homeland. Now, it's either fight or flight—and since flight is not an option (given your family, business, and community ties) your only option is to fight. Then again, how does one fight such a formidable foe when one's time, reinforcements, and financial resources are so limited? For starters, you'll need a war-tested general, as in the "right" war-tested attorney, to chart a strategic, long-range battle plan for you.

Question is: Is there such a thing as the "right" attorney when the accused is facing a federal criminal case? There certainly is such a thing as the right attorney when battling a civil case, or a family law case, or even when battling a state criminal case. But the right attorney for defending a federal criminal case is a different story altogether. It boils down to that one rare attorney who informs you of at least one of these three awful truths before he or she discusses their fees with you. The three awful truths are as follows:

1. That according to Department of Justice statistics, the federal government's prosecutors have enjoyed a better than 92% total conviction rate over the past 10 years, equating to only an 8% acquittal/dismissal rate in favor of you the accused.

2. That the odds of being acquitted is within that razor-thin 8% figure.

3. That if you dare choose to exercise your Constitutional right to a fair and impartial trial by judge or jury and you lose, your term of imprisonment could be three times as long as the prison sentence offered to you (through your

attorney) by the prosecutor early on in his or her so-called "deal" (aka: the "plea agreement negotiations," which we will discuss in greater detail later).

Should you be so fortunate to find such a federal criminal defense attorney, let us know right away. Point being, we have learned that such an attorney is most difficult to find. As such, the appropriate adjective in the lead title should be "adequate," as in: Choosing The "Adequate" Attorney instead of the "right" attorney.

Make no mistake. All attorneys are businesspersons first, lawyers second. And no businessperson, regardless of profession, will work against their own best interest by eagerly exposing certain negatives such as items 1 – 3 above to you, although I'm certain that there are a few exceptions out there somewhere. So how do you find an adequate attorney? After all, this is your life on the government's altar:

First Strategy: The "Free" Federal Defender: Take heed. Experience teaches that if you have yet to be formally arrested, don't spend a dime just yet or live to regret it. That is, unless you are the Martha Stewart/Michael Milken type with mega-bucks to burn. Instead, when you appear in court, request the services of the Federal Defender (who's usually present for all arraignment and bail proceedings), and a Federal Defender will be temporarily appointed to you, on the spot, per the Fourteenth Amendment of the Constitution.

Once you have entered your plea and bail has been established, you will then be directed to the Federal Defender's Office for a financial evaluation before a formal appointment of the Federal Defender's Office; and it is then that you can request an in depth consultation with the Federal Defender. During your interview, inquire into items 1 – 3 above. Then listen carefully as the interviewing attorney's awful truths prove to be dauntingly consistent with ours.

Usually before your next court appearance, a formal judicial decision will be made regarding your eligibility, or ineligibility, to receive the free (or partially paid) Federal Defender's services for the duration of your pre-trial and post-trial proceedings. Or, in the alternative, the court will grant you a reasonable extension of time to freely shop around for private counsel if you possess the economic means to do so. Should that be the case, at least you will be armed with the right information and statistics before doling out five to six-figures to retain an adequate private attorney.

Second Strategy: The Paid Private Attorney: If you do not have an attorney as a friend, then consider asking your single most influential friend or acquaintance for the name of an attorney with whom they have a trusting relationship. The deeper the relationship, the better. And it doesn't matter what type of law he or she practices. At this juncture, it's all about a relationship built on trust. Again, the attorney's specialty is not the point here. It's trust.

Now, without revealing the core criminal nature of your case, make an appointment for a paid one or two hour consultation and referral session. Paying for the attorney's time makes it worthwhile for them to see you, especially if he or she is not a criminal attorney.

During your session with this attorney, discuss your indictment, along with the awful truths from Items 1-3 above. Then insist on a "qualified" referral to a federal criminal attorney who he or she knows and trusts for their integrity—and remind this attorney of the trust relationship you have with your friend who made the referral in the first place. A qualified referral is when an attorney employs his or her best effort toward finding you an honest, forthright criminal defense attorney, now that their good name, upstanding reputation, and best of all, his or her relationship with you and your friend are at stake. Therein lies the power of relationship.

Here's The Skinny . . .: Let's go back to the awful truth, Item number 1 above, regarding the government prosecutors enjoying a minimum 92% conviction rate. How is such an unconscionable conviction rate even possible? Or asked another way: How are federal criminal defense attorneys able to sleep at night after charging their emotionally devastated, irrationally frightened client tens of thousands—even hundreds of thousands—of dollars, all the while knowing that the client stands a mere 8% chance of acquittal?

Consider my plight. I also had a Constitutional right to a fair trial. And I exercised that right—and, as mentioned on our website home page, I lost. In other words, I refused "to cooperate" (meaning "snitch" on someone else to save my own skin), nor did I agree to plead guilty to "pile-on" charges I did not commit in exchange for a term of imprisonment of eight years[4]. By exercising my Constitutional right to trial, and for having made the government take me to trial, I received a term of imprisonment of twenty-four and one-half (24½) years, plus five more years of supervised release (probation) for a non-violent, white-collar (securities fraud and money laundering) crime(s). So why are we rehashing this? Because, even I, an educated, trained in law (though not criminal law)

> **Experience Teaches:**
>
> Demand a written retainer and fee agreement before parting with one dollar to a defense attorney.

[4] Glenn Harlan Reynolds, a professor of law at the University of Tennessee, suggested the banning of plea agreements due to prosecutors grossly overcharging those accused. The professor stated, "Our criminal justice system, as presently practiced, is presently a plea bargaining system with actual trials of guilt or innocence a bit of showy froth floating at the top" (Source: Wall Street Journal, June 8, 2013).

professional, I did not learn of the government's 92% conviction rate until ***after*** my trial! This is not to say that I still would not have taken my case to trial. However, it does mean that, considering my awful odds, I surely would have thought long and hard about the rationale of going to war with a BB gun when my opponent has a Howitzer 50mm aerial machine gun.

Fact is, most people plead guilty to a lesser charge because they are tired of, and naturally frightened by, being locked away in jail. Or their legal fees are skyrocketing out of control; or perhaps the fees are altogether out of reach; or they fear the possibility of losing at trial where three times the punishment awaits them. These are the cold hard equations of crime and punishment in America today. So it is crucial that you set aside your pride, your ego, your denial, your fear, and think long and hard about the role you played in the offense with which the prosecutor indicted you. If you are guilty—not by way of denial, but by the government's clear and objective evidence against you—quickly have your public or private attorney negotiate the best possible "deal" you can muster and be done with it. Or, if you are so inclined, do what I did: Lace up your boots, strap on your helmet, and polish up your BB gun. Go ahead, exercise your Constitutional right to a fair trial against a 92% conviction rate adversary and live with the consequences.

Analyzing Your Indictment

No, I'm not implying that you, in any way, shape or form, play attorney on your own behalf. That's like playing Russian Roulette. Foolish indeed. Instead, what I am suggesting you do is take time away from your emotions and analyze every word for dictionary clarity (you'll likely also need a law dictionary) for a clear, definitive understanding of the government's charges against you. Why is this exercise so important? Because in your indictment, every "and," "with," or "or" has significant meaning, which could result in irreparable harm against you. For example:

The Devil's In The Details: Does your indictment refer to "you *and* someone" or "you *with* someone" or "you *or* someone?" Believe me . . . with a federal indictment, the devil really is in the details; and the devil's known for showing up later on in the proceedings, hell-bent on sending you straight to prison. How about this: Does your indictment use words or phrases such as "on or about," referring to appropriate dates certain events supposedly happened—events involving you? How about "approximately" or "on or before?" Analyze your indictment. Your freedom is at risk. Point being, if your indictment is inaccurate, unclear, or overly general, document it, correct it, and then outline your corrections in letter form. Then deliver a copy of the letter to your attorney for counsel. But hold on. There's another step . . .

Material Accusations: Take another fresh look at each Count in your indictment — Count I, Count II, etc. Are the material accusations correct or incorrect? Material accusations are ill-deeds that only *you* know—or perhaps your co-defendants know—are really not accusations, but truths. Example: If Count I of a hypothetical indictment reads:

> **On or about January 1, 2010, John and Mary Doe conspired to steal a blue Range Rover . . .**
>
> But here's what you know *really* happened:
>
> **On January 4, 2010, John and Mary Doe conspired to steal a black Range Rover . . .**

Of course, document the inaccurate date and the inaccurate color of the Range Rover. Although the date in the first example is incorrect, the indictment read "on or about," which renders the date's error as immaterial in the grand scheme of events—at least in the beginning. But the Range Rover's color is definitely material because the prosecution might have the wrong Range Rover in evidence. In my 77-count indictment, these types of errors existed, which resulted in the dismissal of 23 counts.

Again, analyze your indictment for material accusations that are incorrect. Then document them, correct them, then outline them in letter form to your attorney. **Also, it is imperative you keep copies of all correspondence between you and your attorney for future reference! And there definitely *will* be a future reference as experience teaches.**

One might be inclined to ask, "How could you be so bold as to make such a claim?" Great question. Here's how. After twenty years of sifting though thousands of prisoners' post-conviction cases and court documents, I have discovered how pretrial attorneys, or sentencing attorneys, or appellate attorneys (oftentimes one in the same) have made one or more constitutional errors during one of the above-stated proceedings—the kind of error that could reduce your prison sentence, or overturn it altogether, pursuant to 28 U.S.C, §2255. So yes, keep copies.

Advice About Federal Criminal Attorneys: Those of us who are trained in the law are taught to put everything in writing that benefits and protects our interests. Conversely we are trained to avoid putting in writing that which opposes or threatens our interests or the interests of our clients. To prove my point, analyze the "Retainer And Fee Agreement"[5] provided to you by your private attorney (federal

[5] "In each state, there exists a licensing body known as the State Bar Association. Within this licensing body, there exists a "Client Security Fund Office" (or the equivalent) that arbitrates client-attorney disputes relating to unearned attorney's fees that the attorney either (1) refuses to return to you, the client, (2) that the attorney is unlawfully withholding funds due you, or, (3) the attorney used trust funds belonging to you without your consent. When arbitrating such a dispute, this agency's first request from you is for a copy of the written retainer agreement between you and your attorney. Why? Because everything starts there. Such an agreement, in advance, greatly protects the your rights. Plus, it binds the attorney to a set of predetermined obligations from which he cannot deny."

defenders are not paid by the defendant; therefore, retainer agreements are not applicable).

I'm assuming, of course, you do have in your possession a retainer agreement between you and your attorney, right? I'm also assuming you received the Agreement before you paid your attorney. If not, my point is made. Case closed. However, should you have a retainer agreement, it is likely a unilateral retainer agreement, meaning it principally protects the attorney—not you. The reality is—as hindsight teaches—it's up to you to protect yourself, irrespective of your private attorney's smiles and reassurances, such as, "Don't worry. I'm on top of things." On the contrary, you had better worry. Worry most when the attorney tells you not to worry; and ultimately it is up to you to remain on top of your own case and case documents. Therefore, it is crucial that from the beginning you document *everything* between you and your attorney—as if it were a journal—per my suggestions in the Subsections of this chapter. You might very well need this documentation should you lose your case and later discover that your private or public attorney(ies), or the court, have procedurally or constitutionally violated your rights. Indeed, thousands of us (who have been incarcerated) have come to learn how our attorneys erred *long after* we have lost our cases. Long after we have been sent to prison, and have finally mustered the strength to begin working on, or assisting with our direct appeals or post-conviction appeals.

So analyze your indictment for your own protection while you can. And while you are at it, analyze your retainer agreement, also—if you have one.

Crisis And Strategic Management

There's nothing like throwing bloody "chum" in the ocean in order to excite the sharks into a feeding frenzy. Ask golfer, Tiger Woods or U.S. Presidential Candidate, John Edwards. Similarly there's nothing like a "cordial" federal probe into your business dealings that excites the media into a feeding frenzy.

Frankly, I have yet to see a cordial (aka an informal) federal probe into a company's practices not evolve into a federal indictment against someone—or against the company as a whole.

I, for one, was an example of how hostile the media can be when the announcement of a cordial probe is underway. In retrospect, had I known then what I know today, I would have been able to neutralize much of the media impact on me and my family by proactively running "to" the media instead of reactively running "from" the media.

The key is to go on the offensive—the public relations offensive—by offering exclusive interviews with the most fair and friendly reporter your PR people can find. Here's the strategy that worked fairly well for me.

By granting exclusives to only one reporter, I gained leverage with the news department, while simultaneously tempering what the opposing news organizations would show and report about me and my company.

This strategy worked fairly well. Problem was, I waited far too long before my strategy could take hold and gain momentum. For best results, it is to your advantage to hire a crisis and strategic management firm during the cordial probing stage of the government's investigation. Don't wait for an indictment to fall into your lap before you go on the offensive.

Focus On Your Family

When I first learned that my attorney was served with my 77-count federal indictment on a Thursday afternoon, my initial thought was, "Oh God, my family! What do I tell my family? And how do I protect them?"

With my feet stuck in the morass of fear, denial, and arrogance, I chose to say nothing to my family right away.

Instead, I concluded that a man of my stature could stamp out the federal indictment and make it all go away. After all, I had the best of lawyers. But, by the following Monday morning—a dark and rainy Monday—the Gates of Hell were opened, unleashing the news of my indictment, along with the usual titillating media hype and exaggerations—all for public consumption, all at your expense. Yet by the time I learned of this news, my family was out and about—the kids at school, the wife at the spa—while I was at the office. And within the first hour into my workday, my wife called me. She was apoplectic . . .

From that moment on, I was on the defensive, from which I had lost much of my creditability with my wife and children. Why? Denial. Arrogance. Shame. For the life of me, I couldn't bring myself to tell them what I had done to violate the law and where I had lost my way. Now I was forced to tell my wife and children. But it was too late. The media reports had me in a state of collapse—to the extent where I could not recover.

With that said, here's what organizing a timely, proactive meeting with the family accomplishes:

1. A timely meeting with the family lessens the blunt-force trauma when the news is eventually made public. Moreover, you can dispel most anticipated lies and exaggerations about you by informing your family

of what untruths might be told. Then tell them the truth about how you "screwed up," and the worst of penalties you may face. And, if appropriate, have your lawyer, your spiritual leader, or some other trusted friend present. Whatever your decision, know this: bad news is best when it is revealed early.

2. Next, meet with your extended family. Bringing everyone together—early—will strengthen your resolve, build support and credibility, and lessen the pain that comes with fighting a federal indictment.

3. Then meet with employees, colleagues, and friends. These people are key resources for strength, encouragement, and for character references when you need them the most. Problem is, if you wait to meet with employees, colleagues, and friends after the media portrays you as the next Osama bin Laden you greatly reduce the odds for future support when character-reference letters and possible character testimony in court becomes necessary.

Co-Defendant(s) Gone Wild

Most federal indictments name more than one defendant, simply because most crimes—be they violent or non-violent, white-collar or black-glove—require someone else's assistance to some degree.

Case in point: In my indictment, two of us, who were the top two executives, were named in the indictment and referred to as "co-conspirators" who, according to the indictment, "conspired to sell unregistered securities to investors . . ." hence the white-collar offenses of securities fraud and money laundering. I was the Founder, Chairman of the Board, and the CEO—and my co-defendant was the president of our company. As mentioned on Page 2 of our aafpamerica.com website, we went to trial and lost. Yet, at no time during our brutal battle with the government did we turn informant (or "snitch," as the term is known) on one another.

However, many who are indicted are so intimidated by the possibility of going to federal prison, they ultimately and secretly "cut a deal to cooperate" for themselves. What type of deal? Plea bargains, as in agreeing to turn "state's evidence" against you in order to save their own skin.

Depending on the alleged crime committed and its prescribed punishment, your co-defendant might exaggerate the facts, or even make up lies in order to avoid prison time altogether.

Once the deal is made, your co-defendant will be coached by the prosecutor in anticipation of taking you to trial.

Yes, it's a very ugly game. But that's the way the game is played in the Federal Judicial System.

So what can you do to hedge against a co-defendant gone wild?

First, be honest with yourself. If you know you are truly guilty of, for instance, Counts 1, 3, and 5, but not guilty of Counts 2, 4, and 6 of a six-count indictment, communicate your feelings, in confidence, with your co-defendant. Get into his head. Learn what he thinks he is guilty of. If you know he is also—without a doubt—guilty of several of the counts, but denies it, or toys with legal technicalities to dispel guilt, guess what? Your co-defendant is likely planning on serving you up to the government on a Thanksgiving platter first chance he gets. Another angle is to engage your co-defendant in private plea-agreement discussions. See where it leads. The problem is the more fragile and frightened your co-defendant is, the more likely he will turn on you. If that is the case, contact your attorney fast. Discuss the "what if's" and come up with a protective plan that will tame a co-defendant gone wild.

In my case, my co-defendant and I had several heart-to-heart discussions. I even went so far as to suggest the following:

> "Hey look, the government is really targeting me, the Founder, the Chairman. You, on the other hand, are simply in the line of fire. You are in the way. Trapped in the house fire. How about we engineer a 'deal' for you so you can stay out of prison and help take care of my two young daughters? Go ahead." I encouraged, "Testify against me. Your testimony can't make matters worse for me if you simply tell the truth. How about it?"

We discussed this strategy on two separate occasions. Yet my co-defendant never wavered. On the contrary, he stood fast and firm. He was determined to take our case to trial. And even though we fought and lost and went to prison, I knew early on that my co-defendant was a stand-up kind of guy. Instead of running for the hills, my co-defendant took it on the chin with me, and never wavered once.

Of course, there's no way of knowing if this strategy will work for you or not; for there are risks, especially if your co-defendant is weak. He might be induced to lie on the witness stand. Believe it or not, it happens. Especially with a headline-grabbing prosecutor hot on your trail.

All-in-all, you should discuss these strategies with your attorney before engaging in sensitive talks with your co-defendant. Perhaps your attorney will not approve of such a bold strategy. However, should you suffer a conviction, you are the one who gets to do the orange-shoe shuffle into prison, while your attorney gets to go home.

Leveraging Your Inner-Circle

Isn't it astonishing how just one bad decision or unfortunate mistake can completely overshadow all the good deeds you have bestowed on others over your lifetime?

Unfortunately, that certainly appears to be the case when we find ourselves pinned under the weight of a federal indictment. However, depending on your social, economic, and business status, your circle of influential friends and acquaintances can prove to be of significant assistance to you, should things turn out for the worst.

Your circle of friends in high places can greatly assist you with invaluable character reference letters at the time of sentencing. And now that the Federal Sentencing Guidelines are no longer binding on district judges (but advisory), the judge has broader discretion when sentencing convicted defendants. In addition, your attorney will be better positioned to argue for a form of alternative sentencing should he be so inclined to use the status of your inner-circle as leverage.

Below are some mitigating strategies you should consider when planning to leverage your circle of influence:

Leveraging Your Circle of Charities: Think back over the years of the many charitable causes to which you contributed your time, talent, and treasure. You've probably forgotten the number. In any event, begin making a list of organizations you have supported. Then, at the appropriate time, contact them—or better yet, meet with them—and secure the best possible character reference letter(s) you can muster.

Leveraging Your Circle of Business Friends, Colleagues, and Associates: Much like your circle of charities, your business friends, colleagues, and associates can be a treasure trove of character references. In fact, you might be surprised just how many of your friends, colleagues, and associates would be happy to come to your aid, being that they themselves are likely guilty of the same or a similar offense as you.

They just have not been caught yet. So helping you would likely make them feel better about their own wrongdoings.

Leveraging Your Political Contacts: Political affiliates are a great source for character references. Problem being, politicians are so fickle and narcissistic and self-serving, they often abandon anyone—absolutely anyone—they believe might become a liability of sort in the next election. Then again, some politicians can prove to be an exception to the rule, depending, of course, on the relationship you have developed with them over the years. Regardless of the depth of each specific relationship, it's in your best interest to leverage them to your advantage. Because believe me, political leverage could go a long way if or when you find yourself standing before the judge at time of sentencing.

Leveraging The Second Chance Act of 2007: Although we will discuss The Second Chance Act in greater detail in Chapter Two, it's worth noting that The Second Chance Act provides white-collar defense attorneys with a potential tool to combat the draconian sentences suggested by the Federal Sentencing Guidelines for economic crimes. In other words, should you be convicted and face prison time, your attorney should argue at sentencing that Congress has established a national policy of promoting early release and community confinement for the kind of crimes that pose little to no violence or harm to the community. Your attorney should argue that Congress has also endorsed the notion that age, rehabilitation, and fiscal responsibility are all relevant to determining the appropriate sentence. Furthermore, the message to judges is that the rigid, punitive, deterrence-based approach to white-collar sentencing should be discarded. In fact, the new perspective, formed in the terms of the ever-relevant sentencing factors set forth in 18 U.S.C., may preclude some courts from crafting the sort of individualized sentences that were abandoned under the Federal Sentencing Guidelines when they were created back in 1986.

Do I Man Up Or Draw Down?

One of the most difficult decisions that many of us defendants have to make—usually within the first month following the indictment—is: "Do I plead guilty and get it over with? Or do I take it all the way to trial?"

As you know, the Fourteenth Amendment of the Constitution grants us the Right of Due Process, the right to remain silent, the right to bail, the right to an attorney, the right to be tried by a jury of our peers, and the right to appeal the trial verdict. That's all fine and good. But the awful truth is, as stated in the Section above, entitled: "Choosing The Right Attorney", the U.S. Attorney's Offices have enjoyed a better than 92% overall conviction rate over the past 10 years—and counting. Such a statistic translates into an 8% chance of you prevailing at trial.

It may prompt you to wonder: "How on earth could the playing field of justice be so tilted in the government's favor? Are private attorneys that inferior to government attorneys?

The answers to these questions are complex and multi-faceted at best. But for the sake of simple straight talk, here are the indisputable facts:

Power to Accuse: The Fourteenth Amendment of the Constitution does not protect a defendant from the might and power of the federal government's ability to "pile on" charges of which the defendant must defend against. As such, we, the accused, are immediately disadvantaged if we possess limited financial resources with which to defend ourselves—which forces the average defendant to accept sub-par legal representation from day one.

Power to Bargain: Also, the Fourteenth Amendment of the Constitution does not permit the accused to hire counter-informants or to pay counter-informants; nor does the Fourteenth Amendment grant the accused the power to give or to take away the single most precious right desired by all Americans: one's liberty. In other words, the government has immense bargaining power by granting an informant their freedom if he or she testifies for the government; or, in the alternative, the government can throw them in prison should they refuse. Yet, we, the accused, have no such power at our disposal.

Power to Tax: Lastly, the Fourteenth Amendment of the Constitution does not afford the accused equal resources with which to defend ourselves, insofar as it affords the government endless resources with which to prosecute us. For example, the government possesses the power to tax its citizens in order to finance its prosecutorial endeavors. Whereas we, the accused, must rely on our limited life savings for attorney fees; or, if funds are not available, then we are at the mercy of an overworked and usually unskilled federal defender. . . unskilled, that is, when compared to a seasoned assistant U.S. Attorney.

Armed with this information, what guideposts should the accused look for when trying to decide whether to entertain a plea agreement or go to trial? Looking back through the lens of experience, here are my suggestions for your consideration:

Consider A Plea Agreement When Or If:

1. The government has reliable, unimpeachable informants and witnesses who are willing (or, perhaps forced) to testify against you,

2. The government offers you 1/3 or less of what you could receive in terms of prison time should you go to trial and lose. (Remember my deal? I was offered eight (8) years. But I received twenty-five (25) years after losing at trial),

3. You received a multi-count indictment that exposes you to a prison sentence that by statute could run consecutive in lieu of running concurrent,

4. You received a multi-count indictment that could carry ten (10) or more years in prison, and yet you have not the resources to hire an adequate attorney,

5. The evidence against you could be explained to a jury with relative ease,

6. You have family members who were indicted with you, yet the government is willing to dismiss them if you plead guilty,

7. You know you have a co-defendant who's gone wild, a co-defendant you strongly believe will turn state's evidence against you, thus foreclosing your opportunity to negotiate a deal with the government. That is, short of turning on or testifying against someone yourself, against your own will, or,

8. You have prior criminal convictions for similar bad acts that could be used against you at trial.

9. Should you fear that your health and safety—or the health and safety of your family become a concern due to those you must testify against at a trial.

10. If you know for certain you have other "indictable offenses" out there for which you can be prosecuted.[6]

---

[6] Oftentimes a federal indictment will omit certain indictable offenses for which could be used to (1) supersede your instant indictment, (2) be used at sentencing to enhance (as in "slightly" increase) your prison sentence, or, worst of all, (3) upward depart (as in "greatly" increase) your prison sentence. Should this be the case, make sure your attorney structure a plea agreement that precludes the government from prosecuting you for undiscovered indictable offenses that might be discovered later.

Consider Going To Trial When Or If:

1. The government's allegations in the indictment can in no way be supported by your conduct or by the evidence the government purports to possess,

2. You possess the financial resources to hire the most experienced criminal defense team possible—as in attorney(ies), paralegals, investigators, etc.—a team that is not only reputable in federal criminal defense matters, but is also forthright with you about your odds of acquittal,

3. The net prison sentence from the proposed plea agreement with the government bears little difference with the net prison sentence of going to trial and losing,

4. The evidence relied on by the government has been destroyed or compromised in a manner that deems such evidence impermissible in a court of law, or that the production of this evidence from the government is not possible; and/or,

5. The witness(es) relied on by the government has a conflicting story, or is easily impeachable; or, for reasons beyond anyone's control, the witness—including a co-defendant—refuses to, or is unable to, testify against you.

Given these generalized suggestions, you now have some logical options with which you can discuss with your attorney when weighing your options of taking a plea or going to trial.

Pretrial Services

Following your arraignment—which is usually your first or second appearance in court—and you are released on bail, you may be ordered to report to pretrial services immediately after court. You may also be ordered to continually report to a designated pretrial services officer on a daily or perhaps on a weekly basis pending the disposition of your case. In fact, depending on your case, your pretrial officer may insist on your submitting to a urine test at random, or insist that you wear an ankle bracelet (electronic monitoring device) while on pretrial release.

In essence, you will be treated as if you were on parole or probation, except this stage is before trial, pending the final disposition of your case. Usually, formal probation or parole follows a conviction, and when required, a term of incarceration.

As for me personally—similar to that of other white-collar offenders—I was required to appear in person and sign-in daily, except for weekends. But I was permitted to travel the country on business and on vacation in Hawaii with my wife, provided I: (1) submit my travel itinerary in advance,(2) agree to call in to pretrial services on a daily basis, and(3) report my specific whereabouts.

This begs the question: Specifically, what dangers should one be mindful of while under supervision of a pretrial services officer?

Should you have contact with law enforcement in any manner—even a simple traffic infraction—and fail to inform your pretrial services officer that same day, or first thing the next morning, you could find yourself in court for a bail-revocation hearing. And if the judge is having a bad day, you could go straight to jail. So, the lesson: regardless of how "nice" a pretrial officer might appear, look again. Take nothing for granted, because if you do, you do so at your own peril.

FREQUENTLY ASKED QUESTIONS

Choosing the "Right" Attorney

Q: ***What is the best method of obtaining reliable, objective information on how "right" a criminal defense lawyer is as it relates to defending a federal criminal case like mine?***

A: Ask the attorney a simple question: What is his (or his firm's) win-loss record in federal criminal defenses? Then ask him or her how many cases have they defended in their career, then do the math. (**Note**: Forget about his or her standing or ranking with the State Bar or with any other "fluff" group. Focus on what matters: results). Also, Google their name. Look for past articles that feature them. In other words, do some serious homework. Lastly, go to our home page and click the button titled "Attorney Meter" for a list of qualifying questions. Then invite us to help you analyze your options.

Q: ***Should I pay the attorney's retainer fee all in one lump sum, or pay over time?***

A: How astute a negotiator are you? Try this: Upon concluding you have found an adequate attorney, seek to make payments at four or more stages. For example, if the total fee is, say, $100,000 offer $25,000 now, $25,000 once a trial date is set, $25,000 at the conclusion of the production of trial discovery, and $25,000 on or before the day of the trial. Also, demand a written retainer and fee agreement prior to paying one dollar to the attorney. Otherwise you will not receive an agreement at all.

And, above all else make sure there is language in the agreement that spells out how and when you will receive itemized bills for services rendered.

Now, beware of much resistance from the attorney, in that he or she might:(1) insist on the entire fee upfront, and,(2) refuse to obligate themselves by providing you with detailed billing on anything.

Attorneys love obligating others but they despise obligating themselves. Take it from experience. You'll be kicking yourself in the butt down the road if you do not insist on a retainer agreement that includes detailed billing practices that fully account for every dollar billed against the retainer.

Another note about defense attorneys. Experience teaches that when dealing with criminal defense attorneys on behalf of yourself, or on behalf of a loved one, emotions run high while good judgement runs amok. With someone's life and liberty on the line, your brain needs to be firing on all cylinders at all times. Naturally you will be gripped by fear. And naturally, the attorney sitting across from you knows this. For these reasons, I advise against settling in on any attorney on the initial go around. First, settle down and clear your mind. Second, talk to a level-minded professional (or even us) about your options prior to making that most crucial decision. Third, when you are ready to make that decision, insist on a detailed retainer agreement before paying out one dollar towards the attorney's retainer. This is far too important a decision to take any chances with an inadequate attorney.

Analyzing Your Indictment

Q: ***What is a superseding indictment? And why is it sometimes necessary for a prosecutor to obtain such an indictment?***

A: A superseding indictment is simply a revised indictment that replaces the originally filed indictment. A superseding indictment is sometimes necessary for a host of reasons. The primary two reasons, however, are because (1) the originally filed indictment has been deemed defective and thus it poses a legal problem for the prosecution if the defect is not rectified, or(2) newly discovered evidence that adds additional names of co-conspirators or adds additional charges, or both.

Crisis And Strategic Management

Q: ***Doesn't too much negative press taint my jury pool should I decide to go to trial?***

A: In most instances, no, not really. By the time a jury pool is purged down to the twelve jurors plus the alternates, skilled questioning by your attorney often times counteracts any media impact—unless you are a JefferyDahmer-BernieMadoff type of defendant.

Focus On Your Family

Q: ***Should I consider transferring assets into certain family member's names should the worst happen?***

A: Such a sensitive question requires legal advice, which means you should consult a professional. However, I can tell you what I did when I realized my fate. Since I was not subject to forfeiture proceedings nor indebted to a secured creditor, I did the following:

> (1) established a family trust and transferred assets into it,(2) encumbered my fixed assets, and,(3) liquidated other non-essential assets in an orderly fashion.

Every case, however, is so vastly different. As such, there is no way to standardize how one should proceed in this matter, other than through customized advice of an estate planning attorney.

Co-Defendant(s) Gone Wild

Q: *What if there are multiple co-defendants, as in six, ten, or eighteen? How does one strategize when there are so many who can turn on me at once?*

A: Unfortunately, this becomes a bidding war. Every man for himself. The problem is, the more co-defendants there are, the easier it will be for the government to obtain a conviction against you, depending, in part, on your alleged role in the offense(s).

In any event, you have to think about yourself, you family, and your freedom. Upon assessing the government's case against you, upon assessing the risks associated with losing at trial, and upon assessing the mounting expenses associated with your defense, making a deal with the government may logically be your best—if not your only bet.

Leveraging Your Inner-Circle

Q: *What if I have no significant circle of influence from which to draw? Will that reduce my odds towards a favorable outcome at sentencing?*

A: It doesn't matter if your circle of influence consists of three or four people of little to no social stature. What matters is the fact that there is someone in the community who's willing to shine some much needed light on your good character. After all, the U.S. Attorney and members of the probation department have colored you in darkness from the very beginning. So yes, anything positive about your character not only aids in the sentencing process, but it also gives your attorney more to work with when arguing for leniency at sentencing.

Do I Man Up Or Draw Down?

Q: *If I decide to go to trial, but then later decide to change my mind and seek a plea agreement, will the government reinstate the plea agreement originally offered?*

A: Most prisoners I have interviewed regarding this subject reported that the government accepted their willingness to enter into a plea agreement. However, the terms of their latter agreements delivered a deeper bite than their originally proposed agreements. Then again, there are reported instances where the government's response was simply, "Thanks, but no thanks. We'll see you at trial." For these reasons, you should discuss strategy early on in the process with a competent attorney.

Pretrial Services

Q: *What if I need to move from one city or state to another while I'm under pretrial service supervision? Will they allow me to move?*

A: Every case is different, therefore this question cannot be answered with a simple yes or no. In my case, I had two homes; one in Southern California, the other in Central California. Pretrial Services permitted me to travel back and forth due to the ongoing nature of my business. Later I sought permission to consolidate my homes into one as my trial drew near. The court granted my request without contest from Pretrial Services. Again, every case and circumstances are different.

Q: *Do you have other questions for Mr. CEO?*

A: Go to our website: http://frenchcuffsblog.com. Fill out the contact form with your question and we will get back to you as soon as possible.

frenchcuffsblog.com

"Ninety-seven percent of federal convictions [do not result in a trial, but] are the result of guilty pleas."

—U.S Supreme Court Frye Decision, 2012

In this chapter . . .

Protecting Yourself And Your Family

Do You Have A Last Will And Testament?

Powers Of Attorney

A Handy Man Is Dandy, Man

Presenting: Stage One Of Facing Your New Reality

Facing Your New Reality

Think Flexibility, Think Liquidity

Pre-Sentencing Documentation: Curse Or Blessing?

Beware Of Time-Sensitive, Specific-Performance Documents

Pending Traffic, Civil, And Family Matters

Pre-Sentence Investigation Report (aka PSI or PSR)

Hire A Private Firm To Prepare Your PSI Report

Pre-Existing Medical Conditions

Establish Fine And Restitution Payments At Sentencing

Frequently Asked Questions

CHAPTER TWO

PRESENTENCING PREPARATION

Protecting Yourself And Your Family

Hopefully you are reading this chapter before you or your loved one receives his or her sentence from the federal district judge.

Conversely, if you are at the presentencing stage of the court proceedings, your case has gone the course, which means one of three things has occurred:

1. you are now among the highly-coveted seven percent of those who won their freedom back by defeating the government at trial,

2. you are now among the seventy-six percent who lost their freedom by losing to the government at trial, or,

3. you are among the ninety-three percent of those who knuckled under and took a plea deal. You plead guilty in hopes of receiving little or no prison time.

Well if you're in category 1, congratulations! Do celebrate. But know this: somewhere lurking amid the recesses of a strewn government office is your U.S. prosecutor. And he's livid. Given another opportunity, he would swallow you whole. So watch your backside, if you know what I mean.

On the other hand, if you fall in category 2 or 3, it's time to man up and stop the sniveling. It's time to stop feeling sorry for yourself. It's time to begin the process of building a wall of protection around yourself and your family before the scavengers start moving in. And believe me, they ***will*** move in.

So let's discuss a few planning options you might want to consider during your presentencing stage.

Do You Have A Last Will And Testament?

Relax. This question is not to imply that you will die in prison as a result of prison violence (though anything in prison is possible). Instead, this question goes to the fundamental principle of prudent estate and financial planning for you and for your family. Of course you know that, right? But did you know that should you die in federal prison without a last will and testament, the federal government can supersede[7] the rights of your heirs? Did you know that the federal government can assess the cost of incarceration, the medical expenses (and other costs associated with your death) against your estate, and therefore receive priority over your heirs if you do not have a will?

For reasons beyond the garden-variety estate planning purposes, having a last will and testament offers you and your family that added layer of protection against the state and federal governments, especially if you are exposed to a term of federal incarceration.

---

[7]The death of a federal inmate while in federal custody is administered pursuant to BOP Policy Statement entitled "Escapes/Death Notification, Number 5553.05", 9-17-97. In large part, most federal prisoners are classified as "indigent". However, if the deceased inmate's case manager or the office of the U.S. Attorney possess financial information to the contrary (i.e. existing assets of former executives, business owners and politicians), the federal government may file a claim against the estate of the deceased inmate for the cost of incarceration, including all medical expenses, pursuant to BOP Policy Statement Number 2100.07 entitled "Cost Of Incarceration". In such cases, should the inmate die in custody without a last will and testament, the federal government will have "general priority" over the deceased's family, and "creditor priority" over other the deceased's creditors. For these reasons, you should make sure that your financial affairs are protected and in order prior to entering federal prison. (See CFR 28 CFR 5553.07)

And if for some reason you are presently incarcerated pending (or even after) formal sentencing, and you do not have a last will and testament, get one. Leave nothing to chance. Sure, it's going to be a bit more difficult and costly to secure a will and a notary public if you are presently incarcerated. However, the peace of mind is worth it.

Powers Of Attorney

With or without you, life goes on. Tomorrow the sun will rise. Adults will go to work. Children will go to school. Others will travel to the desert lows, and to the mountain highs. Life goes on and things must get done.

The question is, who's going to take care of your things should you go to prison? Your attorney? That's all well and good. We applaud you if you have the means to keep a high-priced attorney on retainer for the duration of your sentence to take care of things. Unfortunately everyone's not able.

But even with an attorney at your continued service, what about those basic, yet sensitive matters your spouse will need to accomplish on your behalf while you are away? For example, the sale, the transfer, or the encumbrance of real or personal property? Perhaps there are banking, insurance, or legal matters that require your signature, or the signature of your appointed power of attorney, should the need to act swiftly and efficiently arise. Waiting to act while you're in prison would be costly and outright foolish. So while there's time, make arrangements to appoint a trusted loved one as your limited or a general power of attorney to handle part or all of your affairs. Because once those prison doors close behind you, it's over. You're helpless. Paralyzed. That is, when it comes to getting anything important done out in the free world. And in prison, being helpless and paralyzed are tantamount to being tortured. So do yourself justice. Secure your power of attorney *before* you are sentenced.

A Handy Man Is Dandy, Man

Oh, the things we take for granted, our freedom being one of them. And nothing known to man makes taking our freedom for granted more painfully and acutely pronounced than losing one's freedom to a physical illness or to a prison sentence. Believe me, I know. I've been in prison for 15 years and counting as of the date of this writing. So I know the pain all too well.

What's worse, however, is when the pain of prison is vaulted into the forefront of my mind when the slightest of challenges at home pop up.

Think about it. If you left a family behind, who's going to take care of the incidentals that were once your responsibility? Or what if there's an emergency during your absence? Guess who bears the brunt of a raging spouse? You do!

Before the threat of prison, such incidentals were no-brainers. They were automatic. They were part of a normal day. But once you are closed in behind prison walls, your spouse's flat tire could easily set the stage for World War III (hopefully you are single with no children when encountering prison circumstances). Point is, every routine, everyday problem gets magnified tenfold. And you'll be constantly reminded of how you are to blame. Of course nothing or anyone can completely satisfy all the needs that will pop up at home.

However, below are a few suggestions that have worked well for me, as well as for others, who have served lengthy terms in federal prison:

1. Independent Housekeeping Agencies: From time to time, reward your spouse with an on-call, as-

needed housekeeper, provided you have the economic means to do so. Not full-time, but on call. Say two to four times a week. Or during those times your spouse is due to visit you. Or at times when the stresses of home life pile up. During the first four years of my incarceration, I employed this strategy—one that I learned from a fellow-former executive who was serving a six-year sentence for tax evasion. The strategy worked extremely well.

2. A Bookkeeper: Note that I did not say "CPA" or "Accountant", even though these titles are often used interchangeably. So let me be clear: I'm referring to a competent, cost-effective bookkeeper with whom your spouse can work. Case in point: Prior to coming to prison, I was heavily invested in the stock market, in addition to other less-volatile investments. With confidence in my wife—who was a university graduate—and my full-service broker by my side, I believed my investments could remain on auto-pilot for quite some time. Wow! How misguided I was. Once the prison doors closed behind me, I quickly discovered that, in spite of my many historical successes, my wife cared nothing for the workings of the stock and bond markets. As such, the expectation of training her to act in my stead proved disastrous.

3. A Handyman Is Dandy, Man: Above all others, our trusted handyman named Mario outlasted and outperformed all of our professional and semi-professional contractors. When there was a problem with the plumbing, Mario was there. With the swimming pool, Mario was there. Moving furniture in and out of storage, Mario was there. Tenant problems with our rentals, Mario took care of it—regardless of

the time, be it day or night, Mario was there. Of course, Mario was with us long before my legal troubles. Keeping him on, however, was, by far, the best presentencing- preparation decision I could have ever made.

Let me be clear. While in prison, you run nothing. And in spite of what you may think, you control nothing. Ultimately your spouse knows you control nothing. Your family and friends know you control nothing. And your colleagues surely know you control nothing. How's that? Because they know you are vulnerable. They know that if you say the wrong thing the wrong way, they could simply tell you to go "get bent" and you could do nothing about it, other than huff and puff hot air. Fact is, you're in prison. And certain people, including family, have a cruel way of reminding you of that.

Be that as it may, strategic presentence preparations afford you a bit more leverage and peace of mind as you do your level best to push through these difficult times.

Presenting: Stage One of Facing Your New Reality

With every trial in life comes a rude awakening. Unfortunately, facing federal prison time can be an existential experience, like you're a walking ghost of the living dead attending your own funeral. In fact, it's eerily surreal listening to friends and relatives make future plans without you, divvying up the spoils as if you were already dead and buried. Even still, there's a deeper, darker side of Stage One of your new reality which you must be made aware:

1. The Wounded-Shark Effect: A school of sharks swim and hunt in harmony, so long as none of them are wounded or bleeding. But the very moment a fellow shark is injured and a hint of blood flavors the water, he too becomes the meal of his fellow schoolmates. Similarly, the moment you are accused

of a crime, the most unsuspecting people—oftentimes those closest to you—begin to smell blood, and thus they begin to circle you in secret. And what you will discover, to your dismay, is that somewhere along your dreadful journey, a turncoat (aka a snitch) or two have been voluntarily and systematically aiding the government prosecutors with destroying you. The odds of this happening, of course, are greater if you are an individual with critical mass or with a high-profile image. Irrespective of your economic or social stature, one or more turncoats will emerge. My point? Be mindful of what you do, say, or give to those closest to you, pending the full resolution of your legal matter. For you never know who federal investigators are seeking to interview next. And you never know who might end up on the witness stand to testify against you.

2. <u>Friends Wear Wires, Too</u>: Depending on the government's case (or lack thereof) against you, a family member, a friend, or a close associate could be facing intense pressure from a prosecutor, forcing them to turn on you. But at times, force, per se, is not always necessary. Sometimes it's sheer envy towards you. Sometimes this "so-called" friend needs a criminal conviction against you more than the government does, thus clearing the way for some sort of civil action against you (as was the situation in my case). In any event, friends wear wires too. And the goal behind wearing a wire is to get you to talk yourself into a solid criminal conviction for the government. For good measure, particularly upon discovering that you're being targeted, pay close attention to social and conservational pattern changes

among friends, associates, employees, and new comers. Beware of small talk or prying, sympathetic questions designed to get you to relax and open up, or perhaps explode into an angry tirade.

3. Civil Action: When you find yourself accused of a criminal offense, civil suits often follow, particularly if you are a business owner or a white-collar professional. Suddenly everyone becomes a victim. And interestingly, every civil suit will, in one way or another, design its causes of action around the alleged offenses for which you are criminally accused. Moreover, do not be surprised when you discover who some of these sudden "victims" are. Some will be individuals who owe you money. Others could be tenants, vendors, current employees, past employees, ex-wives or ex-husbands, the neighbor and her sheep dog—you name it. The bigger you are, the more blood you have for the leeches. And get this: the criminal investigators and U.S. Attorneys love civil-suit action against you during the course of a criminal investigation. Their reasoning? Civil discovery makes for easy, free, silver-platter evidence—evidence that is unimpeachable and acquired under oath. So, in essence, when an active civil case mirrors any part of an active criminal case, the accused runs the risk of waiving his or her Fifth Amendment Constitutional Right against self-incrimination. Procedurally what I did when confronted with this exact situation was file a series of motions to "stay" all of my civil cases pending the outcome of my criminal case. With much contest from the civil petitioners and little resistance from the state civil judges, my motions were granted. The civil cases were stopped cold in their tracks.

Immediately discuss this strategy with your criminal defense attorney should you encounter a similar situation.

4. Unindicted Co-Conspirators: Interesting term. But what does it mean? Well, in my federal indictment, unindicted co-conspirators meant all of my employees and any of my family members who worked for me at one time or another. In essence, unindicted co-conspirators are persons to whom the government refers throughout an indictment as "aiders and abettors" to a crime, but are unindicted; that is, for now. How do you think that would make them feel? And what do you think will happen once these unindicted co-conspirators receive an alarming telephone call from government prosecutors when investigating you? And finally, what do you think will happen should the government prosecutors dislike these unindicted co-conspirators' answers about you, or should they—the co-conspirators—refuse to cooperate altogether? Like you, they will get the hammer. There's too much at stake. Your job is to immediately inform your criminal attorney of who these unindicted co-conspirators are, including any dangers they might present due to past relations or unpleasant business dealings. Especially if problems existed between you and them. The key here is to be proactive, and, of course, truthful with your attorney in order to anticipate and countermand the government's attacks against you.

5. Ex-Wives, Ex-Partners, Ex-Lovers: Perhaps one or two of these people are already listed in your indictment. If not, that's a good start. But federal investigators, federal prosecutors, and federal

probation officers will do their level best to find as many of your ex's as possible, either before or during

> **Experience Teaches:**
>
> Federal prosecutors will not hesitate to indict your son, your daughter, or your spouse as leverage to compel you to plead guilty to a crime you did not commit.

the prosecutorial proceedings. For example, before my trial, 15 ex-employees and 2 ex-business partners were interviewed by prosecutors. During my one-month trial, the same number of ex-employees and ex-partners testified for the government. Following my trial, but before sentencing, my ex-wife was contacted by federal probation officers who were in the process of preparing my Presentence Investigation Report (aka "PSI" or "PSR") for my sentencing judge's consideration. Of course, I did not learn that the probation office contacted my ex-wife until *long after* they had already done so. Fortunately, no further harm was done. But one slip—just one strand of vengeance in the heart of my ex-wife—could have buried me even deeper into the bowels of federal prison.

Facing Your New Reality

Surely by now you should have a fairly solid indication from your court proceedings and from your attorney as to where your fate lies. Prison time or no prison time. Which is it? If you managed to escape prison time, congratulations! Now quickly email your attorney's name to us. If you are headed to prison, however, keep your attorney's name to yourself. Now let's move on . . .

As you prepare to face your new reality, I cannot stress the utmost importance of properly and sufficiently winding down your affairs as though you were an enlisted soldier—and a civilian business owner—who has recently received his orders to deploy overseas. You would likely think, of course, that a business owner, or one with substantial holdings of sorts, would naturally make provision for his or her departure. However, there must be other overarching considerations that even a soldier facing deployment need not worry about:

1. he's not a convicted felon,
2. he's not a federal prisoner-to-be who has lost most of his Constitutional Rights, and,
3. he will not be restricted or punished for calling home offering guidance and direction towards running his business.

For these reasons, we offer the following suggestions, along with grievous lessons we have learned as business owners who assumed far too much about what we "thought" we could do, or get away with, while in federal prison.

Loose Documents: Upon facing a term of imprisonment, every business document I had signed or co-signed 5 years prior to my indictment was put to the test. No stone, as is said, was left unturned. From my Articles of Incorporation to my Last Will and Testament, every deal and every document was scrutinized ad nauseam by federal prosecutors. Every one. And according to the government, every document was either a sham, or, by its nature was an indictable offense. Keep in mind, by the way, I had chosen to go to trial in lieu of accepting a plea bargain and accepting guilt. Point being is that had I accepted an early, easy-for-the-government plea bargain, my business documents would not have received such prosecutorial and investigative scrutiny. Bottom line, prosecutors can twist any business deal or document into a criminal offense at will. And I mean ***any*** document.

For these reasons I propose the following questions:

1. Are your foundational business documents (i.e. sole proprietorship, partnership, or corporate—*especially corporate*—documents) valid, properly recorded, and up to date? If not, you're at risk of facing another criminal offense.

2. Are your professional or vocational licenses and permits valid and in good standing? If not, you're at risk of facing another criminal offense.

3. Are your taxes—both personally and businesswise—paid in full? Or if your taxes are unpaid, have you been granted an official extension of time in which to pay? If the answer is "no" to either question, you are at risk of facing another criminal offense.

4. What about your banking records, such as your loan applications, loan renewal applications, corporate resolutions to borrow, financial statements, submitted tax returns, and appraisals? Do they all coincide? Do your numbers on your banking documentation tally with the "real" numbers found inside the file cabinets at your office? If not—well, you get the picture.

Problem is, whatever was done is done. You certainly cannot go back and change the fact that you might have "fudged" the figures somewhere along the way. Attempting to alter or correct a document to avoid prosecution only leads to more aggressive prosecution and even stiffer criminal penalties.

In the alternative, inform your attorney should there be a series of improprieties in your business or personal documents, especially if you are determined to go to trial. Because the absolute last thing you want is for government investigators to start down a paper trail and uncover certain improprieties of which your attorney is not aware. Should you make such an error in judgement, you only strengthen the government's position. Plus you increase the possibility of serving a much longer prison sentence.

Going To Prison With Insurance: What active insurance policies do you currently have in place? Business and personal? Life, health, or casualty? Perhaps all of the above? And do you plan on maintaining your insurance coverage through the duration of your term of imprisonment? If so, I advise you notify your insurance agent and inform him of your imprisonment (in the best possible light, mind you) prior to the commencement of your prison sentence. Here's why. All insurance policies include "Materiality Clauses" and/or "Exclusionary Clauses" that, in essence, may relieve the insurance company of any and all liability should you, the policy holder:

1. Suffer a criminal conviction,

2. Engage in conduct that exposes you or your insurance company to adverse, above-average risk, such as sky diving, mountain climbing, whale riding, and the like,

3. Permit a change in, or a transfer of, ownership or control of your business, or,

4. Permit any other material changes that are defined in the insurance policy's subsection pertaining to "denial of coverage."

By notifying your insurance agent of your legal situation, and, of course, continuing to pay your requisite premium, you shift the responsibility to them. In other words, pursuant to the "notices" subsection of your master policy, your policy remains in full force and effect since your agent was duly informed by phone (and hopefully by certified mail)—and continues to accept your predetermined premium payments.

Usually, however, an insurance underwriter or examiner will forthrightly respond, informing you of their position on your material change.

Unfortunately for me, I failed to notify my insurance companies following my conviction, and even after being sentenced to federal prison. "*Why bother?*" I thought, "*so long as I am paying my premiums, I'm covered. So all is well and good.*" Truth is, I could not have been more wrong.

I learned that even though I continued to meet my monthly and annual premium obligations (while serving time in prison), I was, by contract law, not covered by my insurance companies. For 23 months I gave away premium installments—that is, until my wife filed a business insurance claim for inventory that was damaged during transport.

Within days following the filing of our claim, the insurance company wrote back, denying payment on the claim on the grounds of a "material breach" due to my failure to notify them when I, one of the business's principal owners, "had been convicted of a federal criminal offense, which incapacitated a principal owner and operator of the insured business."

Yet when we then demanded the refund of the 23 months of premiums, my wife and I were advised, in relevant part, that, " . . . although the claimant forfeited coverage for operational and personal property segments of [the business], general liability coverage had remained in effect for the 23 months in question . . . therefore a refund is not warranted . . . "

A week later my wife received an official cancellation notice, along with a check for the reimbursement of the single 24th premium installment.

Following that debacle, we carefully examined two additional policies from a different national insurance carrier. Hence the policies contained the same twisted legal language.

And yes, as you might have guessed, we cancelled.

One month later we repurchased business insurance coverage from a different company. This time, however, my name was removed from the business and my wife and daughter were named as principals.

So here's the lesson: Insurance companies will sit back and allow you to ostensibly breach the policy contract, but say nothing. So long as the premiums continue to flow in with regularity. Yet the moment a substantial claim is filed, let the games begin.

Active Agreements By Contract: Do you still have an active business? If so, what is your business's legal structure? And how does going to prison materially alter that legal structure?

Below are a few presentencing challenges I experienced for your presentencing consideration:

1. Sole Proprietor: This, of course, is the simplest, cleanest legal structure for a business if you must serve some time in prison. However, certain creditors—especially secured creditors—could be problematic due to specific language contained in the creditor's security agreement regarding your death or incapacitation. For this and other business preservation reasons, take an inventory of your time-

sensitive, specific-performance (hereafter referred to as "TSSP" documents) and closely examine any and all performance and covenant clauses that detail your responsibilities to the creditor. Following your assessment, should you deem the clauses overly restrictive or punitive (as a result of your absence), you should consider (1) closing the account, (2) transferring your business to a trusted family member, or, (3) notifying the creditor, in writing, of your leave of absence; and in your notice, include the name and contact information of the person(s) who are operating the business in your stead.

2. Partnerships: Here, you have two primary contractual issues with which to contend. First, the agreement between you and your partners. Second, the agreements between the partnership and its principal creditors. Even though most well-written partnership agreements include clauses pertaining to a partner's "incapacitation," with remedies addressing the incapacitated partner's lack of legal, physical, or intellectual abilities, many of us federal prisoners still own businesses. Thriving businesses I might add. But while in prison we are strictly prohibited from running the business, be it by phone (which is monitored) or by mail (which is opened and screened). Moreover, prisoners lack the legal and physical capacity to enter into or prosecute a free-market contract. Additionally, prisoners lack the legal and physical capacity to renegotiate pre-existing contracts established prior to entering prison. As such, if you are a partner in a business, you may want to consider the following measures before you begin serving your prison sentence: (1) Write a certified

letter to, and later meet with, each of your partners, informing them of your legal situation along with the possibility of what your time-in-prison exposure is, and, (2) In your letter, and during your meeting, make mention of the incapacitation (or similarly situated) clause(s), and how you would appreciate the partners' waiver of the incapacitation clause(s) along with the appropriate amendment to your partnership agreement.

3. Corporations: As the owner and an officer of a business that is a private, closely-held corporation, you may wish to consider the following recommendations should prison time appear inevitable: (1) Maintain your ownership, but resign as an officer of the company. Of course, upon resigning, follow the appropriate corporate protocols to ensure a clean transition, or, (2) maintain your ownership, but take a leave of absence if your prison exposure is a relatively short sentence. Whatever your decision, the worst decision is to do nothing—as in going off to prison and leaving your name on corporate documents as if nothing has happened. In essence, from the day you go to prison, each act that the corporation engages could be illegal, simply because the corporation has not duly notified the Secretary of State or the Department of Corporations (or the equivalent agencies) of a "material change" in its corporate structure. What change? One of the corporation's officers and/or directors has been convicted of a federal crime and is serving time in prison. Hence, the corporation, by operation of law, has no standing, which means everything your company is doing and has done since

your conviction is invalid and illegal. Now you—and whomever is running your company—may face an entirely new strand of felony conspiracy offenses.

Think Flexibility, Think Liquidity

One of the most difficult realities to face while awaiting your sentencing date is having to get rid of your "stuff." Rich or poor, young or old, we all have our attachments, our keepsakes, our prize possessions—all of which we generally refer to as "our stuff." Some stuff we store away, some stuff we entrust to others until we are released from prison.

Well, in case you haven't heard, here's your new reality. Unless you are wealthy enough to hire a staff of bonded overseers for your stuff, most, if not all of it, will be pilfered away by those with whom you left it. Point being, when you go to prison, people know—family included—that you have no power to do anything about it. Not that day anyway. Everyone is well aware that you control nothing, all of which becomes painfully evident to you once you are actually in prison.

So my advice is to sell your stuff and start anew upon your release from prison. Save yourself the grief and anguish. More importantly, save your relationships. Sell your stuff and get liquid, for liquidity offers you more flexibility, independence, and peace of mind while you serve out your sentence.

Consider my story: Not only did I have two homes that were filled with stuff, but I also had three storage facilities and a small 2000 square foot warehouse that was also filled with stuff valued at over $320,000. That was just the warehouse! There were automobiles, jet skis, artwork, antique furnishings; the list goes on and on. Making matters worse, I continued to pay storage fees for almost three years into my prison sentence in an attempt to hold on to my stuff.

Ultimately everything was sold for pennies on the dollar by my now ex-wife who kept all those pennies-on-the-dollar.

Seriously, how does one who is schooled in the law and trained up to be a CEO make such a juvenile error in judgment? Denial is the answer. Blinding denial, yes, even though I was at the pre-sentencing stage, I suffered from an asinine illusion that someone would realize that I was a harmless little fuzz ball, a really good guy, and thus I would not "really" go to prison per se, but sentenced to a more rational place like home confinement. So I refused to part with my stuff.

Well guess what? That was 15 years ago. And I am still in federal prison—completely stuff-less.

So look, get rid of your stuff while there is time to do so in an orderly and equitable fashion. You can always get more stuff. Besides, there is no way of getting a fraction of a fair price for your stuff when you are trying to fire sell it while sitting inside a prison somewhere. My advice is this: think flexibility, and get liquid fast.

Pre-Sentencing Documentation: Curse or Blessing?

The answer is both. First a curse. But later comes a blessing. Permit me to explain.

From first-hand experience, I know the last thing you want to talk (or read) about is the retrieval and organization of your presentencing documents from the court and especially from your attorney. And yes, if you are reading this Survival-Chapter Subsection during the presentencing stage of your legal proceedings, while still uncertain of your fate, I know your grief. But your freedom, your rights, and, perhaps, the restoration of your good name rest principally on the timely collection and preservation of your presentencing documents.

How so? Constitutional errors made in your case by federal investigators, federal prosecutors, your own defense attorney, the judge, or a combination of these noted actors. Problem is, any constitutional errors made will not be discovered until long after you are sentenced. So other than a direct appeal—provided you didn't waive it when you knuckled under to a plea agreement—there is nothing you can do right now.

However, oftentimes such mistakes are uncovered by a pair of fresh, objective, and post-conviction legal eyes as someone inspects your presentencing documents that are hopefully in your possession.

Conversely, let's take the position that you've ignored my suggestion of collecting your presentencing documents while you are currently able to do so. Then six months, one year, or three years down the road, while sitting in prison, a circuit court or Supreme Court ruling is made on someone else's case with exact or similar convictable components as were in your case. Say this someone else's case is overturned. Now you thrust into action to reclaim your freedom. So you contact your defense attorney who represented you back then. Now you desperately need your documents. But the attorney has died, or moved, or simply will not take your calls because you're old news. Now you're stuck. Stuck without documents. Stuck with a bad rap. Stuck in prison.

How do you get your hands on your case file documents? Why chance this scenario happening to you? With this unacceptable scenario in mind, let's discuss these essential documents, their purposes, and other important nuances you may find instructive. We will discuss these documents in their natural order of progression:

1. The Indictment: This is the document that will change your life forever. It is the government's charging document that accused you of committing one or more federal offenses. Perhaps the indictment named only you. Or perhaps it named you along with others whom the government referred to as "co-

conspirators," or as "aiders and abettors." Whatever the instance, keep a copy of the indictment in safe keeping for future reference. Following your indictment, you either secured private defense counsel, or you were appointed the services of the federal defender's office.

2. Journal/Retainer Agreement: In Chapter One, I offered "Advice About Criminal Lawyers" wherein I stated, in relevant part, ". . . it is critical that from the beginning you document everything between you and your attorney, as if it were a journal . . ." after all; your life, liberty, and freedom are (or were) under frontal assault by federal prosecutors. Maintaining a journal (in addition to copies of letters and email messages) is your first line of defense. My principal point here, however, is the document called a Retainer Agreement. I trust you were prescient enough to insist on having a signed retainer before writing that check to defense counsel. In fact, through the retainer agreement, you would have a back-up journal, so to speak, of your attorney's actions (or inactions) through his or her billing records. Billing records are essential should it later become suspect that your attorney's representation fell below the constitutional standard of professional responsibility. Therefore when fresh, post-conviction legal eyes are examining and reconstructing your case a year or two after the dust settles, you can produce your journal, your retainer agreement, and your detailed billing records that will greatly aide in your post-conviction defense.

3. Trial Transcripts: If you went to trial, be it by judge or by jury, a court reporter was present, documenting every word spoken by and between

every party involved in the trial. Consistent with my earlier "docket sheet" advice to you, the court itself maintains a detailed account of every matter that comes before it. Why? To protect itself against you should you later claim (by way of an appeal) that the court abused its power or discretion when presiding over your trial. In like manner, the court's detailed account of every matter could also become *your* detailed account of every matter. Difference is, you're required to go through your attorney in order to acquire these most-important documents, including a copy of your trial transcripts. Believe me, you'll need them.

4. Presentence Investigation Report (aka "PSR" or "PSI"): Whether you went to trial or whether you opted to knuckle under to a plea agreement, the formal proceedings are over. If you went to trial and were acquitted, congratulations. But if you were found guilty, or if you accepted a plea agreement, the judge ordered the federal probation office to prepare what is referred to as "The Holy Grail" of all court documents: The Presentence Investigation Report. Yes, your PSR is considered "The Holy Grail" as far as the judicial system is concerned. But to the accused, the convicted—to you and me—the PSR is synonymous with the Scarlet Letter. One of the investigative components of the report itself begins with an interview with you in the presence of your attorney. Without fail, the PSR report is written with the clear intent of placing you in the worst possible light. For it is written by a probation officer, but ostensibly edited by the prosecutor with the intent of inflicting the greatest possible pain and punishment

on you at time of sentencing. Prior to sentencing, however, you're given 72-hours' time to review an unofficial copy of your PSR. At that time, you and your attorney are to make corrections, as well as preparing written objections to errors and gross exaggerations, which is often the case. In any event, secure a copy of the final draft of the probation officer's PSR, along with a copy of your attorney's written objections. (**Note**: There is much more to discuss about the all-important PSR that is inappropriate for this section.

5. Judgement And Commitment Documentation: Usually within 30 days following your sentencing, your sentencing court will file its Judgement and Commitment (J & C) Documents with the Clerk of the Court. The Judgement and Commitment is the court's official decree and disposition regarding your legal fate. The J & C primarily decrees the terms and conditions of your sentence, the terms of your supervised release (or probation), your restitution, court assessments, fines, and any special restrictions that the court may deem appropriate. Once the J & C is filed with the Clerk of the Court, certified copies are then forwarded to the probation office, the U.S. Attorney's Office, the U.S. Marshal's Office, the Bureau of Prisons (if you were sentenced to a term of imprisonment), and to your attorney. With this in mind, I would recommend you inform your attorney of your desire to have a copy of your J & C immediately following your sentencing proceeding. Then follow up with your attorney to secure your own copy. Most important.

6. Direct Appeal: At this juncture of your legal proceedings, jurisdiction has changed. Jurisdiction of your case (or your direct appeal, should you be eligible) would shift from the District Court level (or the lower court) to the Circuit Court (or the higher court) level. In other words, your case—by operation of law—is removed from the hands of the District Court and placed into the hands of the Circuit Court. Your direct appeal, however, could be prepared by your original attorney or by a different attorney who specializes in appellate work. In any event, follow up with whomever prepares your direct appeal and insist on a copy of the following: (a) your direct appeal, (b) the government's response to your direct appeal, and, (c) a copy of your traverse, which is your rebuttal to any of the government's responses that opposes your direct appeal's points of contention.

7. Docket Sheet: The docket sheet is the official yet abbreviated district court journal that records every hearing, every motion, and every proceeding that comes before it. As such, the docket sheet provides a detailed overview of everything the court (not your attorney) received, acted on, and filed—as its own paper trail—as they relate to your case. With that in mind, you should insist on a copy of your docket sheet from your attorney or simply visit the criminal court clerk's office with your name and case number and request a copy.

In conclusion of this subsection, let me attempt to make myself emphatically clear when you're dealing with criminal defense lawyers: If you fail to make your expectations of him or her crystal clear, in writing, in the attorney's retainer agreement, *before* you pay them, you're screwed. There's no other way to put it. Screwed! And no, it does not matter that you paid the attorney $50,000, $100,000, or even $200,000. It does not matter if they're the biggest, most prestigious law firm in America. No detailed retainer agreement, you're setting yourself up to get royally screwed. This is what experience has taught me (Consult Chapter One for more information on retainer agreements).

Beware Of Time-Sensitive, Specific-Performance ("TSSP's") Documents

What are TSSP's? Simple answer, they are negotiable instruments. Documents of value you hold as evidence that a debt or other consideration is owed to you, which, by law, would make you the holder in due course of the TSSP's.

For example, a TSSP document could be a promissory note, a bank's certificate of deposit, a lease or a rental contract, a UCC-1 Financing Statement, a check, etc. Some TSSP's are secured, others are unsecured. Bottom line, I am referring to money owed to you—and will continue to be owed to you during the term of your prison sentence. I am referring to a lump sum or installment payments due to you as evidenced by a valid, enforceable contract.

Many of us business types seldom, if ever, give much thought to the number of TSSP's we have outstanding at any given time, especially when we're free to roam the world. Unfortunately for you, however, your freedom card, so to speak, is about to be (or has been) revoked. Until then, I urge you to be proactive. Not reactive as most of us were. Get your affairs in order now.

Consider my situation: When I initially entered prison, I had a small, but thriving consultancy. And with my consultancy remained scores of TSSP documents just dangling in the wind upon my departure to prison.

This begs the question: Why? Why would I leave my TSSP documents open and active as I did? What was I thinking? Answer: I ***was not*** thinking . . . because I was a blind ding-bat—blind with denial. Yes, denial was the cause of my ignoring the inevitable fate of my having to face federal prison, and of having to leave my precious family and my thriving consultancy behind. And then at times I would think: "No need of rocking the boat. Leave everything in play until the TSSP documents expire. Or I'll renew then while in prison."

Well . . . foiled again.

Problem was, when I arrived at my prison designation, I was informed, in no uncertain terms, that operating a business from prison was strictly prohibited. However, upon further investigation into the matter, I learned of a stipulation in the Bureau of Prisons' Policy Statement[8] that permits an inmate "to assist" with maintaining his or her lawful assets by "advising or consulting" with family members, or with your attorneys-in-fact (those who hold your power of attorney or a licensed attorney.

Given this stipulation, I recommend the following strategies for your consideration before you commence serving your sentence:

If You Are The Bearer Of Negotiable Instruments: I recommend you *not* engage your wife or close family members in the administration of, and the collection efforts towards, your negotiable instruments; namely, promissory notes, deeds of trust, assignment of rents, UCC-1 Financing Statements, etc. Why? Because, as mentioned earlier, should the debtor or obligee learn of your imprisonment, you

[8]It's well known by the Bureau that many of its federal prisoners have existing businesses; and, in many cases, substantial assets that were not subject to his or her criminal proceedings. Therefore, in the instance when an inmate finds the need to consult with a family member, a business partner, employee, or the trustee to his trust to preserve or protect his assets, he may do so, provided the inmate is merely "counseling" these individuals and not "directing" these individuals in the running of a business (Source: BOP Policy Statement No. 5381.04 entitled "Inmate Organizations").

can rest assured that payments to you will become less of a priority to the obligee and thus those payments would likely cease flowing in altogether. I have experienced this behavior from my obligees in the past, in that such behavior is similar to the mortgage meltdown phenomenon that recently swept across our country: many people who were perfectly able to pay their mortgages simply stopped paying them just to see what would happen. I call it "piling on" due to a wave of bad news. Unfortunately, good people go bad rather quickly when they learn of others' misfortunes.

Be that as it may, if you are prescient enough to hire a professional, or a third-party representative, such as an accountant, a property manager, or a business attorney to act in your stead, you would be ahead of the piling-on curve. A paid professional will keep your obligees on the straight and narrow, regardless of your whereabouts. As an added benefit, the professional can forward reports to you regarding your projects' performances while you are serving your prison sentence. Plus, when deemed necessary, your professional can visit you in prison at will. Additionally, if you have an attorney on your payroll, he or she may have "special attorney-client visits" with you should you be so inclined.

Point being, when a prison sentence is inevitable, you should not leave anything to chance where your TSSP documents are concerned.

Pending Traffic, Civil, And Family Law Matters

As this chapter prepares you for sentencing, I ask: What legal livewires have you left dangling in the winds of chance? Are there any law-enforcement wants and warrants anywhere in the country with your name on them? How about civil actions against you? Or are you going through a divorce? Let's address them one-by-one and discover the adverse effects these matters might have on you while you serve your prison sentence.

Pending Traffic Warrants: Of course it is always wise to satisfy any pending motor vehicle violations before you begin serving your prison sentence. But don't panic if for some reason you are unable to do so.

Oftentimes it serves to your financial and judicial benefit to actually wait until you are at your final prison designation before challenging your pending traffic warrants. I know that sounds crazy, but allow me to explain. For starters, judicial economy, which translates as follows: the state doesn't want to spend its precious and very limited resources on sending two officers to pull you out of federal custody and bring you to court to answer minor legal infractions, such as traffic tickets or other minor misdemeanors.

Therefore, for purposes of judicial economy, coupled with your Fourteenth Amendment right to a speedy trial, the state routinely dismisses minor offenses when properly challenged by you—the defendant—who is incarcerated in federal custody. In fact, there are specific state statutes specifically available to federal prisoners who wish to challenge state violations in general. And these state statutes and requisite state pleading forms are well known by inmate law clerks throughout the federal prison system nationwide.

With that, the state invariably dismisses traffic infractions within 60 to 90 days following your challenge. I have witnessed hundreds of dismissals over the span of my many years of incarceration, without costing the defendant anything more than photocopies and postage.

That said, I leave you with this warning: Challenge all state violations *shortly after* your arrival in prison. *Do not wait until near the end* of your sentence. For I have also witnessed scores of inmates remain in prison past their release date due to a lingering state infraction that the prison staff discovered shortly before the inmate was scheduled to be released to the halfway house. So take heed.

Pending Civil Matters: Are you currently in the midst of being sued in state or federal court, or are you in the process of suing someone? In either case, avoid, settle, or defer all civil actions until you are released from prison. But if getting sued or having to sue someone cannot be avoided, please hire a lawyer to advocate for you. Here's why: First, federal prisoners are not exempt from being sued civilly, nor are federal prisoners granted much latitude by a state or federal judge on civil proceedings simply because he or she is in prison. In fact, my experience is judges do not really give a rip about your being in prison, primarily because there are little to no Constitutional Rights that are subject to violation when adjudicating garden-variety civil matters. So if you lose your civil case out of ignorance or by default, too bad. You'll just have a judgement debt waiting for you when you get out of prison.

Second, federal prison law libraries are not required to stock a single law book pertaining to state law and civil procedures whatsoever. Therefore, you would have absolutely no way to defend or prosecute a civil case on your own. In short, you are rendered helpless, that is, unless you can hire a lawyer—or better yet, put it off (provided the statute of limitation permits) until your eventual release from prison.

Pending Family Law Matters: Here we will focus on two areas of family law that weigh heaviest on a prisoner's heart: 1) receiving a divorce while in prison, and, 2) losing his or her children to adoption (or foster home through Child Protective Services if both parents are subject to incarceration). Let's examine both scenarios:

Divorce Proceeding: Much the same as civil matters, divorce proceedings are of little difference when compared to the court's attitude toward federal prisoners: they don't give a rip. However, when there are children involved, the court yields to what it deems to be in the best interest of the children. But the proceeding itself? It's just another case number to the judge. To you, however, it could mean everything if there are significant community assets in the marriage. If so, hire a divorce lawyer without delay, because as it relates to civil matters, federal prison libraries are not required to carry family law books for all fifty states. So you would be completely and utterly helpless without a family law specialist.

Conversely, if you have a no-asset marriage (or very little in assets) it is probably best you not contest your spouse. For peace of mind while in prison, let it go. Trust me, I have been through the divorce-in-prison bit. It is not worth the grief and mental anguish. Let it go and be done with it. Or you can let it consume you as though it were a malignant form of cancer.

Losing A Child To Adoption: Now it gets rather precarious for the court, in that there are Constitutional Rights of the biological mother and father (regardless of prison status), and Constitutional Rights of the minor children—each of which are at stake. Therefore, the court proceeds with extreme caution, beginning first by making sure both parents and the minor child are represented by separate counsel, especially the incarcerated parent who is at risk of losing his or her parental rights to adoption. Accordingly, if the incarcerated parent cannot afford an attorney for such proceedings, the court will appoint one, so long as the incarcerated parent contests the adoption in a lawful and timely manner.

As such, should you be exposed to the threat of adoption while in prison, and you do not want to lose your children to adoption, your best pre-emptive method for blocking an adoption is indisputable documentation evidencing your past and present involvement in your child(ren)'s lives. For example, records of child support payments, or receipts for educational or medical expenditures; or even birthday parties and Holiday expenditures. Such documentation from you demonstrates your unyielding love, support, and the over-arching dedication to the welfare of your child(ren).

The bottom line here is if you are served with adoption papers while in prison, and you cannot afford an attorney, here is what you should do: 1) Go to the prison law library and immediately explain your situation to one of the inmate prison law clerks. As a fellow prisoner (who likely has children of his or her own), he or she will find the help you need. The key, however, is a timely and properly documented response once you are served with legal papers. So do not delay! 2) Notify your family. Have them prepare a "care package" of items such as the above-mentioned documentation, character letters from family and friends regarding your historical display of interest in your child(ren), and, 3) A well-written letter to the court—strongly—yet respectfully—objecting to the adoption; and in that letter, request the appointment of counsel in order to protect your parental and other relevant Constitutional Rights.

Pre-sentence Investigation Report (aka "PSI" or "PSR")

More about your Presentence Investigation Report. Much More.

From the onset, let me preface this subsection with this warning: Beware of the PSR. As stated in the above section entitled "Presentencing Documentation, Item 4, the PSR is ordered into existence by your sentencing judge immediately following your conviction, which means weeks, if not months, before you are actually sentenced. During this interim period, mind you, an appointed federal probation officer begins her investigation into your character and background. To begin, she first notifies the U.S. Attorney's Office (which is likely in the same federal building where the probation office is located) where your prosecutor works. She is then briefed by the prosecutor on how extraordinarily awful and heinous you are. And then she's offered the prosecutor's work-product file from which your PSR will be framed and ultimately drafted for the judge, and ultimately for the Bureau of Prisons should prison be your designation. Put another way, your PSR will be written by a probation officer whose mind was colored by a government prosecutor—and this is *before* your formal interview with the probation officer. With that in mind, I urge you to beware of 5 things:

1. Beware Of Being Excluded: During the interim period between your conviction and your actual sentencing date, the probation officer will request an interview with you (provided you are still free on bail) through your attorney. Following your attorney-supervised interview, a draft copy of your PSR will be provided to your attorney. But defense attorneys routinely exclude you from the draft-reviewing process. Why would an advocating attorney exclude his or her client from the PSR-draft process? Because it's too much of a hassle to involve you in the process. You might make the attorney work too hard with all of your objections to the errors and exaggerations discovered in the draft. So the attorney takes it upon him- or herself to contest the errors and exaggerations on your behalf. Problem is, how could that be possible? Sure, your attorney will catch some of the inaccuracies, but not as many as you would catch. Therefore, I encourage that you "not" be excluded from reviewing the unofficial draft form of your PSR. After all, it's you who would have to live with the PSR's final content. Not your lawyer.

2. Beware Of Errors And Exaggerations: I touched on errors and exaggerations above. Now, however, let's examine the deeper, more dangerous reasons why errors and exaggerations must be nipped-in-the-bud at once. Your PSR—once made official—in essence becomes the holy grail to the Federal Bureau of Prisons and to future law enforcement agencies should you encounter legal problems long after your

present legal situation has passed. And as for federal prison, mistakes and exaggerations come with a steep price. Say, for example, the probation officer spoke to your ex-wife during the course of the probation officer's investigation. During their conversation, your jilted ex-wife makes a false statement by claiming you beat her during a heated argument years ago. But there was no complaint filed with the police. So there's no evidence from which to draw a conclusion. Yet still, the false allegation makes it onto your official PSR. As a result, you will never be designated to a minimum-security federal prison camp where there are no razor-wire fences. Instead you would be arbitrarily classified as "violent" and thus you'd be designated to a fenced-in, higher-security federal prison. Yes, just one oversight in your PSR could be extremely costly—with no legal standing to correct or contest the ex-wife's falsehood. Get the picture? Your PSR is the sole collection of data upon which every correctional decision is made, decisions that seldom, if ever, play out in your favor.

3. Beware Of The Internet: Following a criminal conviction, your life—including wants, warrants, warts and all else—becomes an open book. And although your PSR itself is not web-available, most of the information contained in your PSR could be obtained from the government by way of the Freedom of Information Act ("FOIA") request. Once the information about you is made available to the FOIA-requesting party, voilà, it's on the internet—accurate or not. And know this: prisoners' families have access to the internet, too. So if you are a government informant—accurate or not—inquiring

prisoners will know. In fact, anything about you—accurate or not—prisoners will know. So it behooves you to do your level best to fight with vigilance towards the accuracy of your Presentence Report before it becomes etched in stone.

4. Beware Of Probation Officers: In Beware Number 1 above, I vaguely touched on how "the probation officer will request an interview with you through your attorney." And yet I did not touch on the why and the how such an interview plays an essential role in mitigating or exacerbating the anguish associated with doing time in federal prison. First the why: As part of your Constitutional Right to Due Process, an attorney-supervised interview with an investigating probation officer is required because the criminal proceeding (which means anything you say could be incriminating) is still in process. You are still live bait for government prosecutors. For that reason alone you should never engage the presentence investigation probation officer without your attorney being present. For one slip of the tongue could instantly result in an "upward departure" (more years in prison) or designation to a higher-security prison facility. Second, the how: How does the interview mitigate or exacerbate your anguish associated with doing time in prison? As for mitigating your anguish, let's say, for instance, you had a substance abuse problem during the 12 month period leading up to your conviction, be it alcohol or drug abuse. When properly revealed to the probation officer, you could be eligible for the prison's Residential Drug Abuse Program (RDAP), which could reduce your prison sentence by one year. Of course the probation officer

would never know this nor would your attorney know to the fullest extent. Only the prison will know upon your arrival, during your orientation process (more on the prison's RDAP program in Chapter Four). Conversely, you can exacerbate your anguish by, for instance, over-exaggerating a medical condition you might have, resulting in being designated to some prison medical facility three thousand miles away from your home, friends and family.

5. Beware Of The 72-Hour Rule: By law you are supposed to have a copy of your "unofficial" PSI report 72-hours (three days) before you are to be sentenced; and it is your attorney's duty to ensure that you receive it accordingly. But beware. Many attorneys are overbooked and overworked, meaning you will likely receive a copy of your own official PSI report one day before, or, worse yet, on the day of sentencing. Knowing what you know now, do you not see the danger of such a delay? If you overlook an error or exaggeration made by a probation officer, you own it. That is why the law gives you 72-hours in which to review your PSI report. Even still the law goes farther. The sentencing judge must—absolutely must—*ask you in open court*, "Have you had an opportunity to review and discuss the PSI report with your attorney?" If you answer "Yes, Your Honor," the PSI report goes from being "unofficial" to "official." In other words, you now own it. Every word of it. But if you answer "no," the judge will halt the proceedings and inquire into your concerns. But until you say "yes" the PSI report remains unofficial. To avoid this problem from occurring in the first place, insist on reviewing your PSI report for a full three days *before sentencing*. And should you discover an error or exaggeration, do not ask, but ***demand*** of your attorney that it be removed or corrected.

6. Beware of Prison Officials: Due to the sensitive nature of PSI reports, the Federal Bureau of Prisons prohibits you from possessing PSI reports while in prison. However, you would be allowed to examine the prison's central-file copy of your report should the need arise. So receiving an actual copy from your central file, or even from your attorney, is strictly prohibited.

For the foregoing reasons, you want to arrange for your attorney to make an official copy of your PSI report available to you for safekeeping at home. Then, should a legal challenge arise later on, you will have an official copy of your PSI at home ready to aid in your cause.

Hire A Private Firm To Prepare Your PSI Report

If you possess the financial means to do so, discuss with your attorney the possibility of hiring a reputable investigation firm to produce your PSI report. An independent report could be prepared in conjunction with the PSI report being prepared by the probation department. The purpose? To level the playing field. Consider this: the probation officer's report is always written with a serious slant toward the government's position of making you look like the spawn of Satan. Why? Because they (probation officers) are working from the prosecutor's file—with a prosecutor's point of view. Conversely, a private firm would write a report with a slant toward you. Now, with both reports, the sentencing judge will have balance, if you will, from which he could draw in order to arrive at a fair and equitable sentencing decision for you. Of course, judges' opinions and views on privately prepared PSI's are often unfavorable, but the privately prepared PSI must be considered.

In the least, you should mention this strategy to your attorney, but do so *immediately after conviction* so he has time to secure a qualified investigator should he concur. But whatever you decide, do not allow your attorney to flatly disregard this strategy without giving you a compelling reason for doing so. Do not roll over simply because he's your lawyer!

Pre-Existing Medical Conditions

For the last 15 years, I have been under the care of the Federal Bureau of Prisons' medical care. And, naturally, I have witnessed how the Bureau administers medical care to a broad spectrum of medical conditions of ailing inmates. But first, I need to make this dual disclaimer: 1) Blessedly speaking, I do not have, nor have I ever suffered from, a serious medical condition while in prison. Instead, my medical ailments have been considered garden-variety, i.e. moderate hypertension, high cholesterol, losing teeth, etc. Otherwise I'm in good health; 2) Even though I am a federal prisoner, I have no gripe, per se, with the government, in spite of its many faults. That said, I believe my assessment and advice are fair and objective.

So here is my objective assessment: Medical care in federal prison is tantamount to receiving healthcare in a socialized country. But for a heart attack, a stroke, or an injury from some sort of prison violence, work-related accident, or a sporting accident, there are long waits, long lines, no choices, and no one else (private doctor) is permitted to help you; and, of course, it is all paid for by taxpayers. Keep in mind, this is not Kaiser Medical, this is prison.

If you have a pre-existing medical condition that warrants special attention or special medication, be prepared to do battle with the government. Why? Because "special" needs demand more resources, and more resources cost more money per prisoner.

So here is what you must do to prepare yourself for a potential battle with the government—via the prison—should you insist on receiving better-than-substandard medications and treatment while in prison:

1. *Early Preparation Before Sentencing*: Following your conviction and *well before you are sentenced*, have your attorney contact your personal physician and request a physician's letter pertaining to your medical condition and requisite treatment be incorporated into your PSI report. The letter should be written with great specificity relating to your condition and the doctor's recommended ongoing treatment. With that, the letter from your physician becomes an exhibit to your PSI report, which follows you into and out of prison. It is not a silver bullet mind you, but it makes denying your specified treatment more difficult for prison officials. There is, however, one caveat I alluded to earlier when discussing your PSI report: **Your medical condition directly affects where you will be designated, which could be quite a distance from your home and family**. So it is very important to keep that potential trade-off in mind when strategizing with your attorney.

2. *Articulate Your Medical Condition(s) As You Would With Your Doctor*: It is all too common for medical staff at the prison to downplay the seriousness of your medical condition. On the other hand, embittered inmates often exaggerated the seriousness of their medical conditions also—to the point of grossly abusing and overburdening the system because it is free to them. I have witnessed both extremes.

   The great equalizer, however, is your ability to articulate your condition(s) to the prison's medical staff when being interviewed during medical orientation. It helps to show that you are extraordinarily informed pertaining to your condition(s) by articulating medically and clinically-based information when challenged. Avoid arguing your case with Internet pseudoscience or non-clinical herbal concoctions (even though they might work). That could discredit your argument. Stick with hard science consistent with the Physician's Desk Reference. More important, knowing such information on command is also helpful should you need to seek administrative remedies or even legal action against the BOP.

3. *Surrendering With Medical Devices And Equipment*: Herein lays another important reason why a letter from your physician detailing your medical condition *and* the equipment needed to assist you with the quality of your daily life is suggested. The Federal Bureau of Prison's inmate receiving policy prohibits the introduction of certain medical equipment, such as canes, walkers, wheelchairs, crutches, etc. into its facilities. All equipment deemed medically necessary by the prison staff will be provided from inside the prison. No exceptions.

But non-equipment related aids, such as eyeglasses, dentures, prosthetics, etc. (considered as "extensions of the body") are permitted, so long as the value (for items such as glasses) are not excessive or could be used as a weapon. Otherwise, it will be confiscated or ordered mailed home upon your arrival.

Establish Fine And Restitution Payments At Sentencing

Interesting how many dangling live wires are left hanging, hot and deadly, following your sentencing proceedings, only to then wrap around your neck once you are in prison. Fines and restitution are ideal examples of such live wires, if left without a clearly defined payment schedule, the prison staff will gladly initiate a payment schedule for you. And believe me, you do not want to give prison officials any more power over you than necessary. Here's why.

Because they will use it. Then they will punish you. So before you are sentenced, make sure your attorney is aware of, or seeks to secure, the following payment plans during your sentencing proceeding:

1. *Payment Schedule Plan "A"*: First, as part of your sentencing, seek a court order deferring both your fine or restitution until *after* you are released from prison and are gainfully employed. Otherwise the prison will demand an onerous Financial Responsibility Program (FRP) payment schedule that far exceeds the $0.12 per hour prison wage you will earn. And if you fail to comply, the prison will level a number of sanctions against you. Or, in the alternative, you can satisfy the entire court-ordered fine and restitution amounts *before* you enter prison, thereby eliminating any need for prison-official intervention. Should you choose to pay your fine and restitution, or any part of the two of the court-ordered obligations, do take a copy of your receipt to the prison with you when you self-surrender. Otherwise the prison officials will insist on you paying it again, or else. Regardless, until you can prove that all or part of your court-ordered obligations are paid, you will be required to make FRP payments.

2. *Payment Schedule Plan "B"*: If neither of the above is workable, seek a court-ordered payment schedule of $25.00 a quarter (consistent with prison wages) until *after* you are released from prison and are gainfully employed.

With either plan incorporated into the judge's sentencing order, you would not be subject to the prison's unreasonably punitive demands upon your eventual arrival.

FREQUENTLY ASKED QUESTIONS

Protecting Your Spouse And Children

Q: What if my spouse or my son, or even my daughter—or a combination of us—is indicted along with me? What, if anything, can I do to protect them from doing time in federal prison?

A: Yes, oftentimes indictments are a family affair. Protecting your family from conviction or even prison has much to do with their roles in the indictable offense. If you all were what the government calls "major players" in the offense, your options are severely limited. Let's assume for the sake of argument you were the "main player" and the others in your family were "minor players," your options are increased.

Bottom line: the government plays hardball. At day's end, all you can offer the government that would lessen your family's exposure would be "substantial cooperation"—a term any attorney, any attorney worth their salt, would explore with you early on in the criminal proceedings.

Q: Would my family member(s) and I have the same lawyer?

A: That is highly unlikely in criminal cases due to conflicts of interest and a myriad of constitutional protections afforded each indicted individual. Therefore, each of you would likely have your own attorney.

Know Who Your "True" Friends Are

Q: Could a one-time good friend who happened to turn state's evidence against me be sued if he or she out-and-out lied against me?

A: Anyone can be sued for almost anything. But prevailing in a lawsuit is an entirely different story. Here's the deal: It is said that the best defense against slander or defamation lawsuits boils down to one word: Truth. In other words, if you are convicted of the crime of which your lying friend testified, his or her words would be judged as "the truth." Conversely, if you are acquitted of the crime, your chances of prevailing are greater; however, you would now have the "burden of proof" of malicious intent along with an "accounting of damages" in order to prevail in a civil action. In any event, prevailing in a civil matter is a tall order.

Winding Down Your Affairs

Q: Would creating a family trust be an effective way of winding down my affairs?

A: It can be. It ultimately depends on the size, scope, and complexity of your business or your personal estate. In my case, for example, I established a family trust and an irrevocable trust for the sake of my intellectual properties that will produce a continuous stream of royalty revenue. And over time, my consultancy will likewise be converted into books—written in prison with permission, mind you—and assigned to the trust, which works well for my unique situation. Your situation is also unique, which means there is no one-size-fits-all answer to this question. I therefore suggest you speak with a certified financial planner or an estate attorney who is qualified to design a strategy that is conducive to your situation.

Think Flexibility. Think Liquidity

Q: What if I have received a stiff fine or have been ordered to pay restitution? Wouldn't "getting liquid" mean that I would have to turn that liquid cash over to the government?

A: Only if ordered by the court to do so. Usually, however, if your abundance of assets are at issue or in some way at the center of your criminal offense—such as drug trafficking or a large-scale fraud case—your assets would have been subject to civil forfeiture proceedings early on in your case. Not later in your case. Especially during the sentencing phase where fines and restitution are argued and settled. In my particular case—which was securities fraud and money laundering—the government was so fixated on our parent corporation's assets and its subsidiary companies' assets, they either chose to, or simply forgot to, inquire into my "personal" assets. And since I had a right to remain silent, I simply remained silent. No one ever asked, so no one was obligated to tell. So when I went to prison, my personal assets remained intact. And from talking to other similarly situated inmates, my situation was not that unusual. But whatever you do, or whatever your situation, do not attempt to hide, deceive, lie, or commit perjury for the sake of a few replaceable assets. Do not volunteer, but definitely do not lie . . . because it is not worth it in the long run.

Presentencing Documentation: Curse or Blessing

Q: Why should I seek out or even retain the documents in this section when my case and all of its related documents are a matter of public record? If I should need them, can I simply notify the clerk of the court and arrange to get the needed documents?

A: For a copying fee, most court documents are indeed a matter of public record. But correspondence between you and your attorney is not. That aside, not all documents are assured to be with the clerk of the court. Nor are there any assurances that you will receive your documents when you need them most. Lastly, one must weigh the risks: would you want to risk spending one day more in prison than necessary simply because you did not want to bother securing your own documents when you had the early opportunity to do so? Hopefully not.

Securing Wills, Powers of Attorney, And Time-sensitive Negotiable Instruments

Q: How does one execute essential business or family-related documents while they are in prison should the need arise?

A: All federal prisons offer an in-house or a contract notary public service to any inmate who has a need to execute sensitive documents. One would simply visit the prison's law library for details. Keep in mind, however, you are not allowed to operate a business from prison.

Pending Traffic, Civil, And Family Law Matters

Q: What happens if the state in which my traffic or other state-related infractions are located decides to exercise their right to pull me out of federal custody to answer to state charges?

A: Should the state decide to exercise its right to bring you to court, the state judge will likely adjudicate the matter as "time served"—being that you are already in prison. You will then return to federal custody. On the other hand, if the state deems it necessary to come and pull you out of federal custody to answer to a charge, that would mean your charge(s) are surely deemed as serious. As such, the state might very well want its pound of flesh from you through some other form of consecutive sentencing.

Your Presentence Investigation Report: Beware!

Q: Since court documents are a matter of public record, could I freely obtain a copy of *anyone's* PSI report including my own?

A: No. Not all court documents are available to the general public, especially if a certain document contains information that could place you, your family, and others in harm's way. For example: if you provided the government with "substantial" assistance, that specific information surrounding your assistance would be in your PSI report—along with the names of every member in your family, including your children's names. For this, and for similar reasons, certain documents are kept out of the public's domain.

Pre-existing Medical Concerns

Q: Should I become seriously ill in prison and taken out to a hospital, would my loved ones be able to come and visit me?

A: Sadly, no. Under no circumstances would prison officials allow anyone near a patient-inmate other than the relevant hospital staff who is attending to your medical needs. The reason? Security. Security for you, the prisoner, security for the officer(s) guarding the prisoner, and security for the public in general. For example, let's assuming you "snitched" on someone who received a very long prison term; and, say his brother wanted revenge and somehow learned that you were at a hospital. Who knows to what extent an enraged brother would go in order to get at you? Then, if you are injured and killed, your family would sue the government for failing to protect you. Plus the guards' families and an innocent citizen's family would sue should their loved ones get injured or killed in the process. For these and other reasons, your movement outside the prison is considered classified.

Confront Fines And Restitution At Sentencing

Q: As it relates to restitution to the victim(s); in my case, is it possible for me to make a discounted cash offer to the victims much like I would make a discounted cash offer to the IRS pursuant to an Offer In Compromise provision?

A: Yes, simply because the actual funds attributed to the court-determined restitution belong to the victim(s). Not the government. But understand this: should an agreement be reached between you and the victim(s), the agreement would not be binding on the government, meaning that the government would not be obligated to reduce your prison sentence at all, though it often would, provided you make application to the court for an appropriate sentence reduction.

Q: Do you have any other questions for Mr. CEO?

A: On our website: http://frenchcuffsblog.com. Fill out the contact form with your question and we will get back to you as soon as possible.

frenchcuffsblog.com

"There's no such thing as too much war-time preparation, especially when you consider the war that lay ahead is well prepared for you."

—General George Patton

In this chapter . . .

How Prison Designation Works

How Appeal Bonds Work

Judges Recommendations Often Overrated

Mistakes Made When Self-Surrendering

Facts About Prison Consultants

Secure Your Personal Information

Secure Your Professional Licenses And Permits

It's Prison. Not The Chamber Of Commerce

The Top 10 Things Business Owners Should Establish Before Prison

Frequently Asked Questions

CHAPTER THREE

POST-SENTENCING PREPARATION

How Prison Designation Works

So now that the sentencing process is final, the one question among many questions in your mind is, "Yes, I know what my attorney asked for, and I know what the judge recommended, but where am I *really* going?

Your designation to a specific prison destination is determined by two steps that are spelled out in the Bureau of Prison's Policy Statement. The two steps are "scoring" and "public safety factor." These two processes are determined by a Bureau employee called a Community Corrections Manager/Coordinator (CCM or CCC). Every judicial district in the United States has a CCM who scores a sentenced and prison-bound defendant to determine his or her security level, which determines the specific prison facility where you will be received.

The first step considered by the CCM for **scoring** you includes, but is not limited to: 1) the existence of any type of impending detainer (meaning outstanding wants and warrants from unresolved traffic for criminal infractions), 2) the severity of your instant offense, 3) months to release (female prisoners only), 4) type of prior conviction and criminal history, 5) history of the escapes or attempts to escape, 6) your history of violence, and 7) your pre-commitment status.

The second step and its criteria considered by the CCM for establishing your **public safety factor** include 1) determining if you are a member of a destructive group, i.e. gangs, Mafia, militias, or terrorists, 2) greatest severity offense, meaning you are found guilty of arson, assault, organized drug trafficking, carjacking, robbery, prior escape, kidnapping, homicide, etc., and 3) sex offenses, i.e. rape, sex with a minor, the sale, distribution, possession, or mailing and e-mailing child pornography, and 4) months-to-release, meaning "how much longer" must the inmate serve in lieu of his gross sentence length.

Of course, there are other important classification steps taken by the CCM to determine your ultimate destination. In fact, if you are still free on bond pending word on where you are to self-surrender, the CCM is probably reviewing your PSI report right now. Then when the CCM makes his or her decision, the U. S. Marshal and your sentencing judge's clerk will be notified, informing them of the CCM's decision as to where you will be designated. Your attorney will then be notified by the court or by the U.S. Marshal. **WARNING**: In case you do not receive your designation or self-surrender instructions at least ONE WEEK prior to the court's order for you to surrender (which you and your attorney should have received directly from the judge at sentencing), call your attorney at once. Point here is this: you definitely want to avoid a communication breakdown between the court and your attorney that could result in you having to turn yourself in at your local U.S. Marshal's office. Why? Because you will be unnecessarily exposed to and dragged through a living hell (i.e. violent and filthy county jails or federal detention centers) before you arrive at your ultimate prison destination a month later. However, if you self-surrender as planned, you will avoid this horrible experience altogether. So make sure your attorney does his or her job. Otherwise, you suffer while your attorney goes home.

How Appeal Bonds Work

Of course, we are all afforded an opportunity—and a Constitutional Right, mind you—to advance an appeal following a conviction, unless we knowingly, willingly, and intelligently waived our right to appeal as part of a plea agreement with the government.

However, if you proceeded to trial as I did, your right to appeal remains intact and thus you are eligible to apply for an appeal bond. But let's not fool ourselves. Truthfully, the odds of remaining free on appeal bond are equivalent as were the odds of defeating the government once you were indicted. And if you recall, the odds were grim. But for a rare few, it does work.

Here's how:

1. A Blemishless Record: To qualify for an appeal bond, you must be clear of any and all court infractions and arrests, including any Failures to Appear on traffic violations. If you have suffered any of the above, you need not bother to applying for an appeal bond.
2. No Delaying The Inevitable: The court must be clearly convinced that you are not delaying the inevitable, and that in your appeal you have raised a substantial question of law. And in that question, the court must deem that there exists a reasonable expectation your argument will prevail.
3. Reversed And Remanded: The court deems your case will be reversed and remanded back to the lower court, or that a new trial would be ordered, or that a new sentence will be handed down that would not warrant prison time, or that the reduction from its decision would result in "time served."
4. Appeal Bond Requirements: The process of you posting a bond that meets the court's requirements, i.e. probational clearance, financially entrusted, and community anchored.

Judges' Recommendations Often Overrated

From the moment we step foot onto the marble-titled floors inside the federal court building, we know, without a shadow of a doubt, that the person in the black robe—the federal district judge—holds the key to our freedom or to our incarceration, depending on the day's events. We also know, at any time following our first appearance in court, how following our first appearance in court how we cringe at the sound of our phone ringing, in fear that we have again been summoned by the judge for some sort of "special hearing" of which we knew absolutely nothing about. Happens every time.

Yes, the federal district judge runs his courtroom with an iron fist. However, when it comes to the Federal Bureau of Prisons, (B0P) the judge is, in essence, rendered powerless. The judge's recommendations carry no compelling legal power over where the federal prison system places you. In particular, there are two principally consistent recommendations judges make in the process of pronouncing your sentence, recommendations that the BOP certainly take judicial notice of, but the BOP is in no means bound by such recommendations.

Case in point: Due to your judge recommending the 500-Hour Residential Drug and Alcohol Program (RDAP) at sentencing, you'd likely believe you are in good shape. As you await your designation and self-surrender order from the BOP—or perhaps so while in custody at mid-transit—you are probably thinking: "Hey, well at least I can get a year reduction on my sentence because the judge ordered me to take RDAP."

To my amazement, many have come into prison, only to painfully discover that the judge's order was, in fact, a recommendation for RDAP, and that the judge's recommendation didn't mean squat. That's because the Congress vested the BOP with the sole authority to determine policy as to who they (the BOP) would admit or deny access into the RDAP program. For this reason, the judge can only make a judicial recommendation, for he realizes he has no power to issue a court order that would compel the BOP to admit you into RDAP. In effect, you were (or are) the one who singlehandedly held the power to compel the BOP to admit you into RDAP. How so? Had you informed your PSI probation interviewer about your drug or alcohol abuse problem, you would have (or will be) admitted into the RDAP program. (Consult the subsection "Residential Drug Abuse Program" on page 196 in Chapter Four).

Again, we have the word "recommended," which we now know does not really mean squat when it comes to the BOP. Sure, the BOP will take judicial notice of the recommendation, but the BOP is by no means obligated to honor it. Another point: Say your judge recommended a prison facility closer to your home following sentencing. Which, of course, means you can find yourself on a federal-prisoner air lift (known to insiders as "Con-Air") heading to the East Coast even though you may live on the West Coast! However, experience teaches that the BOP makes an earnest effort to keep a prisoner as close to home as possible (within a 500 mile range) based on BOP policy. That said, mind you, I have also observed how certain crimes induce the BOP to move prisoners farther away from home. So what does the BOP consider when routinely designating an inmate? Let's take a look at key factors used when making a designation decision:

1. The Offense: White-collar cases, low-level drug cases, and political corruption cases and similar non-violent cases are ideal candidate cases for near-home designations without much of a problem. That is, so long as the requisite facility is within the 500-mile, near-home range.

2. The Length Of Your Sentence: Again, the lower the length of your sentence, the better your chance is of being designated closer to home.

3. Your Medical Condition: Once again, we come to that famous "PSI" report, and the wide range of uses and effects it has on you. Point being, if your PSI report indicates that you are healthy and do not require chronic care, you are an excellent candidate for near-home designation.

4. Separation-From-Co-defendant Order: In many instances, defendants have hostile co-defendants who may have provided some kind of "assistance" to the government that sealed your conviction. And in the sensitive instances, the U.S. Attorney's office will request a "Separation Order (known in the BOP as a "Separatee") that instructs the BOP to keep the two of you separated. Absent such an order, you would be an excellent candidate for near-home designation.

Experience Teaches:

Remember, it's prison, not the chamber of commerce.

Keep in mind, the BOP is its own separate entity, totally independent of the courts. The BOP's only obligation to the court and ultimately to society is to safely and securely fulfill the judgement and commitment issued by the court. And should you receive anything recommended by your sentencing judge, it is because the BOP saw fit to grant it.

Mistakes Made When Self-Surrendering

Unfortunately for me, I was not afforded the opportunity to self-surrender, even though self-surrender was recommended by the probation officer who prepared my PSI report. Instead, I was remanded to the custody of the U.S. Marshal per the judge's order.

However, throughout the years I have encountered hundreds of self-surrenders who time and again have chronicled their horror stories about the screw-ups they have made (even life-threatening screw-ups) when self-surrendering. Below are six serious blunders you **definitely want to avoid when self-surrendering**, along with some advice on how to make the process less onerous:

1. Avoid Weekends, Holidays, Or Fridays: To avoid being confined to a 6 x 8 solitary confinement cell (a.k.a. "the hole" and officially as "Special Housing Unit (SHU)") for several days while you await intake processing, do not self-surrender on weekends, holidays, or on Fridays. Instead, self-surrender between Monday through Thursday to receive immediate processing and intake. Otherwise you could find yourself sitting in solitary confinement (which is extra, but unnecessary torment) for up to 7 days or more. So you might wonder, "What if my self-surrender order directs me to surrender on a weekend, a holiday, or on a Friday?" No problem. Self-surrender a day or two before the official surrender date. And do so before 12 noon and begin serving your sentence early. After all, a self-surrender order specifies an "on or before" date. Besides, the sooner you check in, the sooner you check out. So avoid the unnecessary grief of several days in solitary confinement. Trust me. You'll be glad you did.

2. Avoid Surrendering At The U.S. Marshal's Office: We briefly discussed surrendering at the U.S. Marshal's earlier in this chapter. Now we will discuss it again—in greater detail. If you want to be treated and transferred as if you were one of the 9/11 terrorists, then make the mistake of self-surrendering at your local U.S. Marshal's Office instead of self-surrendering at your designated prison facility. Defendants are sometimes instructed by their attorneys to self-surrender at the U.S. Marshal's Office when (a) your attorney fumbled the ball and forgot to call you with surrender instructions he received from the U.S. Marshal's office days earlier, or, (b) there is a clerical mix-up with your self-surrender documents amid the pipeline. Should that be the case, you always must follow your attorney's advice. But you can certainly avoid the U.S. Marshal by making sure your attorney stays on top of your designation and your self-surrender order from the BOP. It usually takes 7 to 10 days following your sentencing date for your attorney to receive your self-surrender instructions. So don't wait too long before pressing the issue with your attorney.

3. Don't be late or Miss Your Surrender Date: Being late or missing surrender dates altogether is probably more common than being atypical. However, if you are late or miss your date of surrender, there will be hell to pay. Let's begin with being late to self-surrender. First, you will be routinely processed in, then immediately taken to "the hole" and sanctioned. Second, now you are off to a bad start; and thus, from then on you will be on the prison officials' "hit list" for the duration of your sentence. That means

you lose your future eligibility for family furloughs, extra halfway house time, appeal bond consideration and other privileges offered to prisoners later on in their sentences. So why risk it? Wouldn't it just be easier to get there not less than 3 hours early to be extra safe? My advice: Don't be foolish. Get there on time if you do not want your name on that list. So be where you're supposed to be not less than 3 hours early to be extra safe. Get there on time!

4. Missing Your Self-Surrender Date: Should you miss your self-surrender date altogether, here's what happens: First, before the change of shift at your designated prison facility, the Warden is notified of your failure to appear for surrender. Second, the Warden's legal staff is ordered to notify the U.S. Marshal and the sentencing court, where, were collectively each agency coordinates their data for clear and consistent self-surrender and facility designation orders to ensure that they themselves have not screwed up somewhere. Third, if all is confirmed, a federal warrant is issued for your arrest. Simultaneously the U.S. Marshal will prepare an armed unit to apprehend you as though you were Scarface. So do yourself a huge favor and self-surrender on time.

5. Avoid Arriving Later Than Noon: Besides being economically efficient, a self-surrender process also exists to lessen the trauma of entry in the prison system, that is, so long as your offense is, in relative terms, minor, non-violent, and that you are not deemed to be a flight risk. However, none of these things matter to a prison staff member who is close to a shift change—that being at 2:00 PM—when

suddenly you come bobbing in between 12 noon and one o'clock. Well there is a good chance you will sit in the Hole for hours before being processed in and taken to your living quarters. Should you arrive at the ideal hours 8:30 a.m. and 10:30 a.m., you will likely be efficiently and expeditiously processed in without much delay. It makes a huge difference where your peace of mind is concerned.

6. Avoid Taking More Than $750.00 Cash: Why $750.00? Good question. If you have a fine, or court assessments, or restitution—or like me, all of the above—the prison staff assigned to your Unit Team will greatly increase your Inmate Financial Responsibility Program (FRP) payments. When your inmate trust account (a.k.a. Commissary Account) exceeds an aggregate of $750.00—not including phone money—every six months an increase in FRP payments is triggered. To avoid this hassle altogether, your attorney should secure a Schedule Of Payments at sentencing. Otherwise, the prison will have full discretion to increase your FRP payments based on the aggregate of your inmate trust account. And should you fail to comply (or as prison officials refer to as "volunteer"), you will be deprived of certain living and working privileges afforded to other inmates. However, if you have no fines, no court assessments, or no restitution, you'll have no problems. You can have as much money in your inmate trust account as you desire.

7. Avoid Wearing Anything Remotely Expensive When Self-Surrendering: When you arrive at your designated prison facility, you will be stripped of everything you are wearing and given a prison

uniform to wear. As for your personal belongings, you will be asked to mail them home or asked to have them donated (which really means "thrown away"). All that you will be allowed to bring into the facility are your prescription eyeglasses and a very basic wedding band. Some institutions will permit a modest religious necklace or headpiece into the facility. It varies.

Bottom line, it makes no sense for you to show up wearing pricey apparel—expensive underwear included—only to send it all home or throw it away.

Facts About Prison Consultants

I chuckled when I first read the title "prison consultant" in a caption beneath a photograph of a prominent California-based lawyer who was promoting his book and law firm. I then asked a fellow inmate, "Who does he consult?" I asked that question after reading the impressive academic and professional association background of this lawyer, to which my fellow inmate replied, "People like you and me, former CEO's, executives, business owners, doctors—those of us who have money and stature, but find ourselves facing federal prison time for some white-collar offense." I paused, shook my head, and followed with, "How the hell can he counsel me on doing time in prison when he has never had to suffer through a term of imprisonment himself?"

I later learned, first-hand, that the same lawyer charges $50,000 to advise CEO's like me on how to "successfully" do time in prison. And amazingly there are others just like him cropping up around the country who simply parrot outdated correctional theories and so-called empirical evidence they learned from other sheltered academics. Problem is, most of these university "experts" and book-writing lawyers and academics have spent precious little time inside prisons or talking with men like me. Frankly, here is how I see it: it is much like the man who professes to be a lion tamer, and then writes books on how to "successfully" tame wild lions. Yet, not once has he ever stood in the unsecured presence of an actual wild lion. And yet he charges aspiring lion tamers $50,000 for his consulting services. Go figure!

And then there are other non-attorney types who are emerging on the prison consultancy scene, several of whom have indeed served time in perhaps one or two federal prison facilities. And per my research, their range of fees is from $1,000-$10,000 for their information.

Problem is, both the attorney types and of the non-attorney types are justifying their fees by making outlandish promises that they have not a snowman's chance in hell of ever delivering. Once you are in prison it is virtually impossible to collect on these promises. Below is a list of promises, from the most absurd to the least absurd:

1. Lower Your Sentence: Patently absurd! A prison consultant has no authority, no special knowledge, nor does he or she have the power to alter, modify, or in any manner, affect your prison sentence. Such authority exists only within 4 government institutions: (1) the court that sentenced you, (2) the Federal Bureau of Prisons, (3) the Congress, and (4) the Office of the President of the United States. And even then, these 4 institutions must follow a strict protocol before your sentence can be reduced by as little as one day. Credible criminal attorneys with solid, long-standing reputations dare not make such promises to their clients or prospective clients.

2. Extend Your Self-Surrender Date: In this instance, your sentencing attorney is the only one who could possibly make application for an extension to self-surrender, provided there is good cause to do so.

Being that such an application sets in motion an adversarial proceeding, you would likely be required to appear in court along with your attorney to argue such a motion. Now, unless your defense attorney is a prison consultant also, I cannot see where the role of some prison consultant comes into play. You know why I can't see it? Because *no such role exists within the context of an official judicial proceeding!* So don't be fooled into believing that there is.

3. Get You Into RDAP (Drug Program):Statutory law now provides for a reduction of sentence of up to one year for a non-violent inmate who has successfully completed a residential drug and alcohol abuse program (RDAP) in a federal prison facility. To qualify for the RDAP program, your PSI report is the sole source on which the BOP relies when using its discretion toward granting or denying the RDAP program to inmates. Absent the PSI report's concrete confirmation of your drug or alcohol abuse (not reporting "socially" but outright "abuse") you are not going to be admitted into the RDAP program. Period. However, some prison consultants have the gall to market phony medical records or rehab-center letters (signed by actual medical professionals) that you have been treated in their facility for drug or alcohol abuse. Guess what? That's another federal indictment just waiting to happen. And no, your lawyer cannot sue to get you admitted—as countless number of prisoners attempt. Why even your sentencing judge lacks the authority to "order" the BOP to arbitrarily admit you into RDAP. So if your lawyer and your judge cannot get you admitted, as countless prisoners have attempted to do—all to no avail. how on earth is it

possible for a mere prison consultant to get you admitted? Come on. Think about it.

4. Designate You To A Prison Closer To Home: In this chapter, I speak extensively on how your judge's recommendations are often overrated. Speaking of recommendations, at this very moment, as I pen these words, I am interviewing a 63-year old fellow inmate who was a former executive with a major East Coast civil engineering firm. He had just arrived less than twenty-four hours prior to my writing these words. The fellow inmate, whose name is Walter, pled guilty to income tax evasion, conspiracy to commit income tax evasion (meaning his accountant also bit the dust), and making a false statement to a federally insured institution. Walt received a sentence of eighteen months. At sentencing, the judge recommended that Walt remain close to home while serving his sentence. Walt lives in New York. But he is sitting here, next to me, distraught and confused, in sunny California. Walt's daughter contacted a so-called prison consultant who claimed to have "pull" inside the power structure of the BOP. He claimed that for a fee of $15,000, he could get Walt an immediate "hardship" transfer to an East Coast prison camp. The prison consultant agreed to act swiftly, provided a deposit of $7,500 gets wired to him immediately. The daughter complied. A week later, Walt's daughter received some cheesy book about "doing time." To date, neither Walt nor his daughter has heard from the prison consultant, nor has the consultant returned the family's calls following a dozen attempts to reach him. The lesson? If a federal judge doesn't have any real "pull" inside the power structure of the BOP, what

would lead you to believe that a non-judicial, non-prison affiliated consultant would have the influence to bend the will of the BOP? Amazingly, fear oftentimes causes us to believe something that would normally be considered absolutely irrational. Unfortunately for Walt and his daughter, this was one of those times.

5. Get You More Halfway House Time: Naturally anyone in prison, especially those of us in low and minimum security prisons, come into these facilities with the halfway house on our minds. Why? Because to us, halfway house, for all intents and purposes, is home. So it's easy to understand why we would find the promise of "more halfway house time" emotionally intoxicating. After all, what's a little money—like $1,000 to $50,000—when compared to going home sooner? Problem is, a prison consultant cannot make that happen either, even if he were paid $500,000. At least not legally. Fact is, an inmate's halfway house allowance is, by BOP policy, partly formulaic, partly discretionary, depending on the inmate's sentence, conduct, and programming (education in prison, etc.) while serving his or her sentence. The halfway house's overall logistics with managing its flow of inmates is also a factor. As such, there is no room in the halfway-house equation for a prison consultant—or anyone else for that matter—in which to enter.

6. More Regarding Prison Consultants: So what do I *really* think of prison consultants? I seem a bit hard on prison consultants, but I am not. After all, I am a prison consultant myself by the mere fact of my offering these Survival books, websites and "proven"

consulting services. My problem involves the promises some of these consultants are making, when they know full well they cannot deliver on those promises. Yet they are charging—and getting—fees ranging from $1,000-$50,000 per client. I will concede, it would be worth every penny if any prison consultant had the ability or legal authority to fulfill just one of the above-mentioned promises. But short of bribing a government official or employee (which is probably not that difficult a feat), it is not going to happen.

The truth of the matter is that a prison consultant's value should be measured by 1) his or her years spent in the federal prison system as either an inmate or as an employee, 2) the number of security levels in which the inmate or employee has served, meaning from the highest security level to the lowest security level of the federal prison system, and, 3) the number of references provided in order that you may independently substantiate the consultant's promises, especially if they are seeking up-front fees in the dollar range stated above.

Secure Your Personal Information

Today, more than ever, identity theft is running rampant, especially against those of us who have lost the ability to technologically monitor our identities and other personal information that may be subject to theft. As federal prisoners, we are often isolated from society for years—and as in my case, for many, many years. Yet our personal information is out there sitting dormant in our attorneys' file cabinets, on our doctors' computers, on our stockbrokers' client lists, and in our families homes—all of which could leave us vulnerable to identity theft.

In fact, many of us white-collar types have maintained some form of business activity with, perhaps, family, friends, or pre-existing business partners; or, perhaps, we are in the process of forming business alliances and new endeavors while currently imprisoned.

In this section, I will reveal the various stages that have worked for me and for others like me, along with a few examples of how an inmate's identity enriched others without the inmate knowing about it until it was too late.

1. Do Not Leave Home Without It: I am referring to your pre-paid membership to a reputable identification watchdog agency such as Protect My I.D. or Lifelock® (no pun intended) who is capable of watching and alerting you of any aberrant activity with your credit or identification files. Both agencies are, in my opinion, quite solid and thoroughly responsive to your identification-security needs. The key here, however, is that you subscribe to one of their "premium packages" with your wife, or a trusted relative, or your business attorney as your "attorney-in-fact" while you are incarcerated. And should there be an attempt to violate your identity, have the sensitive information securely "blacked-out and sent to you in prison. But under no circumstances should you apply for credit or identity monitoring by using the prison's address; otherwise you will be stuck with that address in your credit file. Instead, always apply using your home or office address.

2. What Could Happen With Your Unmonitored Identity While In Prison? True Story. In June of 2008, I met a man who I befriended while taking a wellness class during my incarceration at FCI Lompoc, which

is located on Vandenberg Air Force base in Lompoc, California.

My friend, Mr. Wade, had dated a prominent real estate broker—who he casually referred to as his "Lady-friend"—for three years prior to being sentenced to prison for tax evasion. While in prison, my friend discovered that tenants in his commercial triplex building in San Francisco were becoming increasingly delinquent with lease payments month after month on end, simply because they (the tenants) knew that Mr. Wade was in prison (See Chapter Two for helpful tips on dealing with similar issues).

So his lady-friend, the real estate broker, devised a plan to sell Mr. Wade's property for him, since income properties were still faring well amid the sluggish economy. Reluctantly Mr. Wade agreed, considering his prison sentence and other circumstances. So he arranged with his lady-friend to list and sell the property. But first, she needed his "personal information" for the title company's due diligence—naturally. Thinking nothing of it, Mr. Wade complied. Two months later, the property was sold with the proceeds from the sale being rightly divided to the respective parties. So far, so good.

Or was it?

Eight months later, Mr. Wade arrived at his 12-month countdown date, which prompted him to begin the process of preparing for his release. So with the help of the prison's Resource and Employment Training Center, Mr. Wade applied for a copy of his birth certificate, his Social Security card, his driver's license, and his credit report.

Weeks later, upon receiving his tri-agency credit report, Mr. Wade was astonished to learn that he was a married man, even though he was a single man before and during his incarceration! And, for reasons beyond him, he did not recall being at the wedding, nor did he recall to whom he was married.

As a result, "Mrs. Wade" bought and sold nearly a dozen commercial properties and 14 residential properties. Translation? "Mrs. Wade" made big money on Mr. Wade's identity. Exactly how much is yet to be determined.

However, at the time of this writing, Mr. Wade has contacted the well-to-do "Mrs. Wade" in order to get to the bottom of the matter. As it stands at the present, the jury is still out. However, to this I can attest: Mr. Wade is far from being a happy camper.

3. Order Duplicate Statements On Existing Credit Cards: Should you decide to maintain business and/or personal credit cards open and active, then do yourself a favor. First, have your larger-limit credit cards temporarily lowered to an amount that cannot hurt you, if not, suspend them altogether. Second, order duplicate statements and have them mailed to an independent third-party who will forward them to you (again, do not have any credit-granting or credit-monitoring agency mailed data directly to you at the prison's address).

Bottom line: when you are in prison, significant financial and even criminal liabilities could mount against you without your knowing anything about it. The solution is to stay proactive—with a mild dose of paranoia. Therefore, when considering the dynamics of your unique situation, I suggest you revisit Chapter Two in conjunction with this section before devising your strategy.

Secure Your Professional Licenses And Permits

What special or professional licenses do you have? Or what about special permits or general permits still remaining in your name? And should any still exist, what is the status of each?

In this section, we will discuss the present risks and the future repercussions of not securing your professional licenses and permits.

1. Allowing Others To Use Your License(s) Or Permit(s) During Your Incarceration: To many licensed or permit-holding professionals, this issue would appear, on its face, to be a bad idea. Then again, you would be amazed (or perhaps not) by how many of us are somewhat forced to keep certain licenses and permits active due to the fact that our families' livelihoods—notwithstanding our in-prison survival—depends on the revenue that our licenses and permits generate. Tough legal call. However, the unvarnished truth is, maintaining any license or permit that has been issued by a local, state, or federal agency is illegal and can be construed as fraud against the issuing agency. How so? Because in essence, a licensing contract exists between you and the issuing agency. Thus, incorporated in this licensing contract is language to the effect that you unilaterally represent that you possess the "lawful capacity" to hold such a license, and should your lawful capacity change, the

license is to be surrendered to the issuing agency, unless a waiver of sort is granted by the issuing agency stating the contrary.

Even so, the moment you are incarcerated—or in contractual terms "incapacitated"—you no longer have lawful capacity. Yet should you carry on with "business as usual" without informing the issuing agency of your incapacitation, you would be, in fact, committing a dual fraud: a fraud against the issuing agency, and a fraud against the party(ies) to whom you represent yourself as one who is legally licensed to do whatever it is that you do. Therefore, I recommend you suspend your licenses and permits until such time you have regained your lawful capacity.

2. Allowing Others to Use Your License(s) Or Permit(s) Exposes Them To Fraud Also: They call this act of generosity conspiracy. Then again, if you have purchased this book or consulted our website, I am fairly confident you know what a conspiracy is. Chances are you have likely been charged with some form of a conspiracy in your indictment.

Point being is that if the issuing agency did not grant a waiver of sort, anyone who uses your license(s) or permit(s) is likely perpetuating a textbook fraud against the issuing agency—including against the clients or customers being served. So the objective here is to broaden the scope of your thinking when you are considering how you are going to continue your business while serving your term of imprisonment. Then again, since operating a business is against BOP policy, your scope of thinking—

should you opt to keep your business a going concern—might include the help of extended family, or perhaps the outright sale of the business.

3. Think Long Term: Think Probation: Wouldn't it be a darned shame if you were in violation of your probation before ever being released from prison? Well, that could be the case should you or your associate(s) (who is using your license(s) or permit(s)), or even your corporation become a party to a civil action that unveils the badges of fraud. For example, a fellow-inmate friend of mine maintained his upscale real estate development business in San Diego, California, through which he had long held a contractor's license. Before coming to prison for income tax evasion, my friend—whose company is a valid California corporation—followed the appropriate "resignation and notice" protocol. Plus, as an added precaution, my friend's foreman applied for and received his own contractor's license, which now affords the company two contractors' licenses. As such, all is well. However, eighteen months into a thirty-two month prison sentence, my friend was sued in civil court, both individually and corporately. The reason? A wealthy home-owner couple claimed that they were overcharged by the tune of $365,000 by my friend's construction company's cost over-runs when building their multi-million dollar home in La Jolla, California. The court's conclusion? The homeowner's entire case was thrown out (by way of Summary Judgement) before the matter could ever get to trial. So my friend, the prisoner, won the case while in prison. But when we fast forward to one month from my friend's release date, my friend's civil attorney

received a call from a federal probation officer—the officer assigned to supervise my friend upon his release from prison. The probation officer demanded to review the civil court documents, known as "pre-trial discovery," which, once filed with the court, are no longer protected by attorney-client privilege.

Upon receiving the pre-trial discovery, the probation officer discovered, among other juicy tidbits, that my friend's construction company was operating as an "illegal commercial enterprise" during the months the construction company was "technically unlicensed." Problem was, that was the time period preceding the date-of-issuance of the foreman's contractor's license and the date on which my friend self-surrendered to prison. In other words, according to Probation, the company was operating under the license of a man who was in prison; that is, until such time that the foreman became licensed himself. As a result, the probation officer notified the prison of his findings. In turn the prison swiftly sanctioned my friend for running a business while in prison. To that end, my friend (through the loss of good-time credits) served an additional sixty days in prison for the violation.

4. Best Strategy For Securing Licenses And Permits For Future Use? Early Planning: After all that I have outlined above, you are probably feeling a bit dejected, if not frightened, when it comes to preserving what remains of your business or profession. If so, you should not be. Thousands of us white-collar offenders who own businesses—yet find ourselves in prison—manage to keep our business without violating the contracts we might have with licensing or permit-granting agencies, and most

importantly, without violating BOP policy, or any state or federal laws. How so? Early planning. Yes, early planning is the key. I'll explain . . . but first, I need you in the proper "prison-survival" frame of mind. So please, it's very important that you go back and re-read Chapter One in its entirety, then return to this section for further discussion.

With that, here are the specifics regarding early planning.

5. Lawfully Transfer The Business To A Family Member: Most all of us who own a business or a thriving professional practice, of sort, plan for, if not often think about, how might our businesses continue on should something terrible happen to us, like getting run over by a cement truck. Well, going to prison is, in a sense, like being run over by a government cement truck and living to tell about it. So what does conventional wisdom teach us about preserving assets and protecting our businesses? Estate planning.

Employing the services of a competent estate planning attorney would ensure the proper transfer of assets—specifically your business—to a trusted family member. The transfer could be in the form of a discounted sale with a pre-established "buy-back" provision, for you, or as an outright gift, depending on your attorney's recommendation as it may relate to your specific tax, capital-gains, and your debt-restructuring situations.

At any rate, when the appropriate transfer takes place, the family member may then apply for the requisite license(s) and permit(s) currently held by you, since most licenses and permits are non-transferable. Such a transfer of ownership keeps the business operating, and it secures the license(s) and/or permit(s) necessary to operate the business. More importantly, such a transfer could occur without violating a single law. Then, when you are finally released from prison, you and your family members can reassess your future role in the business.

It's Prison. Not The Chamber Of Commerce

Okay . . . here are the rules as they relate to engaging in commerce in prison, all of which are quite simple and straightforward.

1. All Forms Of Commerce Are Prohibited In Prison: Here I am referring to all forms of commerce by and between inmates. Even though every imaginable form of commerce is in one way or another transacted by and between every federal inmate in the system, it is nonetheless prohibited. According to the Bureau of Prisons, if one inmate sells another inmate a mere postage stamp, both inmates would be in violation of BOP policy. Thus, they both could be sanctioned 30 to 60 days in solitary confinement. However, the truth of the matter is that the BOP staff knows full well that prison is nothing more than a microcosm of the greater society—absent women and children, of course. And within this microcosm there are two economies: the above-ground (or "legal") economy and the underground (or "illegal") economy. And both are thriving, especially the underground economy. Even so, there is absolutely nothing the prison staff can do to prevent it. Why? Because the

BOP is so understaffed, due primarily to the burgeoning federal prison population nationwide, now topping 217,000 prisoners. As such, all that prison officials can do is attempt to curtail the flow of commerce as best they can.

So why am I telling you this? Because you need to do your level best to avoid the underground economic activity. Point is, since inmates "handle" everything, meaning from your issue of underwear to cooking your every meal, somewhere along the way you'll have to pay. It simply cannot be avoided. So do as the prison officials do: attempt to curtail your commerce activities as best you can.

2. Running Your Pre-Existing Business While In Prison: Indeed thousands of us who are in prison still have lawful assets and liabilities we have to manage. Others have legitimate businesses in operation; or, in many instances, we may have pre-existing investments that require constant oversight. This, of course, begs the question: What is a prisoner allowed to do when he has assets and an operating business at risk, when neither was subject to civil forfeiture proceedings? Well, here's the skinny:

3. Running Your Business vs. Consulting Your Businesses: According to the Bureau of Prisons' Official Policy Statement, we as prisoners are not allowed to "run a business" while in prison under any circumstance. The reasons for this policy, as the government perceives it, are: 1) to protect the public from harm as a result of one's further criminal behavior, 2) to protect itself from liability since a prisoner lacks the "legal capacity" to engage in business activities while incarcerated, 3) to preserve

the safe, secure, and orderly operation of the confining institution, and 4) to administer and enforce the policies related to federal incarceration. Of course, I am certain that there are other reasons. But these four reasons are the most important to the BOP.

4. Consulting Your Businesses: Here's the good news. Prisoners with pre-existing assets and businesses are permitted to "consult and advise" those whom the prisoner has chosen to manage his or her assets or business interests. The phrase "consult and advise" is not construed as "running or operating" a business, principally because consulting and advising does not constitute decision-making. Rather, they are merely "recommendations" that will aid in someone else making the ultimate lawful decision that needs to be made to operate the business. Not the prisoner. But let's not kid ourselves. Everyone involved knows that ostensibly we're still in charge.

For 15 years, I have not had one day's problem when advising my family and my associates on pending business matters. However, on two separate occasions I was sternly warned about "certain business conversations" over the prison's monitored telephone system. My first warning was in 1997 when I was writing my first book and dictating parts of it over the phone to my secretary. When I explained to the acting lieutenant that their recordings captured the work product of a book in progress, the matter was dropped. The second warning came in 2007 when an out-of-context phone conversation was apparently monitored midway through, wherein I was discussing the content of a written business plan for a hotelresort project in Las Vegas of which I was merely a consultant. Again, once the questioning Lieutenant inquired into my activities and subsequently shown the actual business plan from which I read, the matter was, again, closed without incident.

That's it. Two warnings over a span of 15 years of "consulting and advising" from over the telephone; and not once have I received an infraction for violating BOP policy pertaining to "running a business." Nor have I received any further warnings. To that end my consulting continues, without my ever breaking a stride. All the same, I'm always careful when speaking over the monitored telephone. Careful, that is, not to use language or a tone that might be construed as running a business. So take heed.

5. Consulting Your Business Is Running Your Businesses: Think about it. You have built a business. You have amassed a pool of assets and a loyal customer base. You were the brainchild, the owner, the visionary who built this business. Later, due to one mistake in judgement, you fall into prison and suddenly become the business's chief consultant. Suddenly, one day you call your office and speak with the "new owner" who has a business dilemma. So the new owner informs you of his three tentative solutions, which are solutions A, B, or C. The new owner is now uncertain as to which decision is best, but has a bent toward solution B. However, you consult and advise that a hybrid of A and C makes more sense, and you explain why. What decision do you think the new owner will ultimately make? Need I say more? Point being is that prior to entering prison,

you likely handpicked your successor who breathes in every word you exhale out. So, in essence, consulting your business *is,* in essence, running your business without ever violating BOP policy.

6. Loose Lips Sink Ships: Many of us sink our own battleships by way of talking too much while conversing over the prison telephones, and by forgetting that we are, in fact, prisoners instead of presidents and CEO's of companies. In other words, we often get careless by giving orders over the prison telephone instead of making suggestions, or by allowing the person we are speaking with to say something that could inadvertently be construed that we are indeed running a business. For example, something as simple as a telephone conversation containing a few recorded lines such as these can subject you to painful sanctions:

You in prison: ". . . In my opinion, solution 'B' to your problem will cost us too much in the long run. But a hybrid between 'A' and 'C' would get the desired results sooner, and cost the company less."

Your successor at home: "All right then. If you insist. I'll proceed today with a hybrid between 'A' and 'C'.

The example above would be in direct violation of BOP policy prohibiting the running of a business. Hence, you would be met with stiff sanctions, which include the loss of telephone privileges (See "How Federal Prisons Sanction Prisoners" in Chapter Four). So what specifically caused the violation? When the Successor said, "If you insist," and when you didn't correct the Successor with the following exchange:

Your successor at home: "All right then. If you insist. I'll proceed today with a hybrid between 'A' and 'C'."

You in prison: "No, I'm not insisting. I'm recommending. I'm not running the business. You are. So you decide."

See the difference? In this example, you caught the "loose lips" of your Successor at home and quickly corrected what was captured on the monitored record by exchanging the word "insisting" with "recommending" which implies the giving of advice. And as an added precaution, you made it clear that the successor is running the business. Not you.

Time and again, I, personally, have had to interject corrective language when a family member, a friend, or a colleague forgets where I am, and thus they dangerously and loosely misspeak. Yes, it happens a great deal. Why? Because they are not in prison with me, which means they (people at home) have no idea what they are saying. Therefore, if you must converse on sensitive matters, schedule a visit and converse in private. Last but not least, whatever you do, keep your prison telephone conversations on the advisory tip, and avoid the sinking of your own ship.

The Top 10 Things Business Owners Should Establish Before Prison

Once a business person, always a business person. Yet when under the weight of an impending federal prison sentence, who would ever think about the next great business deal? Absolutely no one! But know this: that next business deal, or the best-selling book idea, or the next stellar product invention is often right there in prison, just waiting to be discovered. Of course, you would never know this while under the all the stress of waiting to self-surrender to some God-forsaken prison. Here's the deal. Once you are on the inside, and have accepted the fact of being at a camp or a low-security prison, you will quickly adjust. Then as you settle into your new surroundings and establish your daily routine, you will be amazed at what you discover. All too often, while in our suffering, we make the mistake of thinking that life is over. So we fail to plan for that great business epiphany that will come while in federal prison. Sounds crazy, I know. But no one can refute 20-plus years of experience on this subject. So stay with me on this. . .

Unlike state prisons, or what you've seen on television, federal prisons are totally different. In the Feds, you have a high population of upwardly-mobile, high-net worth individuals with whom you will invariably come into contact. These men, many of whom with real wealth, are usually quiet, often staying to themselves. But in secret, their eyes and ears are open, seeking to network with other highly-educated, highly-intelligent prisoners with whom they desire to engage in a future business venture. I, for one, am a substantial benefactor of these hidden opportunities in more ways than one. You can be too if you are willing to take action now, while you are still at home and there's still time.

Below are ten important steps a business person should take before self-surrendering to federal prison:

1. In Prison, Cash Is Still King: While in prison, you need money to acquire the essentials to be as comfortable as possible. According to BOP Policy, inmates are granted a spending limit of $320.00 per month on commissary items, excluding phone calls and postage stamps. However, you are allowed to have an unlimited amount of funds in your Inmate

Trust Account at any time, without any questions.[9] In fact, I have seen account balances of $20.00 to $50.00 in a single inmate's account. Point being, you need to arrange for at least five unrelated people to commit to sending you money each month. Why unrelated? Because you want to remain as independent as possible should one person default on their commitment to you. After all, you are in prison. By maintaining funds on your account, you have control. Therefore when an opportunity comes your way, you can move on it without delay. Plus, having access to these funds permit you to pay for business resources from inside prison, i.e. books, independent research materials, editing services, business lawyers and other outside advisors.

2. Credit Cards: In the same manner, through unrelated parties, you want complete flexibility. As such, you need to have access to at least three credit card facilitators who will pay for your Internet resources, gifts to friends and family, book and magazine orders, college materials, and other essential business resources while incarcerated.

3. A Post Office Box: With a post office box, you are assured of having a stable mailing address for your networking sources. Problem with being in prison is that your friends and family seem to be moving every six months. These days, no one seems to stay put.

[9]"Restitution and court fines can present a potential downside to having a high balance in your Inmate Trust Account (aka "your books") when you are subject to the BOP's Financial Responsibility Program (FRP). Large trust account balances trigger large FRP payments. Conversely, low trust account balances trigger lower FRP payments. Absent a Scheduling Order from your sentencing judge stating otherwise, the BOP has the full discretion of establishing your monthly or quarterly FRP payment amounts. Failure to comply with the program's terms and conditions will result in sanctions against you."

That means your mail will either be rerouted or "retuned to sender" because someone at home forgot to register a forwarding address order with the post office on your behalf. Now you're stuck using your prison address for what should remain "private" matters.

4. Power Of Attorney (POA): We expound on this subject in greater detail in Chapter Two. Here however, we discuss how to effectively use powers of attorney to create new assets and to lawfully move, dispose of, or hypothecate others. As the old saying goes: "I'll have my people call your people?" This is the key go-to phrase between serious business minds in prison. It's key because you are prohibited from running a business while in prison, though nothing prohibits you from "talking" about or "planning" for a business while in prison. That means while you are in prison, your POA representative will have to collaborate with another prisoner's POA representative to some degree. Having a trusted individual as your POA allows you to adhere to BOP Policy. Personally, I have two "limited" powers of attorney in effect, both notarized by BOP staff: one with a trusted friend and another with an attorney friend of mine. For the better part of twelve years, my POA strategy worked like a fine Swiss watch. But slow down and let's be perfectly clear. The BOP permits limited or general POA's to be executed by its notary public staff member or contractor. So the BOP is, in essence, ostensibly advised of what you are permitting others to do for you. So handle your business. Remember though: multiple, unrelated parties is always advised.

5. <u>An Independent Bookkeeper</u>: Without fail, my independent bookkeeper maintains all business activities, while forwarding a bevy of financial updates and interim accounting data to me on a regular basis. I also receive projections, manufacturing and distribution forecasts as needed, allowing me to closely monitor my family's publishing and media interests. For me, this BOP privilege is essential to my successful reentry into society as I plan for my future post-incarceration. All my family's business data comes through the BOP's regular, first-class mail—mail that is reviewed by prison staff and then forwarded to me without delay or questions. By employing this strategy, the bookkeeper keeps everyone in check, while keeping you informed on the inner workings of the company. By being independent of family and friends, the bookkeeper is solely beholden to you. The key point here is this: when cash and assets are of concern, you want to keep everyone—family included—as reasonably honest as possible.

6. <u>A Computer Wiz</u>: Here lays the lynchpin to your success in a full comeback from your hiatus in federal prison. Without an effective computer whiz at your disposal, not one of these ten strategies mentioned in this section can be fully effective. While in prison, your every move needs to be highly effective. Otherwise, you suffer the outright waste of a perfectly good prison sentence. Contrary to other areas of your in-prison business planning, here is where family works best. Perhaps a son, a daughter, a niece, or a nephew—someone who's always on the Internet—could be your answer. Not only must they

have the ability to quickly navigate the Internet while on the phone with you, they must also be prompt and reliable with sending you the printed and downloaded data from which you need to render informed decisions. Without question, you'll need daily access to the Internet, primarily for business and technical research that will shore up your plans as you prepare for release.

7. An Irrevocable Trust: For those of us who are unmarried, one unique thing about being in federal prison is that we quickly disappear from the radar of America's commerce grid, the grid that tracks our every dollar earned and spent, every credit extension, and every debt settled—you name it. Bottom line, someone somewhere is watching and tracking our every move. While in prison, I have discovered that being off the grid from data-miners truly took me out of sight and out of mind. In other words, those who might have had an inkling to sue me are no longer as interested now that I am in prison. Honestly, it's tantamount to dying! But fret not, for those who thought I was "dead" by virtue of my going to prison were ever so wrong. Enter my irrevocable trust. . .

Forming an irrevocable trust while in prison allowed me the needed time to build a clean slate. From this clean slate, my "new business concepts" are protected from potential creditors in the future. I'm not referring to some hair-brained scheme to avoid paying my lawfully-owed debts, though, fortunately for me, none exist. Nor am I suggesting we hide our existing business or assets from lawful creditors. Instead, I am referring to those new concepts you are developing while in prison, those new concepts built from the ground up. I'm referring to business endeavors that, while in their conceptual state, have yet to develop any intrinsic value.

Here's the point. Prior to your concept becoming a going concern (according to Generally Accepted Accounting Principles), it can be assigned to, and become the property of, your irrevocable trust before it is fully matured and develops value. On the other hand, should the concept flop, simply abandon it for nothing is lost. Conversely, should the concept gain value and eventual success as the property of your trust, it is protected from your future personal creditors, so long as the trust is operating in compliance with state and federal laws. Consult your estate attorney for further details. Frankly, there can be no better way to financially plan for your post-incarceration restoration.

8. A Business Lawyer: As CEO's, businessmen and politicians, many of us have business lawyers as friends or acquaintances. Frankly, I'd be surprised if you didn't. Be that as it may, I strongly advise you to have a business lawyer on your team prior to prison. More times than not, you will encounter someone in prison (and their contacts outside of prison) who may very well present an attractive opportunity to you through his or her perfectly helpful and law-abiding contacts outside of prison walls and free of prison influence. When this occurs, you must be ready to act. Through your power of attorney representative and your business lawyer, documents may be drawn up and executed on the concept you have crafted. Equally beneficial, business lawyers can aid with navigating you through those sensitive negotiations

of which you are prohibited to engage while inside prison. Furthermore, your business lawyer is authorized, by law, to send confidential documents to you without scrutiny from prison officials. Here, your legal-mail privacy is protected through attorney-client privilege. Under the same constitutionally protected privilege, your attorney may even visit with you to discuss your post-incarceration business plans in private.

9. A Message Center: Naturally, most federal prisoners use family members as temporary message centers during their term of incarceration. But if you are a former executive, politician or current business owner, you need a professional message center. Or in the least, a means of "sounding professional" to various business associates or constituents. You need a professional message center where new contacts and associates can leave messages for you, contacts and associates who are integral in assisting with building your comeback. A common problem with family is the lack of consistency and reliability. Nothing can be worse than finally making a substantial business acquaintance, only to have them call your sister with her three terrorist children in the background, yelling and screaming as she is trying to take a message for you. Misjudgments like this, you cannot afford. As such, to be effective, you must devise a reliable strategy for capturing those crucial messages. For me, I began with family as my message center, from which a whopping 60% of my messages were lost or mishandled. It was a total disaster. But when Google developed Google Voice, my problem was solved. With Google Voice, you can (1) pick your

custom phone number that complements your new business brand, (2) pre-record a professional greeting with promptings that not only tracks your messages, but directs your callers to the correct departments within your organization, (3) capture 99% of your messages, and, (4) conceal the fact that it's Google Voice facilitating your message center. Great service—and guess what? Google Voice is free of charge! Perfect for a cash-strapped prisoner!

10. A Handyman: Last but not least, you need a handyman. This may sound trivial but you don't want to wait until you're sitting in prison to find out how right I am. Take my word for it. When you first enter into prison, family can be great. Your wife and children will help with those many incidentals that were, at one time, a no-brainer for you or your staff to handle. But now that you are gone, those "no-brainers" may seem insurmountable. That said, experience teaches the following essentials: (1) secure a trusted handyman (or woman) on call, someone who's willing and able to take care of those odds and ends for you (or your wife) and your business. This can save your business and possibly your marriage, (2) secure someone to be your eyes, ears and legs out there in the free world. Let's discuss both.

Odds And Ends: Of course, you wouldn't realize it while living in the free world. When you're at home, everything's in balance. It's easy and automatic. However, when your freedom is snatched away from you, having someone to take care of those household odds and ends is, indeed, priceless. Plus, if maintaining order in your business is important to you, consider my handyman story discussed in

Chapter Two. Similarly, having someone send and receive packages for you is a major advantage. Be it copying old files and sending them to you, or repairing leaks in one of your rental properties. There's also the task of retrieving personal property from your storage facility, or conversely, placing them into your storage facility. I'm speaking on those needs you would never imagine needing—that is, until you're stuck in some wasteland prison somewhere with no way to lift a finger to help your family, your business, or even yourself.

Second, having independent eyes and ears out there empowers you in countless other ways. Just knowing someone is looking out for your best interest will help you sleep better at night. For instance, you might have rental or investment properties that require extra attention or oversight. I have discovered that having independent eyes, ears and legs virtually place you at the scene. Strictly speaking though, it's always best to dissociate your wife and children from these tasks (unless your children are competent and full-grown). Early on in my prison sentence, I outsourced such efforts to my handyman.

At one time, my current handyman was on my payroll for the sole purpose of handling these things I definitely needed done, but chose not to do them myself. For I had far more pressing things to do with my limited time. After all, I too was a CEO. But as years passed, I discovered a more cost-effective approach to my handyman situation. Today I supplement my handyman with the use of a web-based business called Angie's List. From this list, I can custom select bonded handymen or women to fill my needs for a predetermined price. Similar to a temporary employment agency, I can stay with my Angie's List contractor or exchange for another with just a telephone call. Point being, any combination of the above will serve you well should you consider my suggestions to some degree.

At any rate, know this. Prison life for former CEO's, business executives and politicians does not have to be as debilitating as it is for the average prisoner. After all, were we not educated and trained to take on the challenges of the world? From my perspective, the prison challenge are no different. It's just a challenge, not a death sentence. So take a moment and summon that same inner strength you have relied on in times past. Utilize your survival instincts within and do what I have done: turn tragedy into triumph by turning prison into progress.

FREQUENTLY ASKED QUESTIONS

How Prison Designation Works

Q. *What is the process if I would like to arrange a transfer to a prison facility closest to my home or my release address?*

A. As a general rule, the Bureau of Prisons requires that inmates stay put and stay clear of trouble for approximately 18 months before a transfer is considered; that is, unless a transfer is initiated for health or disciplinary reasons. Terms of incarceration less than 18 months, however, will likely not be considered.

How Appeal Bonds Work

Q. *If one is already released on bond during pre-trial, the trial itself, and during sentencing, why can't the same bond carry over into the appeal process?*

A. Three principle reasons: 1) Jurisdiction: Once the district court sentences a defendant, the proceedings end at the district court level and begins anew at the appellate court level, 2) Review: The review process also begins anew—not based on the trial itself, but based on the Constitutionality of the trial's results, and, 3) Flight Risk: Yes, a defendant, now convicted, is a much greater flight risk than he or she was during the post-conviction, district court level.

Judge's Recommendations Often Overrated

Q. ***If a judge's recommendation has no binding effect on the BOP, what is the difference between making a recommendation and saying nothing at all? What would be the net difference?***

A. Well, consider the effect of a character-reference letter from your past employer to an impending employer. Such a letter is by no means binding on the future employer. It does, however, offer guidance and direction as the future employer formulates a decision. In essence, the same principle applies when a judge makes a recommendation on your behalf to the BOP. No, it's not binding on the BOP, but it helps as they formulate their decision.

Mistakes When Self-Surrendering

Q. ***What happens if I become seriously ill or fall victim to an accident that hospitalizes me, which could cause me to miss my self-surrender date?***

A. No problem. When you awaken from the medication or anesthesia, two burly U.S. Marshals will be standing there at your bedside with guns and a sterilized pair of handcuffs awaiting your recovery. However, if time permits, your attorney can contact the sentencing judge and the U.S. Attorney's Office for an extension, provided your doctor confirms the severity of your condition. You would later be required to report to the local U.S. Marshal's Office instead of to the prison where you were originally scheduled to report.

Facts About Prison Consultants

Q. ***Are there any prison consultants for state prisons?***

A. I have not located any state prison consultants. Reason being—as I perceive it—is that many of those who go to state prison are multiple offenders and thus they already know the inner-workings of the system; or that the crime a state prisoner commits is so serious, he couldn't care less about the inner-workings of the system. Lastly, I believe that due to there being such a large number of prisons from state to state, with no uniform method of operation, a market for state prison consulting is not economically feasible. But being that I have no experience with state prisons, I could be wrong on all points.

Secure Your Personal Information

Q. ***If I discover a problem or inaccurate information on my credit report while in prison, can I fight it from prison effectively?***

A. Certainly can. You could be just as effective from prison as you would be from home. Problem is, if you use the prison's address during the course of your challenge, your credit record will be largely blemished by the prison's address.

Secure Your Professional Licenses and Permits

Q. ***Really, what's the use? Once you are a convicted felon, the days of professional and specialized licensing are over. Right?***

A. Not for long. Pursuant to the Second Chance Act of 2007, which was signed into law by President Bush, non-violent, first-time offenders will soon be able to apply for a "restorative expungement" of conviction. Under the Act, qualified offenders may soon apply for this expungement upon satisfactorily completing probation. The offender then becomes eligible to apply for, and upon approval , have his criminal conviction expunged. With this expungement, the offender may then apply for government or professional jobs that require special licenses or permits.

It's Prison. Not The Chamber Of Commerce

Q. ***What about reports, spreadsheets, and copies of contracts and proposals of transactions in the making? Will I be able to receive such data while in prison?***

A. Yes. In fact, I have been receiving them for fifteen years without the slightest of inquiry. Again, let's be clear on a couple of points: 1) You can receive *copies* of the above stated documents, but you are not allowed to sign and return anything willy-nilly, that is, unless you want to get keelhauled by prison officials. My point? You *cannot* be a signatory on anything whatsoever without BOP approval, and, 2) should the BOP approve the execution of a certain document, it will not be a document that constitutes being part of—or the running of—a business. However, should your wife or a friend require a power of attorney of sorts, no problem. But if you push the limits and get caught, you could find yourself shipped to some God-forsaken prison three thousand miles away.

Q: *Do you have any other questions for Mr. CEO?*

A: On our website: http://frenchcuffsblog.com. Fill out the contact form with your question and we will get back to you as soon as possible.

frenchcuffsblog.com

"Nothing could ever be as bad as what can be imagined."

—Author Unknown

In this Chapter . . .

Your First Day In Prison

Top Ten "Thou Shalt Nots" in Federal Prison

The Truth About Prison Violence

Details About Living Quarters

Prisoner's Rights, Privileges, And Administrative Remedies

Telephone Access And Restrictions

You've Got Mail

Educational, Vocational, And Recreational Programming

Visiting Privileges And Limitations

Sentence And Goodtime Computation

Residential Drug Abuse Program (RDAP)

Commissary Privileges: Limitations, Special Purchases, And Religious Accommodations

Race Relations In Prison

Interacting With Prison Staff

Inter-Prison Transfers

Common Inmate Infractions And Sanctions

Frequently Asked Questions

CHAPTER FOUR

ENTERING PRISON DOORS

Your First Day In Prison

It was a warm and muggy day on June 19, 1995, when I entered through the doors of a federal prison for the first time ever, looking and feeling like some sort of refugee from a faraway land. As with all new arrivals to a federal prison (other than self-surrender prisoners), I was afraid, overwhelmed, and dejected—exactly what my judge and the U.S. Attorney ordered; and it is exactly what your judge and prosecutor ordered for you also. But in this chapter, my objective is to shine some much-needed light on this dark and desolate road on which you will soon be traveling, in order that you may see the sharp curves, the deep potholes, and the signs that read "Steep Cliffs Ahead."

Receiving And Discharge (R & D):This department will be your first stop upon entering prison. Here you are processed in, much the same as being "booked" into a county jail: photographed, fingerprinted, physically evaluated, etc. And at some point in this process, you will receive the all-important "Inmate Handbook" that contains the rules and regulations of that particular institution. Upon receiving your handbook, you will be required to sign for it, meaning should you violate any rules and regulations during your stay, you will not be able to claim "ignorance of the rules." So I strongly urge that you to take the time and read your Inmate Handbook before you get too comfortable and violate a rule. It's a painfully boring and agonizing read. But you must still know the rules—both the written and the unwritten rules, if you desire to mitigate the degree of your suffering.

Your Housing Unit: Once you are fully processed, you will be greeted by a receiving officer who will escort you to your next stop known as your "assigned housing unit." You will then be met by the housing unit's correctional officer (commonly referred to as the "CO") who will assign you to your specific living quarters, be it a cell, a cubicle, a barrack bunk, or a room, depending on the security level of the institution where you will be officially designated (Consult "Facilities' Reports" on *frenchcuffsblog.com* for an up to date intelligence reports on all federal prisons).

Your Inmate Handbook will also contain rules regarding your housing unit and your specific living quarters respectively.

Your Bunkmate: Unless you have been to prison before, or perhaps in the military, you will undoubtedly be overwhelmed by the noise of the prison and by the hundreds of men or women confined in such a concentrated area. However, to your astonishment, in a matter of days you will be well into the swing of things. Not because you will want to be, but because you will have to be. And the quickest way to get into the swing of things is to ask your bunkmate about the facility. Whether you like him/her or not, your bunkmate will be the closest thing to being your best friend at that very moment. Your bunkmate would usually be the first person to inform you what is "really" going on inside and outside your housing unit, or clue you in on the myriad of "the unwritten inmate rules" and the "rogue-staff members' rules" not found in your Inmate Handbook. So, for a safe landing, gain the confidence of your bunkmate. How? By being respectful. Introduce yourself. State where you are from. Shake hands if he/she is so willing. But *do not* ask personal questions. It's safest to mirror your bunkmate's demeanor. If he/she is kind and talkative, do the same. If close in and withdrawn, do the same—following your initial introduction.

Next, be respectful of your bunkmate's space, property, and privacy—much the same as you would in any shared-living arrangement. Remember where you are going. It's called prison. The great equalizer. Prison is a place where I, a former chairman and CEO of a $200 million-dollar a year corporation initially bunked with a crack-head street-gang member. And in a prison environment, the crack-head gang member rules, not the CEO's. So for your safety and peace of mind, leave that pompous, self-important attitude tucked away in the wine cellar of your home.

Incidentally, should you be assigned to living quarters where your bunkmate gives you the "cold shoulder" for whatever reason, move about the common areas (not others' living quarters) and search out a kind face and inquire about the facility. For experience teaches that, by in large, fellow inmates will reach out to assist a new arrival, being that we all have been a new arrival at one time or another.

Your Fellow Inmates In General: Regardless of the security level of the prison where you will be designated, fellow inmates are often more than willing to assist new arrivals as alluded to earlier. But on a broader note, prison is no different than many sectors of the free society, in that you should be very selective about whom you seek out for information. For those who take the initiative to volunteer guidance and direction to you, show your gratitude, and then move on. Soon you will intuitively know who you can trust to give you sound advice on how everything works: who to mingle with, who *not* to mingle with, where to go, where *not* to go, what to do, and what *not* to do, etc. Given 48 hours or less, you will find such an individual, or unless your "I'm-better-than-you" attitude warrants otherwise.

Taking Your First Day In Stride: No doubt about it, your first day in prison will naturally be overwhelming; and, all-in-all, it will take about two weeks before you are fully settled into your new digs. So take each day in stride, knowing and accepting the fact that you will be in your appointed place for an appointed period of time. Take some time to reflect on why you are where you are in the first place. Trust me, it will serve you well—in addition to making the process of prison much easier to endure.

Top Ten "Thou Shalt Nots" In Federal Prison

In my many years in federal prison, I have observed—and continue to observe—how inmates engage in conduct or activities that invariably bring them much grief in an environment that, in itself, is grievous. It's like observing a person who is engulfed in flames asking another person for directions to the nearest gas station, as if the circumstances in his life were not hot enough already. It baffles my mind. But time and again, I have witnessed inmates repeat the same old mindless prison antics and insanities over and over again, expecting different results.

Keep in mind, you are not at home, nor in college, nor a night club, nor a country club. You are either going to or you are currently in prison. And while in prison, it will be assumed you will want to avoid the following Top Ten "Thou Shalt Nots", each listed in the order that burns the hottest:

1. Thou Shalt Not Gamble: In my fifteen years of prison, I have seen more killings, stabbings, and outright mule beatings over gambling or gambling related incidents. Why gambling? Because many prisoners—especially uneducated, less-sophisticated prisoners—rely on their gambling endeavors to occupy their time and to make what little money (or "hustle") they can for either commissary or to send home.

   Now I can probably guess what you are thinking: "No problem. I don't gamble." Well, think again. Maybe you don't gamble. But your bunkmate, or a fellow inmate of whom you really know little about—but who has gained your trust and confidence—could drag you into a gambling debt that he/she cannot pay. Personally, I don't gamble either. But on two separate occasions I have had to pay debts (albeit small debts) for inmates who I befriended, not knowing they had gambling problems. This, of course, begs the question: How did I, a non-gambler, become responsible for a debt I did not owe? Well, I became a "debtor by association," meaning I allowed the wrong person to get too close to me; a young man to whom I became somewhat of a surrogate father and mentor. So when the youngster friend of mine couldn't pay his gambling debt, I was approached by a hoodster (my term for a wannabe gangster) and given an implied ultimatum, due to my association with the youngster. Following a week of attempting to rationalize with desperate, irrational prison hoodsters, I later came to my senses and realized that logical and rational reasoning are an anomaly in prison. Either pay . . . or *really* pay. So to settle the matter I gave the money (in the form of commissary) to the hoodster, and then I disassociated myself with the young man.

2. Thou Shalt Not Snitch or "Dry" Snitch: You have probably seen the movie based on John Grisham's novel, *Witness*. A young, innocent Amish boy witnesses a murder. The murderers discover that this young boy becomes Detective John Book's (played by Harrison Ford) key witness.

Suddenly the boy and his equally innocent mother are marked for death. That's great fiction. But it's also a great truth in real life and equally true in prison life.

Call them informants, witnesses, plants, operatives, or even sorcerers. Doesn't matter. In prison terms, you are a snitch. And depending on the security level of the prison where you will be designated, life could be a living hell should your fellow inmates mark you as a snitch.

In fact, the very moment you enter your assigned housing unit, and inmates discover that you are a new arrival, the whispers among the inmates are, "Wonder if he's hot?"—hot being the code word for "snitch." Like a pride of lions, curious inmates will watch you from afar, studying your moves, mannerisms, and demeanor. And when they question you, or offer their assistance too freely, what they are *really* doing is fishing for information as to whether you are hot or not. For this reason, and others, you should not discuss your case with a fellow inmate, at least until you are absolutely certain that you can trust him.

At any rate, if inmates discover that you assisted the government and later received a Motion 5K1[10] departure, the entire institution—prison staff included—will know about it before sundown the next day. And so will you. Hence, you will then be perceived as a "yard informant," meaning that while in prison, you will probably snitch on your fellow inmates in order to curry favor with the prison staff. Or, perhaps, you will "dry snitch," which is a prison term for snitching without actually naming names.

For example, a dry snitcher would say something to

[10] A 5K1.1 Downward Departure Motion was created by Congress for the sole purpose of allowing defense attorneys and the U.S. Attorney's office to enter into a joint motion for a much lower sentence for the defendant than that which is statutorily prescribed for an offense of conviction. Before a motion for a lower sentence can be granted, the sentencing court must find that the defendant provided "substantial assistance" to the government; assistance in the form of testimony that resulted in others being brought to justice for their roles in the offense.

the affect, "I am not mentioning names officer, but it was a black guy on the 'A' League Baseball Team who wears his hair like the boxing promoter, Don King," says the dry snitcher . . .

So here's the bottom line: If you, in fact, cooperated with the government and received a Motion 5K1.1 departure (See your Presentence Investigation Report—PSI), I recommend you keep that information to yourself. However, if your case was published in the caselaw books or in the newspaper, your fellow inmates will know. Moreover, these days, inmates are resourceful enough to have someone on the outside Google your name and, perhaps, uncover certain details regarding your case, including whether you cooperated with the government or not. That said, I will let you in on a secret that could significantly play to your advantage by keeping your "hot" secrets a secret:

(1) a good attitude toward your fellow inmates. If you are a down-to-earth gentleman or lady who does his or her prison time by these rules and principles, you greatly reduce the odds of being a target;

(2) if you did not cooperate with the government, that is all well and good. However, the key now is to mind your own business while in prison, and keep what you see to yourself; and

(3) avoid long, protracted, goody-two-shoe conversations with prison staff. Remember, you are in prison. You are not at home.

Inmates are always on the watch for "inmate cops" who pal around with prison staff. So when conversing with staff—and all of us do from time to time—keep it professional and as brief as possible in order to avoid the appearance of impropriety.

3. Thou Shalt Not Steal: Yes, I know you do not steal. But in prison, there are two definitions for stealing of which you need to be mindful: First, the obvious, as in outright stealing from your fellow inmates. Second, you're being marked as an easy target from whom others would steal. Both pose their own unique potential dangers.

Let's discuss them . . .

Stealing in prison is nothing like stealing in the general free society. For instance, stealing a postage stamp from a fellow inmate who earns a mere 12¢ an hour could get a man killed. Such a violent act is not exclusively about the money, per se, but about a prisoner's so-called need for honor and respect among the other prisoners as well. Irrational? Absolutely. But as for life in prison, the irrational is considered rational in the minds of hoodsters. Another contributing factor to prison theft is one's lack of privacy. While in prison, there's seldom ever any privacy. Everyone can see, or will soon discover, what you have in your personal property and what you are all about. It will grate your every nerve, but you'll have to get used to it. Why? Because it's intentional. It's prison. It's all by design. So get used to having a bunkmate, or two, or three, or eight. It all goes with the territory.

Whatever the number, at times, one or all of you will leave personal property out and about your immediate living area. Perfectly natural. However, if the smallest of articles become lost, misplaced, borrowed, or stolen, everyone in your quarters is suddenly a suspect, some more than others. Now comes the suspect eye, the cursing, the questions, the arguing, and so on and so forth. Suddenly you—the new guy—is labeled a thief. Go figure.

Yes, all of this angst over a friggin' 49¢ postage stamp. So now your free-world rationale kicks in: "What the hell," you reason, "just give the guy a damn stamp and be done with it." Right? No, wrong! Giving in by offering the guy a stamp confirms (in the guy's mind) that you indeed stole the stamp. Otherwise, you would not have offered to replace it. There you have it. Prison rationale.

> **Experience Teaches:**
>
> A prisoner's first line of defense against incompetent or abusive BOP personnel is to know BOP policy.

So my advice is as follows: Never borrow or even touch another inmate's property, unless, over time, you have come to know and trust him well.

Experience also teaches how you could unconsciously project yourself as an easy target from whom others would perpetually steal. Here's how:

Many of us white-collar offenders continue to live in denial for a protracted period of time, even while we are well into our prison sentence—myself included. Admittedly, it is called hubris. Don't laugh. It's really true. I have studied my fellow white-collar offenders for years. We are, in essence, like our own "prison gang" so to speak, in that when one of us sees another enter through the front door—regardless of race, mind you—we gradually adopt him into the fold, so long as he's not a liability. You see, many of us white-collar offenders tend to believe we are "better" than other inmates because (1) many of us still own a business or parts of businesses, (2) many of us are still well-connected, which keeps us in a mindset of "self-importance" while in prison, (3) we are all highly educated, which is in stark contrast to the greater prison population—as well as the greater prison staff population and (4) in many instances we are treated with more reverence and respect by most prisoners, as well as prison staff. In addition, we are provided with the best of prison office jobs available, for example, department clerks, town drivers, teachers, tutors, and other office-related jobs. So of course, we often stand out. And standing out is *not* a good thing among less fortunate prisoners. So to remind us who is "really in charge," some of us become victims of theft, extortion, or even violence.

Therefore, to prevent yourself from becoming a victim of theft or extortion, assess your attitude towards the general population of inmates. Find out how others perceive you before others have to "tell you" or "show you" how they perceive you. Then do what is necessary to immediately change that negative perception.

For example, when I initially entered prison back in 1995, I became a victim of theft within my first ten days, and later learned that I was marked for extortion. To counteract the move against me, I strategically passed word around that I would be teaching a class and writing a book for inmates on real estate. Instantly, the perception about me changed. In other words, my willingness to share my knowledge with the less fortunate inmates suddenly made me "one of the fellas" if you will. Well, it worked. And even though I am still a CEO in mind and in heart, you best believe I now know how to become "one of the fellas," when necessary. Suffice it to say, over the past fifteen years, this being-one-of-the-fellas strategy has served me well. Rest assured, it will do the same for you.

Remember, you are in prison. Not at home. So I urge you to heed to this advice for your own good.

4. Thou Shalt Not Disrespect Others: Yes, I know. You are probably shaking your head as you read this subsection while thinking, "What the hell? You mean to tell me that disrespect is all of a sudden a moral concern of the very criminal that disrespected society when he himself has broken the law?"

Need I again remind you of where you are?

Yes, it is true! Despite the contradiction in logic, respect among fellow inmates is paramount—especially in higher security prisons. But make no mistake. Some higher security inmates eventually work their way down to minimum security levels. As such, should you disrespect the wrong inmate at a minimum security prison camp, you could find yourself choking down a knuckle sandwich before you could say "uncle."

With that in mind, never *ever* underestimate the violent proclivities of any man in prison, regardless of the prison's security level (Consult "The Truth About Prison Violence" later on in this chapter).

5. Thou Shalt Not Engage In Homosexual Acts: Don't flinch.

Do you not recall what I mentioned on our site regarding "the good, the bad, and the very ugly" relating to federal prison? Well, unruly homosexual conduct falls squarely in the "very ugly" category as it relates to prison. Of course, we see it all in prison: homosexuals, transvestites, transsexuals, transgenders, you name it. Every sexual preference, male and female, goes to prison.

For those of us who are heterosexual prisoners, we tolerate the differences in prison, much the same as they are tolerated in free society today. But serious problems arise when any group is promiscuous while in prison, which inevitably leads to pockets of violence.

To stay clear of such violence, simply keep your sexual preferences to yourself; and, as experience teaches, you will make it through federal prison without much of a problem in this area.

Then again, the higher your security classification, the higher the odds are of your being confronted with, or witnessing, abhorrent sexual behavior between prisoners. Even then, unless a man carries himself with a hint of femininity, or associates with someone who does, he will likely escape the problems associated with homosexual violence in prison (Consult "The Truth About Prison Violence" in this chapter for more details).

6. Thou Shalt Not Get Cozy With Prison Staff: Frankly, I am amazed at how oblivious certain inmates are when it comes to realizing how dangerous it is when they get too "buddy-buddy" with prison staff. They are not your friend, nor are they your enemy. They are prison staff whose job is keep prisoners in line. So use common sense. In fact, this is the one and only "shalt not" that could turn a group of mild-mannered inmates into a pack of rabid wolves in an instant. Here's why: (1) You would be regarded as a "yard snitch," meaning you work for "the man" while sleeping, eating, and conversing alongside fellow inmates; (2) should something happen on the yard or inside the living quarters, you would be regarded as the "go-to" inmate of the prison staff's list of reliable informants; and (3) you would be regarded as the "staff pet," meaning you would likely receive favor from prison officials—or even from the U.S. Attorney—when you seek a reduced sentence or perhaps more halfway house time.

Know this: there is a right way to interact with prison staff, and there is certainly the wrong way to interact with prison staff.

In any event, getting too cozy with prison staff—at any security level—is *not* good for your health and welfare.

7. Thou Shalt Not Be Nosy: It is a well-known fact that even a convicted, currently incarcerated inmate could also be an active informant for the government at the same time. And thus, as a prisoner perceives it, once an informant, always an informant. He or she is perceived as one who will turn on his or her own mother in order to assist the government with netting its next big fish. But for the time being, plying you for actionable information on your case or a fellow inmate's case could lead to yet another conspiracy indictment against you.

Such conduct is most common in the higher security prisons where the prison sentences are much higher, and where there is much more to be gained by an inmate informant. But make no mistake. Inmates in minimum-security federal prison camps—most of whom are first-time offenders—have been known to be considerable informants for the government.

So unless a fellow inmate offers, in general conversation, to tell you about his case, stay clear from the subject. And should such a conversation ensue, do not run away or freak out about it. That would only make you sound suspicious. Just keep it simple, like, "Oh, I'm here for bank fraud," and then skillfully move on to another topic.

8. Thou Shalt Not Flaunt Thy Wealth: Yes, you best believe that class warfare is alive and well—and even dangerous—in prison.

Much like free society, prison society has its poor, its middle class, and its very rich prison inmates; and even though the prison system is designed to be an equal opportunity oppressor, those with money, including inmates, always seem to have a way of getting much of what they want, which causes them to stand out among all the other inmates. Even their speech, their walk, their perceived education, rich inmates have a way of standing out among the usual prison fray.

However, standing out in-and-of-itself is not where danger lies. The danger lies with the rich man's "I'm-better-than-all-of-you-miscreants" attitude he brings with him when he enters prison. And many rich inmates will flaunt their wealth in order to prove that they are indeed "better and more important" than those other "scruffy" inmates.

For example: At the time of this writing, there is an inmate who does not eat a single meal inside the prison dining hall with us—the general population—who he considers "the great unwashed." Instead, he has his own personal inmate who cooks his meals three times a day, and then the cook washes the rich man's dishes. This same man has an inmate room keeper (like a housekeeper), a laundry guy, a shopping guy, you name it—and he spends his day watching CNBC and calling his stockbroker son with his daily trades. My point? Such conduct in prison makes you a target by drawing attention to you like bees to pollen. Not only are you a target to the indigent inmate population. Now there is *double-trouble* for you to contend with; hence, you and your money could go up in flames . . . literally.

So, please, do yourself a favor. Refrain from being a rich fool, only to end up as a rich victim of extortion, robbery, beatings, or an administrative transfer to some God-forsaken prison where the sun never shines. Do your level best to simply blend in. Stay low-key, and work toward going home standing upright and in one piece.

9. Thou Shalt Not Use Or Deal Drugs In Prison: Drugs is a growing problem in our federal prison system; and, the irony is, the higher the security level of each prison, the easier it is to obtain drugs. Go figure.

Now, you are probably thinking, “Since I don't do drugs, I can skip this part.”

Hold on before turning this page. You may also be thinking of the garden-variety street drugs, such as marijuana, cocaine, methamphetamine, etc., none with which you have a problem. But what prescription drugs might you be taking? OxyContin, Percocet, or Vicodin? Well, if you are in prison, and find yourself in need of these stylish drugs, they are available for a very steep price. Plus, should you suddenly become ill, or suffer an injury or a tooth ache, it could take weeks before you are allowed to see the doctor or the dentist. Well, guess what? When you are hurting, and an aspirin won’t cut it, to hell with rules and regulations and prison policy. You want relief, and you want it now. So what do you do when you are locked in a building, writhing in pain, with three-hundred domino-slamming, card-slapping, television-watching inmates all around you? I’ll tell you what I did. I found a dope dealer in the building and bought some pain medication and some antibiotics for my infected tooth. So yes, I broke the rules. But as they say: "Desperate times call for desperate measures."

Am I condoning or recommending you break prison rules? Absolutely not. What I did was dangerous, even though I ingested small doses of each medicine.

Well, be that as it may, the medication carried me through a week's wait. But many prisoners have recurring ailments that the prison administrators cannot—nor will not—attend to due to mass rationing and other budget-related problems that go along with operating a prison.

As such, an ailing inmate can run up a huge tab with the resident dope dealer and find himself in serious debt. And a debt to the dope dealer invariably leads to violence; therefore, there must be better ways of solving this problem.

And there are: (1) What I have been doing over the years—following my dope dealer encounter—is maintain a small hidden supply of my own legally prescribed pain medication and antibiotics from previous visits to the doctor in case of another emergency. Now I am always in compliance, even though an officer, during a routine locker shakedown, can confiscate my outdated medication without sanctions against me, (2) Plus, should I experience the slightest of ailments, I sign up for sick call and lobby for more stand-by medication, (3) Should an inmate suffer from recurring pain for whatever reason, he or she should request medical transfer to a chronic-care medical facility in the BOP, or, (4) Seek help through the Administrative Remedy Process pertaining to the health and welfare of federal prison inmates.

What I have discovered is that by being proactive with your health issues in prison, you will stay slightly ahead of the curve. And no, it is not an easy task in the least. But it is safe—and it is legal.

10.Thou Shalt Not Be Overly Opinionated: Opinions. Everybody has an opinion about something or someone. Some people seem to have strong opinions about almost everything, while others are more prone to keep their opinions to themselves, simply to avoid conflict and controversy. That's okay in a free and rational society. But not in prison.

In a prison society, a large majority of inmates are grossly uneducated, or undereducated, and thus they are often bored, bitter, and hell-bent on creating conflict and controversy. So they engage in irrational opinion-swapping about anything and everything, which lead to arguments and even fights. And depending on the opinion and the inmate who spoke it, a prison riot could ensue as a result, particularly if the opinions are centered around race or gang issues.

For example, there were many strong opinions among the black, brown, and white prison population during the 2008 U.S. Presidential race. Why? Because a black man, Barack Obama, a Mexican-American man, Bill Richardson, and a white woman, Hillary Clinton—along with other white candidates—were fiercely battling for the White House. So one could only imagine the race-baiting, smack-talking opinions that were uttered around the prison yard as the campaign heated up. Yet what I found most interesting is that due to the racial implications at hand, the three races (blacks, Mexican-Americans, and whites) kept much of their opinions about the presidential race among their own racial groups, in fear of igniting a race riot.

Being overly opinionated in prison all too often leads to problems, be it the pride of being right, the shame of being wrong, or the embarrassment of being made to look like an outright idiot. And being that most inmates are hypersensitive and easily offended—especially relating to race issues—I have learned that when someone asks my opinion on a sensitive issue, such as race, religion, or politics, I am rather reserved, unless I know them well.

However, while in prison, the best policy is to keep your hot-topic opinions to yourself; that is, unless you have become well acquainted with the person(s) who is seeking your opinion.

The Truth About Prison Violence

When was the last time you saw a movie or a television program depicting life in prison? Could it have been a classic prison film, *Public Enemy Number 1*, from the 30's, or the movie, *Alcatraz*, from the 70's, or that a television series, *Prison Break*, which ended in 2009? Whatever the show, I am certain you have seen the stereotypes consistent with most prison-related programs, such as: (1) big muscle-bound, bald-headed black guys with names like Bubba, Spike, or Ice, or, (2) scruffy, gnarly-faced white guys with eyes as dark as hollowed-out skull sockets, or, (3) a prison riot or a prison escape with blood hounds, guns, flak jackets, and tobacco-spitting prison guards tracking the escapee.

Granted, these and other stereotypes about prisons are unfortunately true for the most part; but, just as producers of big-screen movies take everything to the absolute extreme, television prison movies are no exception to the same extreme.

So what's the truth about prison violence? Because the Experience teaches that being raped in prison by a man named Bubba is the Number One fear of most men. Why? Because of what we've seen on television or in the movies. But that's not true in medium-to-low security federal prisons. The Number Two fear is dying in prison from some sort of targeted violence from a gnarly-faced guy named Scar.

For starters, let's go back and revisit how you were manipulated by the violent, graphic images on television.

Assuming all that you have seen actually does happen in prison, here is what you do not see or know: (1) Rapes and killings are rarely wide-spread acts of random violence in federal prison. Instead you become a target by violating one or more of the "Ten Thou Shalt Nots In Prison" In the above section, (2) Rapes, killings, and riots depicted on television would likely occur at a maximum security or a medium security prison, and, (3) most TV programs you have seen are likely depictions of a state prison facility, not the federal prison facility. Here, our focus is on what we know: federal prisons.

This, of course, is not to imply that the federal prison system is violence free. But there is a good reason why movie and television producers prefer a state prison setting over a federal prison setting. That is, in part, because there is a huge difference between the type of criminals in the state penal system and those in the federal penal system. Likewise, there is a huge per capita cultural and economic difference between the state and federal prisoners also.

For example, unlike state prisoners, federal prisoners are considered the elite of the prison world. They are richer, smarter, better educated, and better connected than state prisoners. They are men and women who local authorities were unable to corner, arrest, and convict. Many of them actually beat state charges with high-powered lawyers, but were subsequently re-indicted under federal law (known as "federal oversight"). Others were simply too quick, too savage, or just too plain sophisticated for city, county, or state police agencies.

As such, the federal government and its Federal Bureau of Prisons' staff and management team must be better educated, trained, and in many instances, better compensated than in a state prison staff and management team.

Now, let's backtrack, shall we, and review my personal, 15 years (and counting) of "boots-on-the-ground" prison-violence experienced by detailing the topics in this section.

Rapes, Riots, And Killings: As for prison rapes, Personally, I have never witnessed one. Neither has anyone of whom I have befriended, mentored, or associated with has ever witnessed an actual prison rape. I have, however, heard of two rapes involving homosexuals when I was serving time at the high-security USP federal prison facility in Lompoc, California.

As for prison riots, I was trapped in three: USP Lompoc in the Fall of 1995 was my first riot. FCI Terminal Island, Spring of 2000, was my second riot, and FCI Lompoc, Spring of 2007 was my third riot. Yet I was never injured, touched, targeted, nor accused of participating in the riots in any way. There is a central reason for surviving prison riots. I touch on that reason below. But the deeper reason is discussed in the Subsection entitled "The Ten Thou Shall Nots" In Federal Prison.

As for killings, there were three: an officer and an inmate during a riot in the Fall of 1995 at USP Lompoc (both targeted), and an inmate killing in the Summer of 1998 at FCI a Terminal Island (also targeted). At that time, FCI Terminal Island was classified as a medium-high security facility. Today, however, FCI Terminal Island is classified a low-security federal prison.

Violence Depicted On Television/Movies: Again, what you see on television is utter sensationalism, much like everything else you see on television or in the movies. But I, as well as countless others, have been able to avoid prison violence by being vigilantly aware of, and pro-actively staying away from, the violent hotspots. Moreover, I was pro-active with my attitude toward every inmate and staff member of whom I have had to interact—be they at my prison job site or in passing. In the simplest of terms, remaining mindful of—and accepting of—where I was for the time being remains to be, by far, my best line of defense against prison violence.

State Prison Violence Versus Federal Prison Violence: It stands to reason that the by the sheer differences between state prisons' populations and the federal prison population, violence in state prisons is more frequent, with greater severity. Notwithstanding the differences in populations the BOP has one unique advantage that a state prison does not have—an advantage that even men with life sentences will take heed before engaging in a violent act. And that advantage? The BOP has the ability to move an inmate thousands of miles away from his family and from the court system where he is fighting his appeal. So if the inmate has an ailing mother, or if he is working on his case, perhaps in search of a lighter sentence, a single act of violence could literally wipe out years of litigation, including the last of his hope for post-conviction relief.

So I suggest you revisit "The Ten Thou Shalt Nots" above, in light of what we have discussed here. Of course, no one can assure that you will completely escape all prison violence. No advice on this subject is fail-safe, but I can proclaim this fact for certain. For 15 years, the "Ten Thou Shalt Nots" have worked wonders for me, considering that I, and many others, have managed to get through four security classification levels without incident. So take heed.

Details About Living Quarters

In federal prison, your living quarters are constructed in one-of-four ways: (1) a cell with metal bars, (2) Walled or semi-walled cubicles, (3) actual rooms, or, (4) open-barrack-style bunks. Let's discuss each of the four in relation to each security-level classification.

Cells With Metal Bars: As time passes and more and more federal prisons are built, we are seeing fewer bars and dungeon-gray prison cells that were seen by prisoners of old. Yet still in operation remains most of the original federal prison facilities, facilities dating back to the "Three Prisons Act" passed by Congress in 1891 (Leavenworth, Kansas, Atlanta, Georgia and McNeil Island, Washington). Only McNeil Island has closed.

Today, most of the other prisons with bars and dungeon-gray cells are used to house medium, medium-high, and high-security prisoners. Even so, these facilities are incorporating modern satellite structures as they expand housing to facilitate increased populations. So unless you have been classified as "medium" or "medium-high" or "high" security, you will see very few cellblocks with metal bars.

Walled Or Semi-Walled Cubicles: Two-, three-, and four-man cubicles have become one of the most popular methods of constructing the living quarters of today's federal prisons. In fact, semi-walled cubicles are more efficient and cost effective to construct, and today's prisoners who are classified as "low" or "minimum" security will likely be housed in a semi-walled cubicle of two-to-four inmates per cubicle.

Rooms: Unless you are on your way to a federal hold-over detention center, actual rooms with doors are a thing of the past.

New construction of low- and minimum-security prisons are cubicles or open-barrack-style living. But, again, some of the older facilities may still have rooms, since several prisons around the country were former living quarters for military soldiers, officers, and staff; which, by the way, is why many federal prisons are on military bases.

Open-Barrack Bunks: Like cubicles, open-barrack-style construction has become the new norm. However, between the two, cubicles win over open-barrack construction. Indeed, open-barrack construction is all-around less construction, but less secure for inmates and staff alike, as prison populations increase exponentially.

Other Details Regarding Living Quarters

Lockers And Legal Files Storage: Back in 1995 when I first entered prison, all inmates were assigned a 36″ x 24″ x 24″ metal locker. Today, however, the BOP has increased the size of most inmate lockers to 60" x 24" x 24" in many of its new prison facilities. All that you own in personal property, and all that is issued to you by the institution must be stored in your locker, otherwise you risk losing your property to officer confiscation.

As for inmates whose cases are ongoing during his or her term of incarceration, such as an appeal, extra-legal-file storage is usually available, so long as your case has been deemed "complex" by the district judge prior to incarceration. Such storage, however, is not a right, but a privilege—a privilege based on storage availability.

So I would advise against pushing the limits for extra storage space.

Living Quarters' Common Areas: Every prison facility, among the 120 in operation, are all configured differently, although the newer facilities have many construction similarities.

Each of the housing units' common areas consists of the usual restrooms, showers, and sink areas, naturally. There are food prep areas for light microwave cooking (not all institutions have microwaves) and eating; and sometimes the cooking area will have a television and, perhaps, some game tables included for pastime recreation.

In the newly-constructed prison facilities, these amenities are placed in separate quarters, but are still rather close in proximity. Then there are the infamous prison television rooms. Why do I employ the adjective "infamous?" I can answer that question with one word: Fights.

Yes, fights. And depending on the security level of the prison where you are designated, fights over the television can evolve into arguments and fights at prison camps, fights and stabbings at FCI lows and mediums, and stabbings and deaths at USP's—all of which I have witnessed firsthand.

Again, I know what you are probably thinking: "You've got to be kidding. Grown men would fight and even kill one another over a stupid television? That's totally irrational! In fact, it's insane!" And yes, you'd be correct in thinking so.

Yet again, let me remind you of where you are going or where you are. It's called prison, where irrational becomes the norm. Where the rational is least understood and practiced—and the higher the security level, the more irrational it gets.

From where does such behavior come? I'm not a psychologist or a psychiatrist, but during my 15 years of closely observing prison inmates, and prison staff alike, I have discovered a consistent pattern (at all four security levels) among certain inmates that support my theory relating to such behavior, and from where it must come.

Here is my observation: The men with the least of education—regardless of race—vicariously live and function through television. They appear to lack the cognitive ability to stimulate their own minds through the educational, spiritual, vocational, and self-improvement programs offered by the institution or from the free world. Not only are their bodies imprisoned. Their minds are imprisoned. Two or three men, for instance, will sit morning, noon, and night, guarding "their" television that broadcasts "their" programs at the exact time "they" choose to watch them. And if you and one hundred other inmates are in the vicinity, all of you must watch "their" program, too; provided, that is, that all of you are all of the same race.

Do you see the lunacy in certain prisoners' logic and rationale? These are the sort of mental cases you must avoid as you do time in prison should you wish to stave off prison violence. My strategy over the years has been simple. When I see them coming, or observe them in a group, I simply go the other way. My advice, therefore, is that you do the same.

Finally, there are the common-area laundry rooms . . .

It was 9:30 p.m. In the Spring of 2007, Memorial Day weekend at FCI Lompoc when a race riot between Black Americans and Naturalized Mexicans erupted. It began in a housing unit's laundry room between one Black man and one Mexican man; then, like a wildfire, the violence exploded throughout the entire 3-story building. The sounds of yelling, screaming, cursing, and breaking glass were heard all over the prison. Total mayhem.

But it was calm in my building as we were cram-packed at the window of the third floor—looking out—trying to figure out what was going on across from us. Seconds later, we heard the exploding sound of breaking glass coming from the second floor below us; and, as if by sheer intuition, everyone knew that it was a Black-on-Mexican race riot.

For about an hour, mass mayhem was everywhere, that is, until the prison staff could man up and establish control over the situation. Once control was established, forty-three men were taken to the infirmary for treatment, while twenty-seven were hospitalized. Where was I when all of this was happening? In my room minding my business and staying out of the way. Prison riots are a unique phenomenon. More often than not, prisoners use riots as an opportunity to clean up hit lists, as in those they've been plotting to take out. By God's grace, I was not on anyone's hit list, nor was I in the stream of violence in progress. Know this: My greatest advantage was that I quickly learned the "Ten Thou Shall Nots" in prison and adhered to them quickly. Knowing these survival rules served me well in times of great duress.

Incidentally, this was the third prison riot I experienced—and escaped untouched—during my 15 years of incarceration thus far. But what does this story have to do with respect and common sense? It has everything to do with a common-area laundry room. In fact, it began with one inmate disrespecting another inmate over a dryer, a simple, no-brainer dispute that any two rationally-minded human beings would have resolved in seconds. Instead, seventy men were injured, twenty-seven seriously. Insane! Nevertheless, that's the kind of powder-keg logic that exists among certain cliques in federal prison. Then again, such a mentality is five-times worse in state prisons.

So the deeper lesson here is three fold: (1) While you do your time, always stay in defense mode. Learn where the hot spots are, and who the hot heads are, and then stay clear, (2) Examine your attitude. Then ask yourself "Am I blending in with everyone else, or am I making myself a target by standing out?," and, (3) Remain mindful of the fact that you are not at home running things as before. You are in prison for a season and for a reason. With that said, take this time and look deep into yourself and learn the reason "why" you are in prison in the first place, then consider making a change.

Prisoner's Rights, Privileges, and Administrative Remedies

There has been considerable societal and legal confusion over the standards to be applied when addressing the Constitutional claims of prisoners, which, of course, begs the questions (1) Do prisoners even have Constitutional Rights as do non-prisoners? (2) If so, to what extent?

Well, as one who is educated in business, and more importantly, in the law—and currently a prisoner for fifteen years—I have studied, and largely experienced, the effects that stem from the above questions. Hence, I am adequately qualified to offer clarity to what has long been a subject of societal and legal confusion regarding a prisoner's rights.

So here's the deal: As federal prisoners we have five fundamental (or "substantive") rights that splinter into twenty-eight or so subsidiary rights. However, the five fundamental rights and their subsidiaries are highly restrictive "to the advancement of a justifiable purpose of imprisonment." *Morales v. Schmidt*, 489 F.2d 1335 (7th Cir, 1973) rehearing en banc, 494 F.2d 85 (1974). In other words, a prisoner's five fundamental rights, in their entirety, must be "watered down" in order to advance the goals of maintaining institutional security and order.

And living with such a vast range of prisoners as I have now for the past fifteen years, I must admit (although I don't necessarily agree) how I certainly understand the rationale behind these restrictions of prisoner's rights, especially at the higher-security federal facilities.

My opinions aside, let's hone in on the point at hand, which are the five fundamental rights prisoners do have, along with their corresponding subsidiary rights.

1. **The First Amendment:**

Right to meet with the members of the press,
Right to receive publications from publishers,
Right to communicate with non-prisoners,
Right to assemble for religious purposes,
Right to assemble with other religious groups,
Right to receive visits from clergy,
Right to correspond with clergy,
Right to observe religious dietary laws,
Right to wear religious insignia.

In contrast, these **nine** subsidiary First Amendment rights pale in comparison to the **forty-six** subsidiary First Amendment rights you had prior to prison.

2. **The Fifth Amendment:**

Right to access the courts,
Right to mail communication to counsel,
Right to receive visits from counsel,
Right to communicate with legal organizations,
Right to consult "Jail House Lawyers",
Right to assistance in filing legal papers.

In contrast, these six subsidiary Fifth Amendment rights pale in comparison to the seventy-two subsidiary Fifth Amendment rights you had prior to prison.

3. **The Eighth Amendment:**

Right to sanitary and healthy living conditions,
Right to reasonable medical attention,
Right to reasonable medication,
Right to treatment per a "Doctor's Order."

In contrast, these **four** subsidiary Eighth Amendment rights pale in comparison to the **thirty-nine** subsidiary Eighth Amendment rights you had prior to prison.

4. The Fourteenth Amendment:

Right to clean food, water and shelter,
Right to protection from predictable sex abuse,
Right to protection against suicide,
Right to protection against foreseeable attack.

In contrast, these **four** subsidiary Fourteenth Amendment rights pale in comparison to the **fifty-one** subsidiary Fourteenth Amendment rights you had prior to prison.

5. The Fourteenth Amendment Right To Due Process (Institutional Punishment and Discipline)

An absolute right against corporal punishment (unless sentenced to such punishment), including a:
Right to notice of charges,
Right to a fair and impartial hearing,
Right to an opportunity for defense,
Right to present witnesses,
Right to a written decision and an appeal.

Again, we as prisoners are afforded **five** out of **fourteen** fundamental Constitutional rights we used to have.

Distinguishing "Rights" From "Privileges": All too often, I've encountered prisoners who have no clue of what his rights are in relation to what his privileges are. Worse yet, many men come to prison with so great an entitlement complex, or so blind to the realities of their fates, they ultimately find themselves in rank devastation when the iron fist of reality smacks them squarely in the face. Indeed, with the wrong attitude and the wrong perspective toward prison, your "so-called" fundamental rights and their subsidiaries could be whittled down to just food, water, shelter, and emergency medical care, especially if you are thrown into the "hole" (a.k.a. "Special Housing Unit—SHU").

In prison, being in what is known as "general population" is the greatest of all privileges, simply because by "being social" and interacting with others is the closest thing to being psychologically free. Plus, general population grants you access to an array of other privileges, such as schooling, recreation, television, commissary, telephones, religious assemblage, and so on and so forth.

As such, these and other privileges can be snatched from you *at any time*, without cause or explanation. So as prisoners, we must remain mindful of what our fundamental rights *are not,* as well as, what our fundamental rights *are*. Do this and your time in prison should pass with relative ease.

Telephone Access And Restrictions

When I entered federal prison back in June of 1995, prison telephone policy was amazingly liberal, that is, when compared to prison telephone policy of today. Prior to August 1, 1998, prisoners were allowed to make unlimited collect phone calls to friends, to family, to whomever else they so choose—without imposed time restrictions whatsoever. But after August 1, 1998, the BOP provided its inmate population with both good news and bad, *bad* news, which affected most institutions nationwide.

The good news was that inmates could now lower their phone costs by placing pre-paid, direct calls to friends and family, along with their existing collect-calling capabilities. The bad, *bad* news from that day forward was as follows: (1) At most facilities, inmate telephone calls were limited to three-hundred minutes per month and four-hundred minutes during the November-December holiday months, (2) inmate calls were automatically terminated after 15 minutes, (3) following each call, inmates must wait thirty minutes to an hour before placing the next phone call, whether the preceding call lasted one minute or for the entire fifteen minutes, (4) inmates were required to fill out a phone call list of up to thirty phone numbers, (5) telephone area codes 700, 800, 900 or 976 were disallowed, (6) unused phone minutes do not roll over into the next month, (7) all calls are subject to being monitored (unmonitored attorney-client calls are available through your correctional counselor), and (8) conference calls, speaker phone calls, and three-way calls could cause you to lose your telephone privileges (other than unmonitored attorney-client phone calls) for up to six months. Each institution's policies may slightly vary per the Warden's discretion.

Now you know why I referred to the above as the "bad, *bad*" news. Yes, a plethora of restrictions for so few telephone minutes. But hey, when it's all you have, you find ways to make it work. With that said, here are some other important things you need to know about inmate telephone use in the BOP:

Immediate-Family Emergencies: In the event of a family emergency, such as hospitalization or death, the Warden may grant you additional phone call minutes upon written request. If not, the prison's Chaplain is authorized to grant you "family-counseling" calls in the event of an emergency, so long as it's your *immediate family* that is under duress.

Losing Your Phone Privileges: It's easy to lose your telephone privileges for up to *one year* should you be found guilty of a) running a business over the phone (Consult page 127 – subsection: Secure Your Professional Licenses And Permits, for the definition of "running a business") b) allowing another inmate to use your unused phone minutes, c) using the phone during your work hours, and, as stated above, d) engaging in a conference call, a speaker-phone call, or a three-way phone call. My advice? Don't do it! Resist the temptation or risk losing the privilege of speaking to your family and friends for as much as *one year*. Frankly, it's not worth it.

Holiday Phone Time: As mentioned earlier, during the holiday months of November and December, the BOP grants inmates an additional one hundred minutes of phone time with which the inmates may use as added time to converse with family and friends. But come January 1, it's back to prison as usual. Your four hundred phone minutes revert back to three hundred phone minutes for the next 10 months.

You've Got Mail

All incoming mail to you will be opened, surveyed, and inspected for contraband before you receive it. So it's important that you inform your family and friends of the mailing rules, or risk having your mail returned to them.

Here are key points to remember:

Regular Mail And Packages: First, all incoming mail must have your name an inmate registration number on it if you want it to get to you in a timely manner; and no, you will not be notified every time your mail, in part or in full, is returned—even though BOP Mail-Room Policy requires as much. But that's the inherent nature of the federal prison bureaucracy with which you must contend.

Second thing: for best results regarding your inbound mail, have your friends and family keep their correspondence simple and straightforward. In other words, use regular U.S. Mail services. Prisons do not do well with FedEx, UPS, or other parcel companies. Your mail might find its way to a warehouse somewhere in Area 51 Mojave Desert before it reaches you a month or two later—if at all. So for the most reliable inbound mail service, use regular First-Class U.S. Postal Service mail.

Thirdly, inform your friends and family to avoid using fancy, glittery, or frilly envelopes with colorful stickers (my youngest daughter is notorious for this). Such letters seldom make it to you due to the prison mail handlers' fear of drugs or other forms of contraband entering the institution. So do yourself a favor and keep your inbound mail cycle simple throughout your term of imprisonment.

Fourthly, do not confuse state prison procedures with federal prison procedures. Federal prisoners are not permitted to receive "care packages" of any kind from anyone. Care packages are packages containing food, snacks, candies, stickers, and articles of clothing, etc. These and other items may be available through the prison commissary, which we will discuss later.

Legal Mail: Mail from an attorney or on an attorney's stationery, bearing the attorney's name and clearly marked "special mail—open in the presence of the inmate," (also "attorney at law") will be opened in your presence, searched for contraband, and then given to you without being read by the prison mailroom staff.

However, experience, as well as observation, teaches that the prison mailroom staff will inadvertently open your legal mail without your being present. Should this occur, notify the prison Warden, in writing, along with notifying the sender-attorney of the same. To avoid this problem altogether, instruct your attorney(ies) on how federal prison legal mail works. Here's an example: Prisoners maintain their

Constitutional right to consult with their attorney and with the courts. And with this right, a prisoner is entitled to attorney-client privilege, which means a prisoner's legal mail is not to be opened by prison staff unless the prisoner is present. However, following the attacks of 9/11, federal prison officials have been taking the liberty of opening and reading privileged attorney-client correspondence due to simple procedural omissions by attorneys and their staffs when sending sensitive legal mail to prisoners. For this reason, a prisoner must clearly inform his attorney(s) of what constitutes Legal Mail and what does not. Otherwise all of your legal mail will be opened and read by prison staff. The most common problem is illustrated in the return address in Figure 1 below. Note the attorney's return address in the Figure 1? Big mistake. Why? It's generic, meaning anyone in your attorney's office "other than your attorney" could have mailed this package to you. However, in Figure 2, it's procedurally clear to the BOP mailroom that the package was sent to you by "none other than your attorney himself" for the sole purpose of preserving the attorney-client privilege. Prison mailroom personnel is trained to look for these small but crucial oversights on your part. WARNING: Failure to follow BOP Legal Mail policy will result in your mail being opened and its content severely compromised every time, from which you will have no recourse.

However, to ensure that a prisoner's legal mail is opened only in his or her presence, it must be addressed as follows:

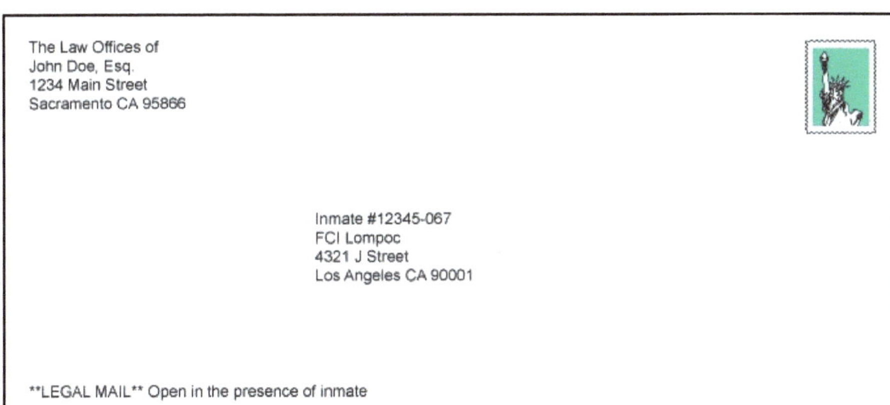

Figure 1

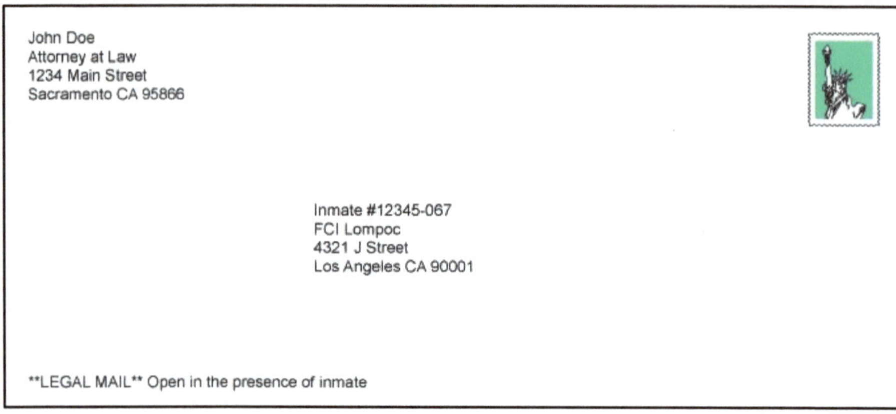

Figure 2

As for outbound legal mail, it is treated with the same level of sensitivity. Your legal mail to your attorney or to the courts should be prominently marked "legal mail" and then sealed by you or by a prison official, in your presence, and deposited in the mailbox. Albeit keep in mind the legal mail process will vary, depending on the security level of your prison facility.

In any event, check with the law clerk at the prison's law library for further details regarding the specific nuances regarding the handling of legal mail.

E-Mail In Prison? You bet! The Trust Fund Limited Inmate Communication System (TRULINCS) is a program currently being conducted by the BOP to provide inmates with limited capabilities to send and receive electronic mail (e-mail) without having access to the Internet, all at the inmates' expense. Email system, of course, will vary if you are designated to a privately-managed BOP facility.

Similar to regular mail, inbound and outbound e-mail correspondence is reviewed by prison staff.

Special Mail: Special Mail is regarded as "mail that is constitutionally privileged, although not necessarily legal mail.

According to BOP policy, Special Mail is defined as mail to the media, to the U.S. Attorney's Office, to the Office of the U.S. Inspector General, to the U.S. Congress, U.S. Senate, and to the Office of the President of the United States. Special Mail is treated similar to that of Legal Mail, in that it may **not be read by a staff member,** but must be sealed in the presence of a staff member for further handling.

Educational, Vocational, And Recreational Programming

As one would reasonably expect, educational, vocational, and recreational programs will vary from institution to institution, depending in part on security level and size of facility.

However, upon entering prison—and once you have had an opportunity to settle in (and you will, in spite of what you are feeling today)—you will discover that somewhere between the educational, vocational, and recreational training departments, 25% or more of your entire sentence will likely be consumed by one or the other. So with that kind of time at your disposal, here are some particulars to consider.

Education: The BOP requires inmates to acquire a high school diploma or equivalency (GED) if the inmate's Presentence Investigation Report (PSR) does not indicate and verify that the inmate has acquired his or her diploma prior to entering prison. The BOP also offers college-sponsored programs, college-correspondence courses, vocational training programs, apprenticeship programs, and even inmate-taught Adult Continuing Educational (ACE) Programs that are offered by skilled and highly-educated inmates, such as accounting, business law, business development, stock market and commodities trading—far too many to list here. Types of classes vary from institution to institution. Oh, and just in case you are wondering: There is no Internet access available at any federal prison. So Internet or online educational programs are off limits in the federal prison system. No exceptions.

Vocational Training: The BOP touts that they offer their inmate population a wide array of vocational training opportunities. Well, the truth of the matter is the BOP does, in fact, "offer" such programs. But such programs are available to a very small percentage of inmates throughout select facilities across the United States. This means inmates cannot obtain certain popular programs due, in part, to: (1) logistical complications with the inmate's place of designation and the suitable vocational training for that inmate, (2) security complications with the prison, which prohibits a technical college or a community college from adequately teaching vocational classes as they should be taught, and (3) the growing budgetary constraints combined with the growing population with which the BOP contend with on an annual basis.

So, in essence, it is not the BOP's fault as much as it is Congress' fault. It's Congress who is shortsighted where real rehabilitation of federal prisoners is concerned. To that end, real rehabilitation is up to the individual inmate.

Recreation: All prisons offer some form of recreation and fitness programs to their inmate population. You will find all the usual sports, such as volleyball, softball, flag football, basketball, bocce, tennis, etc. There is something for young and old alike.

The key to "doing time,"—as goes the term—is to disallow the time from defeating you. Getting fit and staying fit are the keys to successfully emerging from prison. You will be stronger, leaner, and more vibrant than you ever were prior to when you first entered prison.

Visiting Privileges And Limitations

Shortly after arriving at your designated prison facility, you will have to complete and submit a list of persons from whom you desire visits. Only approved visitors will be permitted to visit you during visiting days and visiting hours per your specific prison facility policy. Exceptions, of course, are made for visiting minors who are 16 years of age and younger, so long as they are accompanied by an approved-visiting adult.

Absent security concerns by the Warden that would prohibit visiting, immediate family members (i.e. mother, father, brothers, sisters, spouse, and children) are informally placed on your visiting list if (1) you fill out the quick "Immediate Family Visiting Form" and submit it to your correctional counselor immediately upon your arrival, and (2) the names of your immediate family members are *listed in your Presentence Investigation Report (PSR)*, and if such names have been verified as immediate family. Conversely, individuals who are *not* considered immediate family must submit to the appropriate forms and requisite identification for visitation approval.

Although BOP regulations are adhered to nationwide, each prison facility has its local visiting guidelines, which, of course, are outlined in the inmate handbook you will receive upon your arrival.

For purposes of distinction, the BOP has divided visiting into four classifications: (1) Family and Friends' Visits, (2) Legal Visits, (3) Media Visits, and, (4) Special Visits[11].

---

[11]LEGAL, MEDIA AND SPECIAL VISITING PRIVILEGES can most certainly offer a unique opportunity for highly productive prisoners, depending on the depth of your existing business endeavors. These visits served me well, for they were actually "business meetings." Each visit was manned by my legal team, who navigated and scheduled the parade of individuals who visited me on my terms. Nothing more, nothing less. My end game was to achieve one goal: re-branding myself for future, post-incarceration endeavors.

Let's delve into each classification of prison visits.

Family And the Friends' Visits: As stated above, your immediate family members are automatically approved for visitation provided they are listed in your Presentence Investigation Report (PSR). Friends, on the other hand, must submit the requisite visitation form in order to be approved by the institution.

Legal Visits: Attorney-client visits are available to you by appointment only. Attorneys, however, must arrange such appointments (including attorney-client phone calls) with the prison's legal department (or the Inmate Relations Officer and with your correctional counselor) in advance. Once approved in advance, you will then be notified. Also, there are usually no restrictions on the number of visits or the number of attorneys and law clerks who wish to visit you, so long as they are all approved in advance.

Media Visits: On occasion, the media may flex its First Amendment muscle and thus request to interview you should they (the media) view your case as newsworthy. When such a request is made, the prison's legal department handles the particulars, including, but not limited to, notifying you of the media's request. Should you decline, well, all the better for the BOP, since they (the BOP) abhor the thought of any media exposure. But should you agree to be interviewed, the BOP will do their level best to systematically impede or deny the media's request by (1) claiming that said interview presents a security problem of sorts, (2) claiming a procedural problem with the manner in which the media wishes to conduct the interview with you, or, (3) scheduling the interview so far in advance, the story, by that time, will have lost its value to the inquiring media organization. To that end, the media organization must flex its muscle if they really insist on speaking with you.

Special Visits: On occasion an inmate may develop a unique situation where an individual seeking visitation rights could be denied for the following reasons: (1) the individual marked "no" on the visiting form where it asks, "Did you know the inmate prior to incarceration," (2) an individual may be on probation or on parole, but have special relations with you, the inmate, or, (3) an unexpected relative comes to town and desires to see you, but has yet to be formally processed for visitation privileges. In any event, the Associate Warden has the authority to grant you a "special visit" on a one-time basis only, or as many times as he/she would deems appropriate.

Another Note About Visits: Personally, I have experienced, first hand, each form of visitations listed above, except for the media visit (they sucked my blood long *before* I entered through prison doors).

As you could probably imagine, prison visiting privileges are a joy, even with the restrictions. Visits are our principal lifeline to the outside world[12]. For these reasons, I urge you to remember that family visits are a privilege, not a right. Therefore your family visits can be taken from you at any time. And believe me, there are officers who would love nothing more than to terminate your visiting privileges. So learn the rules. Abide by the rules. And inform your visitors of the rules and consequences should those rules be violated.

---

[12]MULTIPLE VISITS: An effective visiting strategy for highly productive prisoners to consider is multiple daily visits. The strategy here is to have several different parties visit you on the same day, while you are currently in visiting. For example, the BOP permits, say, partner 1, to visit you from 8:00 am to 10:00 am, then partner 2 visits from 10:00 am. to 1:00 pm., then your wife visits from 1:00 pm to closing. You determine the length of each visit. In other words, you are permitted to receive a visitor in staggered intervals throughout the visiting day, or you can have just one visitor. Regardless, the visiting points are the same. There is, however, a catch: should you check out of visiting, you're done for that day. Should a visitor come later on during that same day, the visitor will be turned away. So do not check out of visitation until each visiting interval is complete. (Source: BOP Visiting Policy Statement No. 5267.05).

Sentence And Goodtime Computation

As federal prisoners, we may receive up to 54 days of Good Conduct Time (GCT) credit at the end of each year of our term of imprisonment, beginning at the end of the first year of the term, subject to the BOP's determination that "during that year, [we] the prisoner has displayed exemplary compliance with institution disciplinary regulations" 18 U. S. C. section 3624(b)(1). Under this provision, at the end of each year, the BOP—specifically your Unit Team—determines whether you have been naughty or nice. If the latter, the BOP may reward you credit for an extra 54 days towards the reduction of your gross sentence as declared by your Judgement and Commitment that was signed by your Judge.

The methodology used to calculate your 54 days GCT credit, however, gets a bit tricky due to Congress' lack of legislative clarity in its statutory construction. How tricky? Tricky enough where 54 days of GCT credit morphs into 47 days—seven days a year shy of the 54 days currently authorized by statute. Here's how: Due to Congress' lack of legislative clarity in the statute, 18 U.S.C., §3624(b)(1), and the implementing regulation, 28 C.F.R., §523.20, which is clearly written, a conflict exists. As a result, we as prisoners are deprived of our duly-earned good conduct time credits (seven days from our 54 days).

Example: The statute, 18 U.S.C., §3624(b)(1) states a federal prisoner may receive "up to fifty-four days at the end of each year of the prisoner's term of imprisonment, beginning at the end of the first year of the term" subject to the BOP's determination that "during the year, the prisoner has displayed exemplary compliance with institutional disciplinary regulations."

The problem is, the Congress did not clarify what it meant when it stated "term of imprisonment" as opposed to "time actually served." With that in mind, let's contrast the statute with the implementing regulation on which the BOP relies.

Due to the legislative ambiguity in the statute, the BOP has the implied authority to rely on the implementing regulation known as the Code of Federal Regulations (or CFR's). Relying on this authority, the BOP has adopted a tricky math formula that calculates your "actual time served" 28 C.F.R., §523.20. Consequently, we net only 47 days of GCT credit instead of 54 days.

For many years, prisoners, FAMM (Families Against Mandatory Minimums), and others have asked the federal courts to strike down the way the Federal Bureau of Prisons (BOP) awards GCT credit to federal prisoners. Then in May of 2010, the Supreme Court case (Barber v. Thomas, No. 09-5201) settled the way the BOP calculates GCT credit. The BOP won, hence the matter is closed.

Of course, this matter has been challenged and ruled on across the spectrum of Federal Circuit Courts, all to no avail to federal prisoners, who are statutorily eligible to receive good conduct time credit. So as it stands, the statute grants us 54 days of GCT credit, and the BOP will tell you that you will get 54 days, but when it is all said and done, you will net only 47 days of GCT credit per year, with your last year being prorated per the CFR instead of the statute.

Residential Drug Abuse Program (RDAP)

In 1990, Congress created the outlines for Residential Substance Abuse Treatment for the purpose of addressing two leading causes of recidivism: alcohol and drug addiction. When very few prisoners volunteered for the program, Congress, in 1995, when enacted an incentive of a prison sentence reduction of up to one year for the successful completion of the program. Since then, there has been a back-log of participants willing to take the program. The program is known as the 500-hour Comprehensive Residential Drug Abuse Program (or "RDAP"). Eligible candidates are required to spend nine months in the program at an RDAP approved institution.

Eligibility for acceptance into RDAP is determined by three prison facility groups: (1) institutional case management, (2) the RDAP coordinator, and, (3) the psychology services staff. Collectively, they look for clear, concrete, verification that within one year from the date of your offense you had a bona-fide drug or alcohol abuse problem instead of a mere social or recreational drug or alcohol interlude of which many later claim was a hard addiction. In anticipation of false addiction claims, the BOP relies mostly on your Presentence Investigation Report (PSR) for such verification as mentioned early on in this book. Or, in the alternative, written verification from a medical or mental health professional may be provided to BOP officials indicating such addictions or abuses were clinically legitimate. Such documentation should, whenever possible, be included in your earliest PSR process, undertaken by Probation or by your private Presentence Investigation Consultant.

Those who are deemed eligible for RDAP are generally moved into the program when they are between 27 and 32 months of release. However, if your projected release date is, say, in 18 months, you will likely be given priority over an individual with a longer term of imprisonment, being that there is a long waiting list at all RDAP facilities.

As for ineligibility into RDAP, the following categories of inmates are automatically excluded from applying for and receiving the benefits offered by RDAP:

1. Immigration (ICE) detainees,

2. Pre-Trial inmates or detainees,

3. Military detainees and military inmates,

4. Inmates with prior convictions or enhancements for carrying, possession, or use of a firearm, or other dangerous weapons and explosives,

5. Inmates with prior convictions or enhancements that involve sexual abuse offenses committed upon children, and,

6. Inmates who have prior convictions or enhancements involving homicide, forcible rape, robbery, or aggravated assault.

Upon your arrival at your designated prison facility, you will soon discover scores of fellow inmates either complaining about or filing grievances against the RDAP Coordinator for rejecting their applications for RDAP. For example, if you go to our blog at frenchcuffsblog.com. and enter the words "RDAP grievance" in the search box, you will find an example of a written grievance (formally known as the "Administrative Remedy Process") by an actual inmate. In like manner, you will find the sequential responses from prison staff, justifying their reasoning for denying the inmate's request to enter RDAP. Study it carefully. Then go back and examine your history of drug and alcohol use; and, of course, discuss it with your attorney *prior to your interview with the Probation Officer* who has been assigned the task of preparing your court-ordered PSR.

Commissary Privileges: Limitations, Special Purchases, And Religious Accommodations

All federal prison facilities offer Commissary services to the inmate population. At present, the BOP offers an inmate spending limit of $320.00 during the months of January through October. However, during the months of November and December the spending limit is increased to $390.00, due to holiday items available to inmates and the increased telephone time limit (from 300 minutes per month to 400 minutes per month) for family reunification purposes.

The Warden at each prison facility, mind you, can set the monthly maximum spending limit at or below the above-stated amounts. The monthly maximum spending limit is usually applied to "non-specialty" items under $25.00 in value. Specialty items include: shoes, sports equipment, hobby items, postage stamps, photocopy credits, and, of course, telephone credits. Almost all prisons offer the same selection of the staple items, but specialty items can vary greatly.

As for you, your Commissary account will be established the first week of your arrival. You will then be issued an inmate I.D./Debit card and a Personal Identification Number (PIN) for your telephone credits. Telephone credits, however, are separate from your maximum monthly spending limit of $320.00. So you can spend your entire Commissary limit, plus the full cost of your 300 telephone minutes per month should you choose to do so.

When necessary, your friends or family may replenish your Commissary account, or it can be replenished by your earnings from your authorized prison employment. For friends or family wishing to send funds through the mail, they must send them to the following address:

Federal Bureau of Prisons
(Insert Inmate Name Here)
(Insert Inmate Registration Number Here)
PO Box 474701
Des Moines, IA 50047-0001

I strongly urge the use of U.S. Postal Money Orders, especially if you need your funds credited to your Commissary account immediately. Otherwise, any other money order, or worse yet, a personal check, will be subject to a "hold status" for as many as 14 to 21 days.

In the alternative, your friends and family may send the money via *Western Union* through the internet, (westernunion.com) or through a *Western Union Agent* directly to your account. Funds sent through the use of a *Western Union Agent* should be completed as follows: (1) Complete a *Western Union Quick Collect Program* form, then submit cash or a credit/debit card to the *Western Union Agent, or,* (2) use the telephone and a credit/debit card by calling *Western Union's* toll-free number found on *AAFP America's* website (aafpamerica.com/inmate-locator).

For each *Western Union Quick Collect* transaction, the following information will be required:

> Inmate's name
> Inmate's Registration Number
> City Code: FBOP
> State Code: DC

In Account Number on the internet form enter: The Inmate's Registration Number followed by their Last Name with no spaces. (Example: 12345012SMITH)

Note: *Some BOP facilities are privately managed and may have different procedures for the wiring of funds or the mailing of postal money orders (Consult Prison Intelligence Reports section of our blog at frenchcuffsblog.com).*

Here are some other important considerations regarding Commissary:

The loss of your Commissary privileges: The temporary loss of your Commissary privileges is usually the baseline sanction used by prison officials when it is deemed that you have, in some manner, violated BOP policy. Such policies include, but are not limited to: (1) Not reporting to your job assignment on time, (2) being caught in an unauthorized or restricted area, (3) missing an appointment, known as a "call out," or, (4) minor contraband is found on your person or in your locker—all of which are among the least of infractions possible.

Sanctions of these types can cost you 30 to 90 days Commissary restriction. However, the more serious infractions such as fighting, drinking, or drug use would result in Commissary restrictions—among other harsh sanctions—for up to 6 months.

Commissary As Currency: Why a monthly spending limit of $320.00? It is merely an attempt by prison officials to curtail the unauthorized exchange of goods and services between inmates. In addition, your Commissary account is an intelligence tool for prison officials should they become suspicious of certain activities in which you might be involved. For instance, let's say a random search of your locker reveals an inordinate quantity of one Commissary item, but your Commissary record shows that no such purchase had even occurred. So now, unbeknownst to you, your Commissary account is flagged, your incoming mail is flagged, your phone calls are flagged, and your associations are flagged—solely to establish a pattern of conduct that violates prison policy. Therefore, it is wise to simply resist the flood of temptation that comes with using your

Commissary account as currency; or, for that matter, engaging in activities that could place you in debt with a fellow inmate.

Religious Accommodations: One of the few rights afforded to a federal prisoner is the right (not privilege, but right) to practice one's religion of choice, and the right to religious assimilation with other inmates that share the same or similar religion. But as with all rights afforded to federal prisoners, a balance must be struck between the prisoner's right to practice his religion and the Warden's obligation to ensure the safe and orderly operation of his prison facility. Given the need for such balance, the following question is often posed by civil rights professionals and others who monitor prisoners' rights. The question is: "In case of a tie, who wins?" The answer is clear: the Warden wins. Here's why. The Warden's first priority is to ensure the safety of his staff and the safety of the inmate population. This is paramount. Thus, the Warden's ability to ensure the safe and orderly operation of his prison facility will always trump the right(s) of a prisoner to practice his religion. That said, the Bureau of Prisons (BOP) recognizes the importance of protecting and preserving a prisoner's right to practice his religion of choice. In fact, chapel services in most federal prison facilities play a vital role in the daily programming in which prisoners are required to engage. Moreover, BOP staff, especially the Warden and the chaplains, recognize that religious programming foster the kind of personal rehabilitation the prisoner will need when he or she returns to society. But until then, prisoners benefit from the religious activities because most chapel programs promote the values that build respect for fellow prisoners, respect for prison staff, and the respect for the rule of law in society. Combined, this rehabilitative approach bodes well with a Warden whose aim is to maintain the safe and orderly operation of his prison facility.

Religious Limitations: A prisoner must be sensitive of the fact that Religious Services Departments (or "the chapel") in the BOP face the space and staffing constraints as do other departments within the prison. For these reasons, the major religions tend to receive the lion's share of the chapel resources, major religions such as Protestant, Catholic, Judaism and Islam. That's because these four religions make up the greater population of most prison facilities—usually better than 95% of most populations. Outside of these four religions, it is often difficult for the chapel to fully accommodate the needs of the less populated religious groups. However, BOP policy mandates that the prison chaplains, within reason, make every effort to ensure all religious needs of prisoners are met. Remember, though, each facility's chapel services, resources and capabilities will vary. I therefore recommend when you arrive at your prison destination, pay a visit to the prison chapel and inquire about the services offered to your specific religious preference.

Race Relations In Prison

The primary dividing line in prison is race. With few exceptions, Black prisoners associate with Blacks, Hispanics with Hispanics, and Whites with Whites. However, the lower the security-level, the more educated and culturally tolerant the inmate population, one's race is less of an issue. This is especially the case when a prisoner comes close to his release date.

Much like the free society, there are always those who will race-bait the hook of ignorance and hatred in order to keep strife and division alive. In comparison, prison society is no different. In fact, during my 15 years in prison, and having served at four different security levels—I can attest that rising above racial hatred and bigotry is the first line of defense against racial violence. After all, I have experienced three brutal prison riots and escaped totally unscathed.

How? By abiding by the "Top Ten Thou Shalt Nots In Prison" on page 157 of this book, which deals primarily with one's attitude toward surviving prison.

With that said, below are several strategic tips that will hedge against being targeted for racial and other senseless violence.

Strategic Assimilation: Again, much of what occurs in prison resembles much of what occurs in free society. If you have a bigoted attitude towards other racial groups that are different than yours, you will certainly bring undo attention to yourself. Then again, in free society you can effectively separate yourself from other racial groups. But not in federal prison.

Like it or not, you are forced to assimilate. So why not make it work for you? Begin by opening your eyes to the things that all racial groups have in common, then take the high road and create some sort of dialog. In other words, if you have to be in prison, consider looking for the good in inmates of different races instead of looking for, and therefore dwelling on, the bad.

And no, I am not suggesting that you go all out to be "buddy-buddies" with everyone who is different than you. On the contrary, I am suggesting you simply let it be known that you are not a racist bigot, and that you do not seek to be perceived as the enemy throughout your stay in prison.

Teach A Class: Here's an example of an activity through which all racial groups in prison can find common ground. What is that activity? Going to school. Everyone has a will to learn. And once you earn the respect as "one of the teachers" in prison, you ostensibly rise above the racial nonsense that so greatly plagues our prisons, especially the higher security-level prisons. Teaching a class is an extremely powerful tool in prison. Teaching spreads your name and your expertise throughout the entire prison. And believe it or not, most prisoners—of all races, mind you—are seeking to make a change in their lives when given the opportunity. And your teaching a class represents opportunity to many.

Notwithstanding all of the above, teaching a class or two benefits you in ways you probably wouldn't imagine. I will delve deeper into those benefits in the chapter titled "The Seven Habits of Highly Effective Prisoners".

Interacting With Prison Staff

As stated in detail earlier, when you first enter prison, you will be processed ("dressed out") and escorted to your assigned housing unit by receiving officers. Although they will be wearing varying uniforms, it will not be clear to you what their ranks are, or more importantly, who is ultimately in charge of your care, your safety, and your confinement.

In the federal system, we are ultimately in the custody of the United States Attorney General. But at the prison level, the Warden runs the prison, with the descending chain of command—that being the Associate Wardens, the Captains, and the Lieutenants. Then there are The Sergeants, and the Correctional Officers (or CO's). There's more. All prisons have 2 lines of command structure: The uniformed staff whose job is to guard and enforce, (aka "Custody") and the Case Managers, Counselors, Unit Managers, Program Staff, and Prison Industries personnel, (aka "Administration") who are not uniformed.

So how are you, the inmate, supposed to interact with prison staff? Here's how:

As Little As Possible: If there is one thing you must get through your head from the moment you enter prison, it is as follows: prison staff members are not your friends. Get it? They're not your friends! This remark is not to imply that they are your enemy, mind you, but they are certainly not your friend either. The problem is, all too often, a certain inmate will forget where he or she is. You are not at home. You are in prison. That being said, interacting with staff should be as rare as possible. And when you must, be respectful and professional. But standing among officers, palling around, yucking it up, and sipping coffee with prison staff can get you seriously injured, or even killed by a fellow inmate who quickly assumes you are a "yard snitch." It is crucial that you speak with a trusted inmate about "how to" and "how not to" interact with the officers and staff who are constantly around you. Moreover, never assume that a cordial officer is easy to converse with or is easy to trust. On the contrary. The so-called "nice ones" are the quickest to write you up and have you thrown in the Hole—albeit nicely.

Never, Ever Touch An Officer Or A Staff Member: By this, I mean shaking their hand, patting their back (as a buddy would do), giving them "five," or "hitting the hammer" (as in bumping fists). Sure, I'll admit it. I have shaken hands with a Warden who saw me reading *The Wall Street Journal* on the yard one day. In his suit and tie, he walked over, introduced himself; and, surprisingly he extended his hand as would any gentleman. He then inquired about my choice of reading material, then he moved on. Then there was a Chaplain, who, as any prisoner would attest, is an exception to the "do not touch" rule. Although they are staff, Chaplains are oftentimes the closest thing to having a family member nearby. Chaplains help us through family illnesses, deaths, and through the trials that come with a life of incarceration. So it is not inappropriate to shake hands with or even embrace a prison Chaplain at *any* security level. Most spiritually-hearted inmates do so without a problem from other inmates or from prison staff members.

However, in all other circumstances, touching a staff member in general is considered a serious security violation that could get you written up, thrown in the hole, and or worst of all, an assault charge, which could result in an additional 5 years added to your existing sentence. So watch yourself.

Eyeballing A Staff Member: Can you believe you could get written up and get thrown in the Hole for "eyeballing" a staff member? That's right. In fact there is an Incident Code Section titled "Eyeballing A Staff Member". So what exactly is eyeballing a staff member? Well, there are 3 forms of eyeballing a staff member that would get you in hot water: (1) following an order from a staff member, you scowl at him or her in what the officer deems a threatening way, (2) for staring at a staff member while ganged up among other inmates in a show of intimidation, or (3) for gazing at a staff member of the opposite sex in what could be deemed as inappropriate. Sounds petty? Maybe. But if an officer claims he or she feels threatened or disrespected, you could find yourself shipped to a prison clear across America.

Making one or more of these mistakes can certainly be avoided if you simply remain mindful, at all times, of where you are.

Interacting With Prison Counselors, Case Managers, and Unit Managers (aka "Unit Team" or "Team"):Prison Counselors, Case Managers, and Unit Managers may be male or female, even though the prison may be strictly a unisex facility. They have college degrees, wear suits, and have offices with normal working hours. And best of all—at least for them—is that they sit around and handle inmate paperwork all day. Collectively they are called your Unit Team. Their jobs are to attend to your programming needs and to maintain your existing inmate files, while processing new prisoners in and out of the institution. Your Unit Team is considered middle-management employees who are training to become Associate Wardens or Wardens at some future point. Above all, mind you, is this: These people have a great deal of power over you, since they control your housing assignment, your job assignment, your visitors list, your access to programs, such as education, your vocational training, your furloughs, your halfway house, and your eventual release. So if they like you, they can help you greatly. And I mean greatly. But if they come to dislike you, they can, and will, make your life a living hell. And there's very little you can do about it. So it's important that you are on your best behavior while in their presence. Yes, even when they are dead wrong on an issue concerning you, you'd best stay cool. Choke back your pride. If need be, work your way through the Administrative Remedy process. Because here's the deal. Unless you are transferred to another institution, you will likely be joined at the hip with your counselor, your case manager, and your unit manager for the duration of your stay at that facility. Plus, they are the ones who will be making recommendations for your halfway house time. So it is imperative that you think long-term when interacting with your counselor, case manager, and unit manager.

Inter-Prison Transfers

Once you are designated to a specific prison facility by the BOP, it would almost take an Act of Congress to get it changed to a different prison facility. So I advise you not to bother. However, upon your arrival at your designated prison facility, you may discuss your desire to be transferred to a different facility with your Unit Team. But do so during your "initial Team Meeting" when your Counselor and Case Manager are both present at the same time.

Even then you will likely be denied. But a notation of your desire and your reasons for wanting a transfer will be placed in your file. You will then be informed that BOP policy requires that you serve at least **18 months with clear conduct at your present place of confinement** before an inter-prison transfer will be considered. Therefore, unless you are chronically ill, or, in the interim of the 18 month period, your security classification is either raised or lowered, you are likely not going anywhere.

Common Inmate Infractions And Sanctions

When an inmate commits an infraction in prison, he or she will receive an Incident Report (aka a "Shot"). Depending on the severity of the Incident Report, the inmate may or may not be taken to the Special Housing Unit (aka "The SHU" or "The Hole"). If you go to the Hole, that means all the creature comforts and privileges—and your cozy prison job—will be stripped away from you, whether it's your fault or not. (See Appendix C: "Inmate Discipline Program: Prohibited Acts And Available Sanctions", page 308)

Then upon your release from the Hole, you would have to start all over again as though you had just arrived in prison. Simply put, the Hole and its aftermath is one experience you truly want to avoid if at all possible. But avoiding the Hole is easier said than done. That's because it's all too easy for an inmate to go to the Hole, be it you are in the wrong place at the wrong time, a false accusation, or mere suspicion of some wrongdoing. It's all too easy.

Below are the five most common infractions inmates commit that result in an Incident Report that could get you thrown into the Hole.

Contraband: In short, contraband is considered "an unauthorized item that is deemed in an inmate's possession or in his constructive possession." In prison, contraband is divided into two classifications: (1) soft contraband and (2) hard contraband.

Soft contraband are items such as unauthorized laundry items, food items, reading material, altered commissary items, etc. All in all, these are items that are usually confiscated by the duty officer in lieu of the officer writing out an Incident Report that could get the inmate thrown in the Hole. Hard contraband, however, are items such as razor blades, knives, unauthorized prescription medication, metal or wooden objects of weapons grade, cell phones, or illegal drugs, etc. Hard contraband will get your thrown "under" the Hole. So be advised.

Out Of Bounds: In prison, there are many restricted areas where inmates are not allowed, and when an inmate is found in such areas, he or she is deemed out of bounds. But in prison, there are other meanings pertaining to being out of bounds. Say for instance, you have a dental appointment at 8:00 AM, but you show up at 9:00 AM. Well, you could receive an Incident Report for failing to "be where you were supposed to be," which means from 8:00 AM to 9:00 AM, you were out of bounds. In this instance, the administrative rational is accountability, whereas in prison, accountability among inmates and staff is a major security concern twenty-four hours a day, seven days a week.

Insubordination: Such conduct is also sometimes with, or closely related to, the infraction: "Disobeying A Direct Order". Be it through anger, bitterness, or sheer resentment towards authority, some inmates make the foolish mistake of arguing with, lying to, or outright disobeying an officer. Such conduct will get you thrown in the Hole every time. And many officers (not all) will bait the hook, so to speak, and toss it right in front of an inmate who's a known hothead. These inmates are commonly called "fish" by correctional officers who seek their thrill from others' suffering.

Telephone Violation: It is a well-known policy that all phone calls made by inmates are subject to being monitored. Yet certain inmates forget where they are when phoning family and friends. For example, 3-way phone calls are strictly prohibited. Or allowing other inmates to use your unused phone minutes is strictly prohibited. Inmates all too often go to the Hole for violating telephone privileges.

Disrupting The Institutional Count: The Warden of the prison is held accountable for every inmate who is housed at his facility. Therefore, if you impede the Institutional count, you are seriously imposing on the most powerful person at the prison. So when an officer announces "Count Time," there is no socializing, going to the restroom, making a quick phone call, or running a quick errand. No, you get to your assigned count-time area, be it at work or at your assigned area. Unfortunately, some inmates just don't seem to get it. Get this: Within 12 hours of this writing, an inmate was tossed in the Hole because he decided to call his wife immediately after the duty officer announced count-time. The inmate thought he could slip in a "quick call" once he observed the officer leaving the building following the announcement. But what the inmate failed to realize was that his phone call was being monitored. So guess what? The inmate received an Incident Report for (1) disobeying a direct order when making a phone call following the call for count, (2) being out of bounds, and, (3) the unauthorized use of the telephone. Thus the inmate was thrown in the Hole for 3 weeks.

I am certain that as you read through this section of this chapter you are shaking your head, saying to yourself, "Surely I would never do any of those things." Excuse me, but need I remind you that you thought you would never, ever do anything that would land you in prison either? Yet here you are, doing your level best to prepare yourself for prison. Point is, we all make mistakes. Some more costly, painful, and stupid than others. But all of the costly, painful, and stupid prison mistakes can certainly be avoided if you re-read, and adhere to, the "Top Ten Thou Shalt Nots In Prison".

FREQUENTLY ASKED QUESTIONS

Your First Day In Prison

Q. Will I at least be able to call my family and tell them I have arrived at my prison of designation?

A. Usually not. Here's why. Upon your arrival, you will be interviewed by several staff members. i.e. a custody officer, medical staff, and a counselor of sorts. During this interview, a staff member (usually the counselor) will provide you with a form from which you are to list as many phone numbers as possible (up to 30 numbers). You will then be provided with your personal "PIN" that will permit you to call home within 24 to 48 hours following your arrival.

The Truth About Prison Violence

Q. Does a federal prisoner have legal recourse against the federal government should the prisoner suffer injury or death due to prison violence?

A. Generally, no. But there are always exceptions to the rule, depending on the circumstances. For example, if a riot breaks out, and you are injured or killed, an investigation is ordered as set forth by the Code of Federal Regulations (or C.F.R.'s). And if it is found that prison officials followed procedure before, during, and after the riot, neither you, nor your family, would have legal standing. That is the risk we take when we go to prison. However, if it is found that prison officials were negligent or culpable in any way, the prisoner and his family would indeed have legal standing.

Details About Living Quarters

Q. If I don't get along with my initial roommate, would I be allowed to move?

A. Sure, but not right away. Keep in mind, you are the "new" fish in the pond, so to speak, meaning you get the worst of everything unless you are lucky. Usually, however, bed moves could take weeks. Here, the key is to ask a friendly fellow inmate who has been there awhile. He would probably know how to get you moved much sooner. But if you feel physically threatened, inform your counselor at once. Now the counselor would be compelled to move you on the spot.

Prisoners' Rights, Privileges, And Administrative Remedies

Q. Upon my release, will all of my Constitutional Rights be restored to me?

A. No, not all of your rights. After all, upon your release, you will always be a convicted felon for as long as you live. However, many of your rights will indeed be restored automatically upon your release. But now, there is some good news on the horizon regarding the full restoration of rights for first-time, non-violent offenders and former offenders alike. It is called the Second Chance Act of 2007. For details, go to the Home Page (aafpamerica.com), click the "Inmate Locator" button, then click the "Congress" button for the Second Chance Act of 2007.

Telephone Access And Restrictions

Q. In this subsection, you explain the process the outbound (or outgoing) calls I would make to friends and family. But what is the process if my family needs me (via an inbound or incoming phone call to me) in the event of an emergency at home?

A. Your family is free to call the prison's Chaplain's office should an emergency arise at home. But understand, emergency by BOP standards mean an immediate family member has been hospitalized or has died. Therefore, if hospitalization or death has not occurred, usually you will not receive your family's message. But I have witnessed exceptions to that rule.

You've Got Mail

Q. Is there ever an instance where an inmate's incoming or outgoing mail could be severely interrupted?

A. Absolutely. If an inmate goes to the Hole, or is in the midst of being transferred, an inmate's mail (particularly the incoming mail) could have trouble finding him or her, spanning from days, sometimes weeks. And such interruptions could deal a crucial blow to any legal work in process you might have. As such, an inmate's best bet is to stay as trouble free as possible while in prison.

Educational, Vocational, And Recreational Programming

Q. Do federal prisons permit educational programming through colleges and universities online?

A. No, not at this time. In fact there is absolutely no Internet access to federal inmates whatsoever. The reason? Federal inmates' level of sophistication poses far too great a threat to society where the Internet is concerned. Therefore all educational programming is on-site at the prison through local community colleges, or through a correspondence course offered by select universities.

Visiting Privileges And Limitations

Q. If an inmate finds himself in some sort of trouble and is taken to the Hole, what are the visiting limitations?

A. So long as this 'trouble' to which you refer is not visiting related, you, the inmate, will still be eligible to receive visits. However, one of the sanctions you may receive for this 'trouble' you are in could be the loss of your visiting privileges for a period of time.

How Your Sentence And Your Goodtime Are Computed

Q. How does an inmate lose part or all of his or her goodtime credits?

A. Well, notwithstanding the 7 days a year we are being slighted as it is by the BOP's misapplication of Congress' intent, an Incident Report in the 300, 200 or 100 Series could result in the loss of goodtime credit. Usually up to 27 days per infraction. For specifics, however, refer to the "Schedule Of Infractions And Sanctions" in the Prison Intelligence Report per your prison designation. Consult our Prison Intelligence Reports at: frenchcuffsblog.com

Residential Drug Abuse Program (RDAP)

Q. Upon completing the RDAP program and successfully graduating, can my RDAP-related sentence reduction be taken away from me? And if so, how?

A. Yes, your RDAP-related sentence reduction can be taken from you much like your goodtime credit can be taken from you. However, as a general rule, should you commit a 400-, a 300-, or a 200-series infraction, you will be dealt with pursuant to the provisions set forth in the "Schedule Of Infractions" alone. Not your RDAP credits. But all bets are off if you commit a drug or alcohol infraction, which falls in the most severe of infractions: a 100-series infraction (or "Shot"). In this instance, you could lose *all* of your RDAP-related sentence reduction credits.

Commissary Privileges: Limitations, Special Purchases, And Religious Accommodations

Q. When a family member or a friend visits me at the prison, are they allowed to bring me commissary money?

A. If you are at a BOP-managed facility, no. All commissary funds—in money order form—must be mailed to the Des Moines, Iowa address listed in this section, or sent to you through Western Union. Check our blog at frenchcuffsblog.com on any specific prison facility.

Race Relations In Prison

Q. What does the prison itself do in order to maintain racial harmony among the inmate population?

A. Unlike state prisons, federal prisons are strict on inmates who conduct themselves as separatist leaders and organizers where race is concerned. Radical hate groups are usually disbanded rather quickly and its members are broken up and swiftly dispatched to other prisons around the country. In addition, federal prisons work toward integrating varying races throughout the living and workplace areas. At all security level inmates are encouraged to assimilate.

Interacting With Prison Staff

Q. You laid out in detail how an inmate is to behave in the presence of prison staff. But they are the ones with all the power. What happens when a staff member abuses his power to mistreat or abuse me? What resource is afforded to a powerless prisoner?

A. Great question. First thing: know your rights as a federal prisoner. Go to the prison library and inquire about the Administrative Remedy Process. Here's why. Without knowing the process, a prisoner has no recourse nor any legal standing in court should a prison staff member violate policy or abuse his or her authority when interacting with inmates. Fail here, your lawyer, your congressperson, and your Senator would be rendered legally and collectively impotent. Experience teaches that prison staff respect, and even fear, an inmate who knows how to wield the Administrative Remedy Process. So if an inmate is powerless, it is primarily due to lack of knowledge, poor preparation, or procrastination.

Inter-Prison Transfers

Q. Why would the BOP be so cruel as to send a prisoner a thousand or so miles away from his or her family, knowing full well that the inmate will receive no visits from family?

A. Truth is, cruelty, per se, is not consistent with BOP policy; and I can speak with authority because I have been in the system—at all for security levels—for better than 15 years.

Sure, as with any large organization, there are cruel people who will do evil things to prisoners. It has happened to me. But there are far more good people than bad—even among the rank and file at the BOP. In regards to prison designation, BOP policy aims to keep a prisoner within a 500-mile range of his or her home, provided that (1) space is available, (2) security classification of the prison is suitable for a prisoner's security level, and, (3) the institution is medically suited for that particular prisoner. Unfortunately, some prisoner's individual circumstances cause him to pull the shortest straw when it comes to prison designation.

Common Inmate Infractions And Sanctions

Q. How long does an Incident Report (or "Shot") stay on a prisoner's record?

A. It depends on the severity of the incident. From the lowest severities (say 400-or a 300-series shot), up to one year. A 200-series shot remains for five years. But a 100-series shot remains for up to 10 years.

Q: ***Do you have any other questions for Mr. CEO?***

A: Go to our website: http://frenchcuffsblog.com. Fill out the contact form with your question and we will get back to you as soon as possible.

frenchcuffsblog.com

"Since we were created to be creatures of habit, why not cultivate them into becoming good habits?"

—Og Mandino

In this chapter . . .

Remain Mindful Of Where You Are

No Wasted Time, No Wasted Moves

Your Faith Is Your Friend

Ghost Write Or Edit Religious Or Secular Material For Others

Become A Jailhouse Lawyer

Establish A Blog Or A Website

Establish A Website

Frequently Asked Questions

CHAPTER FIVE

THE SEVEN HABITS OF HIGHLY PRODUCTIVE PRISONERS

Remain Mindful Of Where You Are

In chapter four we discussed the matter and mindset of how you should enter prison, including, but not limited to, the all-important "thou shalt nots" while in federal prison. In this section, however, we will discuss what's necessary for you to get you *through* your sentence in federal prison relatively unscathed. Principally, though, the key here is to encourage you to be smart and well aware of where you are at all times, or suffer the painful consequences. Below are some proven examples of how to do just that:

Do You And Be You: In prison, those of us who have been around for 10 or more years, often advise new prisoners to simply "do you," as in "don't do what other inmates do. Instead, do you. Do your own time by searching for productive pastimes that will put your heart and mind at ease. The colloquial term "do you" also means that you should mind your own business at all times. This is a key survival principal. Otherwise trouble will most definitely find you—and deal with you accordingly.

Being All You Can Be: It is amazing how many men come to prison and, lo and behold, they are self-proclaimed multimillionaires, many of whom supposedly made their fortunes in real estate, manufacturing, software development, law, medicine—you name it.

But it's often easy to discern truth from fiction. And most of the time, these braggarts are fictional characters, legends in their own minds. They made their money illegally. Yet again, there are many of these men who acquired their wealth legally, as evidenced by the mere fact that the Feds did not seize their assets before or during prosecution. The wisest of men are often quiet and very secretive about their wealth, for they maturely and instinctively know the dangers associated with boasting about their wealth in the free world, let alone in prison—at *any* security level. Contrasting the former with the latter, the former are quick to fabricate lies about their wealth and their former stature in society. Like proud roosters, they prance around and crow about wealth and stature they never had. Yet they engage in such conduct in order to curry respect from other gullible, hen-like prisoners. However, in truth, such conduct has the reverse effect. Braggarts commonly slip up and give themselves away, then gradually become the butt of jokes and ridicule. Many, on the other hand, become targets of extortion. Prison is not the Army, where you can "be all that you can be" as goes the Army's old tag line from their recruiting commercials. Yet many insecure prisoners fall into the unfortunate trap of believing that prison is a place where they can "be all that they can be." Granted, prisoners are all criminals. But not all prisoners are stupid or naïve. Not only can many see through your "BS," they can also smell it. With that said, highly productive prisoners will simply be themselves. They stay to themselves. And they do as little as possible to draw unwanted attention to themselves. So why not do the same? It works!

Remain Mindful Of Tribes And Territories: Prisoners become violently tribal and territorial over the most mindless, insignificant things. For instance, if you make the mistake of sitting in Bubba's T. V. -room chair, you could find yourself waking up in the infirmary, with no idea how you got there. Or touch the wrong T.V. and you might find yourself without an arm. Or venture—or even glare—into another man's living quarters, and you could find a steel-toed boot in your mouth. Instead, highly productive prisoners sit back and closely study the hot-heads and hot-spots that, at first glance, do not appear to be hot at all—like a silly T.V. room. But give it time. Listen to your instinct. And when in prison, never assume anything. Ask when you are not certain of a particular issue, no matter how logical it may seem. And when in doubt, just play it safe and leave.

Study Racial Habits Closely: As mentioned in Chapter Four, the BOP strives to discourage and disband racial cliques, However, there are those ignorant inmates who harbor and encourage racial hatred for the sole purpose of keeping the spirit of racial division in prison alive. But, of course, the higher your security level, the higher the racial tension. The lack of race relations is the leading cause of tension and violence in higher-security federal prisons. But civility and reason become the prevailing thought at a low-security prison, and even more so at a minimum-security prison camp. Highly productive prisoners—at every security level—make it their business to study the broader race relations in prison and use it to their advantage—not to their disadvantage. Personally, I used my skills as an inmate teacher of law, finance, and accounting, not only to break down racial barriers between other races of inmates and myself, but also between hard-hearted prison staff members and myself as well. Point being, you will have a tremendous psychological advantage over the small-minded prisoners and hard-hearted staff when your heart and your attitude are fixed on being highly productive, instead of being highly disruptive.

Avoid Controversy: In prison, a high percentage of men live for controversy—all types of controversy—from which contestant on American Idol sucks to the most recent Supreme Court ruling, and everything in between. But highly productive prisoners avoid controversy, simply because controversy leads to arguments. And in prison, arguments lead to fights. Of course, all controversy can't be avoided if you are constantly around groups of prisoners, especially if you are like me, who is the highly-politically-charged type. But time and again, I have had to agree with a fellow prisoner on controversial subjects of which I actually opposed. Why? Because it was the most efficient way to get rid of the Jackass who had cornered me, and, no doubt, it was the wisest thing to do before the cursing and name calling began. So here's the wisdom: Even if the argument, per se, does not lead to a fight, it certainly does lead to hard feelings toward you, especially if you have won the argument. And hard feelings often smolder a long time in prison. So it is best to avoid controversy whenever possible.

Avoid The Idiot Box: It makes me wonder if the term "idiot box" was actually created by some bureaucrat from the BOP's think tank in Washington DC upon touring a prison and observing grown men watching the Jerry Springer Show or Looney Tunes reruns. Wow, you wouldn't believe the audience turn out, or the kind of arguments that arise during and after these shows. I have got to hand it to the BOP psychologists who learned early on that a single television in prison provides the safety and security better than five full-time correctional officers could ever provide. In fact, television consumes more man hours in prison—per prisoner—than all of the available educational and vocational hours combined. But highly productive prisoners, as you will discover, spend their time reading quality material or creating with their hands and minds. As such, little, if any time at all is wasted on watching television—notwithstanding stocks, news, and an occasional movie or sporting event as a respite from hours of intense productivity. For with your new-found rest, relaxation, and focus, you will be stunned by what you produce, or ultimately discover about yourself. Utterly stunned.

Networking With Like-Minded, Highly-Productive Prisoners: Just as I have urged you to study tribal and racial habits closely, I likewise urge you to study the habits of highly effective prisoners as well. And when doing so, inquire into the habits and personality and reputation of these individuals before seeking to network with them. Here's why. In prison, you could be easily deceived by one or two of those prisoners who are "being all that they can be." Remember those guys?

Instead, you want to associate and network with the Michael Milken-Conrad Black types who have decided to take a few months off from Wall Street to visit Fed Street. Yes, they are there, especially if you have been designated to a low FCI or a minimum-security federal prison. These men are just not as public as were Michael Milken or Conrad Black. So take your time in this endeavor and align yourself with like-minded, highly productive prisoners—that is, if you are determined to make your time in prison work smarter and harder for you. Bottom line: There's no need of wasting a perfectly good prison sentence.

No Wasted Time, No Wasted Moves

Highly productive prisoners do not believe in wasting time nor wasting moves, whether they are locked in prison for a relatively short sentence or a relatively long sentence—it doesn't matter. Below are seven proven, reliable "in-prison" strategies that are certain to maximize your productivity, which will avoid wasting time or wasting moves.

1. *Rediscover The Beauty Of Reading*: As former CEO of an asset-based lending and capital development company, and as a father and husband, I lost my way, as it were, when it came to the joy of quality reading. So I decided to embark upon a "rediscover reading" journey. But as a highly productive prisoner, I took the time to plan my reading journey with the bigger picture in mind. And what was the bigger picture? Writing a book—as in writing a novel or two. In other words, I wanted to leverage my time into a minimum 5-to-1 return on investment (ROI) ratio, meaning I

needed at least a 5-times return for every 1-hour in prison invested. As such, I chose a rediscovering-reading strategy that offered such returns. Consider this: (1) I signed up for a Master of Fine Arts (MFA) distance-learning fiction literature course at Louisiana State University (LSU) that taught me the core elements and techniques of fiction writing, (2) The course introduced me to a deeper field of classic writings I had not read while at university, (3) I had to analyze these classic writings in order to uncover the magic that made them "classics," (4) I was then tasked to write short stories in order to complete the class, and, (5) I took those skills and used them to embark upon writing my own 9-book novel series. Yes, I accomplished all of the above and more by simply rediscovering the beauty of reading while in prison.

2. *Taking College Or Computer Courses*: Okay, so you have been to college and earned your degree. So have I, as did thousands of other federal prisoners. But as for me, I knew very little about fiction writing, screenplay writing, or stage play writing. Today, however, I am quite proficient at writing all three—and even more. Highly productive prisoners are constantly searching for ways of (1) expanding on what they already know, (2) incorporating new ideas with what they already know, (3) learning a marketable skill they do not currently possess, or, if for no other reason, (4) making yourself look good with prison officials should you need more halfway-house time or a transfer closer to home. In addition, prisons offer computer access—some more than others. Personally, I wrote five books and two screenplays with my

computer access. So can you if your focus is laser sharp toward being highly productive.

3. *Write A Book Or A Memoir*: Not everyone had to go back to college to learn the elements of fiction as I. Perhaps that's you. Perhaps you possess enough knowledge and skill to write a book while in prison, be it fiction or non-fiction. But get this. There is an amazing bonus to writing a book while in prison: You will have the most attentive, hard-hitting editors, proofreaders, and brutally-honest readers ever found—all in one place—all for free. Equally important, while in prison, you will find nearly every profession and vocation one could think of—and even not think of—all of whom you may call on for research purposes. All of whom are ready, willing, and able to help a serious writer—completely free of charge. So get serious and consider writing instead of sulking in what you coulda, shoulda, or woulda done differently that would have avoided prison. Too late for that. Now it's time to move on. Start writing.

4. *Teach A Class Or Two*: As mentioned previously, I taught a multitude of business and real estate classes to the inmate population. But what I did not mention was that I taught Pre-GED classes (to men who had learning disabilities) and standard GED classes. However, the Pre-GED and the standard GED classes were my requisite job assignment, but the business and real estate classes I taught were on a volunteer basis. In the process, however, I accomplished far more than simply teaching fellow inmates. For example, since I was required to have a job assignment (as every other federal prisoner is required), I secured a job that exemplified my

strengths; but more importantly, it was the type of job I figured beforehand would aid in the fulfillment of my writing desires. So as I taught my GED classes, I began to write my first children's book. And my class of GED students ostensibly became my own personally-assigned focus group for my initial drafts, and so on and so forth. Point is, I made my prison job assignment work for me in spite of my overall circumstances.

5. *Perfect And Patent Your Business Model Or Your Invention*: One of the rare and unknown privileges federal prisons offer is the opportunity to purchase specialized books, classes, drafting tools, hobby crafts, and other supplies that could be used to either make, build, or design a business model or a prototype for an invention of sorts. Of course, there are limitations being that you are in prison. But hey, no problem. Highly productive prisoners often search for—and ultimately find—a way to make gold thread out of hay and stubble. The key is to, again, search out the most innovative and educated prisoners at your designated facility. Explain to them what it is you would like to accomplish, and then watch as they rally about their respective network of outside sources—as well as their in-prison sources—to help you achieve your goals. Therein lies the power of idle intelligence that's just waiting to be tapped.

6. *Learn A Foreign Language*: As a former CEO of a finance concern, I have had the occasion to work with certain manufacturing companies along the U.S. - Mexico border, which are called Maquiladoras. Yet at that time I could not utter one sentence in Spanish. However, today, my Spanish is about fifty percent

proficient. My goal, however, is to become proficient in Spanish by the time I depart federal prison. Why Spanish? My motive is clear, for it is my intention to establish a consulting arm of my finance business in Mexico City, Mexico within 24 to 36 months

following my release from prison. Therefore, I feel it is imperative that my formal Spanish-speaking skills stand ready to take on the opportunities that surely await my eventual release.

7. *Get Healthy, Stay Healthy*: It is a blessing to have hopes, dreams, and a great mind. But what good does having hopes, dreams, and a great mind do when your health has been shot to hell? For instance, when was the last time you ran a full mile, or, for that matter, walked five miles? How is your blood pressure? Your cholesterol level? Your blood sugar level? Or what about that extra person—in terms of being overweight—you've been lugging around for God knows how long? Well get this: In less than one year of actively working out with a highly productive prisoner group (regardless of your age) most or all of those ailments will be history—unless you are permanently disabled. Point being, doing nothing is not an option. Conversely, should you choose the "Do-Nothing" path, you will do it with other "Do-Nothing" prisoners who have embraced failure as their option. Getting healthy and staying healthy is the best revenge for having to go to prison in the first place. Finally, when your term of imprisonment is over, you will be revamped, revved up, and ready to execute your plan of action you have been focusing on during the course of your prison sentence—while looking and feeling good in the process.

Your Faith Is Your Friend

Over my 15-plus years in federal prison, I have observed an amazing truism about a man and his faith—or lack thereof. The truism goes something like this: "You shall know a man's true faith by the manner in which he confronts and ultimately endures life's greatest adversities." For me, the greatest adversity in my life, bar none, was the day I received a 293-month (24 ½ years) prison sentence from a federal district judge for the white-collar offense of securities fraud. Moments following the pronouncement of my sentence, while locked in a holding cell—all alone—my knees buckled and I fell before the Lord. In disbelief, I fell to my knees into the hands of the God of my Faith. Now, some 15 years later, I am standing taller and stronger than I stood prior to my coming to prison. For the Lord had lifted me up and continues to hold me up from my leaning side.

> **Experience Teaches:**
>
> Prison time is like living with an 800 pound gorilla. Either find a way to feed it, or it will not hesitate to eat you alive.

Conversely, along the way, I have witnessed the harsh, bone-crushing effects incarceration can inflict on those prisoners whose lives and faith were built on nothing but sinking sand, prisoners who have allowed prison to maim and mangle their minds, bodies, and spirits. Prisoners whom—I'm saddened to have witnessed—have literally hanged themselves out of hopelessness and despair. Whatever your faith or belief system is, time in prison has a way of putting your faith to the ultimate test, unlike any test you have experienced prior to prison. As such, my objective in this subsection is to plant seeds of thought and encouragement towards the implementation of your faith in order to get you through one of the most challenging adversities ever encountered.

Awakening The Spirit Man Within: Chapter Four, we've discussed how the "First Amendment" touches on one of our principal prisoners' rights that remains in full force and effect—specifically our right to practice our religion, including our right "not" to practice a religion of any kind. Bottom line, the choice is yours. But those of us who choose to practice our faith, prison has a way of awakening the spirit man within, especially if your term of imprisonment is greater than three years. Whatever the sentence prisoner faces, highly productive prisoners soon grasp the importance of recognizing and accepting the greater good for his or her suffering at the moment. A spiritually-minded prisoner knows that suffering often results in a much better life in the future. How so? Practicing your faith awakens the carnal man within, in order that he may finally see the error of his ways—as in the error of his thoughts, judgments, associations, and ultimately his decisions—the very decisions that caused him to crash land inside a federal prison in the first place.

Consider Practicing Yoga: While not a religion, the various practices of Yoga can assist you in becoming a highly productive prisoner in spite of the grim circumstances in which you find yourself. Yoga—in the purest sense of the word—is the ancient practice of harmonizing mind, body, and spirit into a focused stream of energy. Among the array of Yoga definitions, the three most prevalent definitions include (1) Yoga is the harmony of mind, body, and spirit, (2) Yoga is a skill in action, and, (3) Yoga is the process of realizing the essential nature of all things. Many people think of Yoga as a series of contortions and body movements. Traditionally that form of Yoga is known as Hatha (pronounced "hot-ah"), which consists of a series of postures that release tension from the body, stimulate inner organs, while providing greater flexibility and strength. Another basic type of Yoga entails breathing practices known as Pranayamas (pronounced "prŏn-a'-yŏms"). These practices clear the mind and provide an increase in vitality and overall energy levels. Finally, there are a number of different types of meditation practices which allow for the clearing and focusing of the mind. These could be characterized in three main types: (1) Jnana: the Yoga of wisdom for the intellectually inclined who feels the need to know the "why" of things, (2) Raja: the Yoga for those of a strong-willed nature who seek to control things, and, (3) Bhakti: the Yoga of devotional for those whose dominant nature is feeling. Regardless of your choice of Yoga practices, many prisoners of all security levels are permitted to and encouraged to practice Yoga as a form of relieving stress, reducing anxiety, and of clearing the mind.

Spiritual Journaling: The fact that you are in prison is a story in-and-of-itself. So why not keep a daily journal of your prison experiences for further generations to see? Personally, I have journaled for about six of the fifteen years I have served in federal prison. And what I have discovered after the fact is that I have written a book of sorts, be it a personal keepsake for the edification of my grandchildren or as a spiritual devotional for others in society who might be experiencing similar adversities and setbacks in life. Whatever turn the end product from your journaling ultimately takes, keeping a journal is a soothing, cathartic experience amid the course of your suffering, while ultimately proving to be a highly productive, highly beneficial blessing in the future.

Ghost Write Or Edit Religious Or Secular Material For Others

Okay, so you have no material from which to draw upon to write a book for yourself. Fine. But if you possess the skills to write or edit a body of work, use your time and skill to ghostwrite or ghost edit a body of work for a friend, a family member, a colleague, a business, or a religious organization. The point here is to encourage you to do what highly productive prisoners do with huge blocks of quality time. And that is, we look beyond our present circumstances and focus instead on our talent, education, and natural gifts with which to stamp out the dread, the regret, and the guilt that so easily consume us when we serve our sentence. Otherwise you can engage in mindless, useless prison lies, games, and worthless conversations that will lead you into the Great Nowhere.

Become A Jailhouse Lawyer

Don't laugh. Jailhouse lawyering is constitutional, it is legal (in the context of one inmate aiding another), and it is permitted in accordance with BOP policy. However, what is *not permitted* is for one inmate to charge a fee for aiding another inmate with his or her legal work, nor for charging a fee or receiving any form of consideration from another inmate.

Conduct to the contrary constitutes "running a business," which will inevitably result in stiff disciplinary action against both inmates. Surely no one wants that. In other words, what I am suggesting here is that many of you who are highly educated might well be intellectually and analytically drawn to the challenges inherent to criminal law. For example, throughout my many years in prison—I have witnessed, I've worked with, other inmates who were quite artful and very effective at researching and analyzing case law and writing formidable legal briefs. And surprisingly these inmates were not former lawyers. They were business executives, engineers, developers, bankers, and yes, some were lawyers also. And as experience teaches, many of these inmates served their sentences completely enveloped in the law library reading, researching, and helping others. So how would an inmate know if helping others with their legal work is right for them? It's like everything else. Through trial and error. What we do in prison is not planned out, per se, just as many of my highly productive projects were not planned out in advance. In essence, it all begins with "The Big Search" as in how you search for ways to "invest" your time instead of "spend" your time. During my Big Search, I began with where the greatest concentration of knowledge was, which was the prison's Law and Leisure Library.

From there I formulated a tentative plan on how to invest my time—one of which included a time where I aided other inmates with their legal work to a large degree, from which I learned a great deal about Criminal Law and the Federal Rules of Criminal Procedures simultaneously. Once integrated with my business law and finance experience (from my CEO days), I became a formidable criminal law practitioner with whom to reckon. Well, so can you.

Establish A Blog Or A Website

As mentioned earlier, many federal prisons now offer email services to prisoners. However, your prison email account is not what is being alluded to here, in that prison email accounts are restricted to the most basic of family and friend communication. Not to an open-source blog. Such a blog would require the reliable assistance of a friend or family member on the outside. Your blog can be a daily or a weekly post, depending on the subject matter you choose to impart. Of course, you would need to create a month or two of lag-time data in order to keep your blog current and active. Nonetheless, authoring a blog gives you a voice and a platform that you would not otherwise have—especially from a federal prison. Plus, blogs, such as wordpress.com, will establish your blog free of charge; and, if your blog's content draws a substantial following, your family could receive compensation from Google's AdWords Program—a program that allows impression advertisers to bid on keyword placement on high-traffic blogs and websites. This, of course, leads me to my seventh and final Habit of Highly Productive Prisoners: Websites.

Establish A Website

Similarly, you would need a strong support of family or friends on the outside to assist with the development and maintenance of a website. But it is certainly doable, especially if you have developed or currently possess valuable content that is of interest to the cyber public. Oftentimes, highly productive prisoners know and use their genius while in prison, where certain other prisoners' genius ironically develop wings and take flight. Perhaps that prisoner is you. Perhaps through your family you can market and sell your hard copy or an electronic copy of that book you have written while serving time in prison. Whatever the case, even in prison you are limited only by your imagination, your wit, and your desire—in spite of your circumstances.

In closing, it is worth noting that other than practicing Yoga (due to time constraints), I have had the good fortune of **employing every other survival strategy mentioned in this chapter to the fullest extent possible**, including writing and publishing this very book you are reading. And in doing so, not one law or BOP rule was ever violated in the process. So if you have to go to prison for a season, so be it. Even so, being the fighter that you are, you have no excuse for being anything less than a highly productive prisoner.

FREQUENTLY ASKED QUESTIONS

Remain Mindful Of Where You Are

Q. Okay, say I follow your recommendations to the letter, yet still I find myself at odds with someone—especially someone of another race—who simply harasses and provokes me to the point of confrontation solely because he/she does not like me? What steps do I take to avoid a physical confrontation with such an individual?

A. For starters, do not go to a Correctional Officer unless you deem your life or the life of others is at risk. In such an instance, do not hesitate to report your concerns. However, anything short of losing your life or limb, it is imperative that you work out any grievance with your fellow inmate. Here's how. Find out who is literally or ostensibly the so-called unit "shot caller" (or leader) for your race, then explain the nature of your problem to that person. Sounds ridiculous? Well, it is . . . because it is prison. Most prison politics are utterly ridiculous, especially race-related politics. In any event, most conflicts are resolved among inmates, not officers. Consequently, involving an officer instantly labels you as a snitch. And in prison, being labeled a snitch makes you an even greater target.

No Wasted Time, No Wasted Moves

Q. To accomplish much of what is reported and suggested in this section, is it not accurate to say that a prisoner would need substantial outside assistance and a fair amount of financial resources to make much of the suggestions happen?

A. No, It is not accurate. Granted, outside assistance and financial resources are indeed helpful, especially when referencing the

Subsection "Taking College Or Computer Courses". Specialty or high-end distance learning programs can be rather pricey by a prisoner's standard. Granted, but each of the other suggestions can be accomplished through hard work, perseverance, and an unshakable belief in yourself. And as for resources, you will have everything you need right there in prison, i.e. the prison library resources, books, and magazines that are tucked away in fellow inmates' lockers, and the vast amount of knowledge in the minds of other highly productive prisoners in your midst. So I'll say it again: there are no excuses.

Your Faith Is Your Friend

Q. If I write a motivational book or, movie script, memoir, or some other intellectual property while in prison, will I be permitted to publish them and then donate it to my religious organization for fundraising purposes, or, perhaps, assign my works to my family in order that they may market and sell them for my benefit?

A. Yes, however, the key word here is the word 'assign'. Here's what I mean in addition to what I did: According to BOP Policy, we are not only permitted to, but are encouraged to, use our time to self-rehabilitate by writing and publishing manuscripts. That doesn't mean, however, that we are encouraged to engage in the business aspects of bringing our writings to market. That's the job for someone other than you, such as your family, a colleague, or your business attorney—all of which I have on my team of "assignees." So go ahead. Take advantage of your "down time," so to speak, and write or ghost write that killer novel or non-fiction book you've been longing to write. However, in order to stay clear of violating BOP Policy, you must remove yourself from the following business activities: (1) the direct negotiations related to contractual obligations for advances and royalty payments from your writings, (2) the signing and executing of agency or publishing contracts for financial representation of your writings, and, (3) the direct receipt of any payment from an agent or a publisher from the proceeds of your writings. As prisoners, all we are permitted to do is the most important part: write quality content. Then, what our family, our colleagues and our business attorneys do with our writings for the benefit of our future is of no one else's concern.

Ghostwrite Or Edit Religious Or Secular Material For Others

Q. What about copyrights, trademarks, or writers' credits while in prison? Are they as legally binding as they would be had I written the same and not gone to prison?

A. Yes. For the ownership and rights of expression are maintained by your First Amendment Constitutional Rights, those of which prisoners do not lose. That's why the BOP's policy permits and encourages prisoners to write *and* publish their work.

Become A Jailhouse Lawyer

Q. What are the risks to me upon becoming a Jailhouse Lawyer?

A. Historically, I have been able to observe these top three risk factors jailhouse lawyers encounter: (1) violating BOP policy by keeping another inmate's legal documents on his person or in his or her locker, (2) violating BOP policy by charging a fee for legal assistance rendered, and, (3) the irrational, hate-the-government approach toward interpreting important case law, the misapplication of case law, and the rank inability to write a coherent legal brief. Jailhouse lawyering requires at least two years of sound above-average college-level reading, writing, and comprehension skills, which few prison inmates possess. In any event, the top three risks are easily avoidable by simply abiding by BOP policy.

Establish A Blog

Q. You mentioned Google AdWords in this section, specifically how Google would pay me a commission should my blog generate sufficient traffic that would warrant such commissions. Well, wouldn't receiving commissions be considered "running a business" while in prison?

A. No, here's why. A Blog is not a business. It is a Blog. You would not be (or should not be) soliciting for business or selling products. You are simply blogging about your passion or about your days in prison. Whatever you are writing about, Google's actions are completely independent of your writing. Bottom line? You have no control over or influence in the inner-workings of Google's AdWords program.

Establish A Website

Q. Are you saying each of these strategies, including establishing a website, can be implemented from each of the four security levels of federal prison?

A. Absolutely. I didn't say it would be a cakewalk. But yes. Absolutely. So long as you have the ability to write well, and the ability to think outside prison walls. And most of all, the ability to believe that your setback is a setup for your eventual comeback.

Q: *Do you have any other questions for Mr. CEO?*

A: Go to our website: http://frenchcuffsblog.com. Fill out the contact form with your question and we will get back to you as soon as possible.

frenchcuffsblog.com

"One thing about a life committed to a season of solitary confinement. Once you are there, in the presence of Solitary, you will, no doubt, make a change. The question she asks you this: 'Do you wish to change for the better or for the worse? One way or the other, I will accommodate either.' "

—Nelson Mandela

In this chapter . . .

The Secrets To A Successful Exit From Federal Prison

Reinvent Yourself

Using The Internet As A Tool For Reinventing Yourself

Halfway House: Pros And Cons

Home Detention: Pros And Cons

In-Prison Certificates Matter

Frequently Asked Questions

CHAPTER SIX

POST-INCARCERATION PREPARATION

The Secrets To A Successful Exit From Federal Prison

From the very second you enter federal prison, the very first thought that consumes you more than any other thought is your official release date . . . And naturally so. Oh sure, you know what your prison sentence is based on the judge's order and commitment. However, until you hear it from the prison officials themselves, and actually see the words "release date" in writing, you will not be able to rest . . . And understandably so. However, in this chapter—and particularly in this subsection—we will discuss the steps you should take from the moment you enter prison, steps that will ultimately determine just how successful your exit from federal prison will be.

Getting Off To An Effective Start: How long is your prison sentence? Six months? Two years? Five, fifteen, or twenty years? Hopefully not the latter, although all prison sentences, regardless of the term, are terrible. And, of course, a prison sentence is relative to the person who received it, and the crime(s) committed that justified it. Be that as it may, early preparation for release is essential for more reasons than the obvious. How you exit prison has everything to do with your worldview (philosophy), your frame of mind, and your perception of yourself when you initially enter prison. Quick example: I am a naturally light-hearted, optimistic, educated, fun-loving, and a spiritually grounded man—one who received a 24 ½ year sentence on my first serious offense. However, the fact that I received such a draconian prison sentence did not change who I was at the core of my personage. Sure, I was emotionally devastated and afraid beyond measure. But I am who I am. So following my season of fear and despair, the natural, optimistic me emerged without my realizing it. Conversely, the same would have emerged had I been a toxically angry, bitter pessimist. I would have entered prison bitter as hell. I would have served my time bitterly, and would have inevitably exited prison completely scorched by my bitterness. What a waste. Bottom line, one could never expect to have a successful exit from prison if his or her time was squandered away by being bitter. Recently, I met a fellow inmate—who was a new arrival in prison—with a sentence of three years. Shortly after getting to know the young man, he said to me, "Oh well, it is what it is. So I might as well get my college degree out of the deal." And that's the point: "It is what it is," which means prison might as well work for you instead of allowing prison to work against you. My suggestion is this: Yes, fight with a fever-pitched vigor to get out of prison should a legal avenue exist. But if you can't, oh well, it is what it is. Therefore, you might as well plan to get something positive, productive, and life-transforming out of the deal. Look, I received a 25-year sentence, yet I got—and continue to receive—something huge out of the deal. So what's your problem?

Networking From Within Prison: From the very moment you step into prison, be it at the high-security, U.S. Penitentiary level, or the lowest-security, prison-camp level, you are in essence forced to network, that is, if you wish to survive the prison experience. Almost instantly, beginning first with your bunkmate, you will begin to learn who's who among those fellow inmates that live in your unit block. On day one, you will be shown around while being informed of the rules. You will meet a cast of colorful (and colorless) characters, some of whom appear quite pleasant, while others will appear to be noxious. And then, as with any society, you will either meet with or be shown who the "elites" of the prison community are—the doctor, the lawyer, the banker, the CEO, or a prominent politician. In federal prison, you will encounter men or women who were former Wall Street executives, to men or women who were nothing more than a Main Street drug-dealing thug. Given the choice, which prisoner would you like to get to know? Now, as you grapple with yourself over that question, let me explain what I mean by networking from within prison. Naturally, you are going to meet some genuinely wealthy, influential, well-connected people along your journey. And who knows, maybe he or she will take a liking to you; or, perhaps, you might find yourself in some college class where they might be teaching. Under such circumstances, while in prison together, networking for future lawful purposes is all well and good. In fact, oftentimes those who are well connected will make arrangements for you to meet with an acquaintance (upon your release, of course) who is an upstanding citizen with *no criminal record*. When such an acquaintance is made, it is likely because your fellow inmate (the well-connected one) is either assisting you with securing gainful, meaningful employment; or, perhaps he or she is helping you start your own business. Whatever the case, it would be probationally prohibited to network with, or associate with, a known felon while you are on supervised release. For such a violation would violate the terms of supervised release, possibly resulting in your return to prison. So let's be clear on what I mean by networking from within prison. Why, even as a former CEO of a $200 million a year industrial finance firm, I, too, am actively networking with other prisoners of similar backgrounds—whom will certainly aid in my successful exit from federal prison when my term of incarceration ends.

Reinvent Yourself

Following my sentencing date—which was on June 19, 1995—I did not arrive at my final prison destination until August 7th of that same year. Only then was I in a position to begin my journey down this road of incarceration. And only then was I able to look beyond those prison walls toward my future and formulate a plan for reinventing myself. Perhaps, then, you might ask, "How does one reinvent himself after suffering a felony conviction and after serving a sentence in federal prison?" The answer is simple, for in many ways we are no different than any other person who has suffered a major setback in life, be it in health, or an accident, or a financial setback, many people—resourceful, resilient, strong-willed people—do not stop until they discover a way to make some sort of comeback. Yet with each of us, our individual comeback attributes are as unique and distinct as our individual DNA—far too distinct to make one person's method for launching a comeback exactly the same as your method for launching your comeback. Then again, you can glean from my field of factual, real-time comeback plans for reinventing myself, some of which I have put into action before my actual release from prison. Case in point:

From CEO To Author: Before falling from public grace, I was a CEO. Today, I have designs on becoming an author by creating my own genre of techno-thrillers for the Christian fiction market. And, being that I have a 24 ½ year sentence, I have opted to write a 9-book series, two of which are now completed. Plus, I am well into the third book.

From CEO To Ghostwriter And Screenwriter: As augmentation to the subsection above, I ghostwrite novels and screenplays for others in the writing industry. From ghostwriting, I receive two for one. For example (1) ghostwriting expands your productive networking opportunities among other highly intelligent professionals who are serving prison time alongside you. Ghostwriting (2) also increases the odds of getting my own novels and screenplays published and sold. Equally important is when I depart from prison, there will be scores of established individuals through whom I can network in order to advance my work. And, of course, to reinvent and re-establish myself at the same time.

Using The Internet As A Tool For Reinventing Yourself

By chance have you Googled yourself lately? If not, you should. You will find that virtually everything about you is posted, be it fact or fiction. Your crime of conviction, your children, your past and present love interests, you name it. And there is no delete button that avails you an opportunity to correct or delete negative information. So what does one do to reinvent himself if such information about him is already on the web? The answer is to begin by reinventing your reputation before attempting to reinvent yourself, or undergo the entire reinventing process all at the same time. Several internet-based websites have patented, step-by-step processes that will begin the repair and the reinventing strategies for the new you. But first things first. Who exactly are you going to replace the old "you" with? Listen carefully. You must begin the reinventing process early in your prison sentence in order to create a new you. Because, keep in mind, whatever you were doing (your day-to-day vocation) prior to prison, you probably cannot, or should not, do again. Moreover, you are now a convicted felon who served time in a federal prison, which means it's going to take that genius buried deep within you to discover that one product, or that one service, or that one artistic talent powerful enough to overcome the stigma of prison. That is, unless you already have an existing, long-established business or talent or a market niche that's powerful enough to withstand the fallout from having a felony conviction—as did Martha Stewart. For most of us, however, that is far from being the case. So where does one begin the process of using the Internet as a tool to reinvent one's self? Well, keep reading.

Brand Yourself Anew: While in prison, deeply, seriously contemplate this question: "*What gift or gifts do I have, or what idea do I possess that will launch me into orbit, thereby making me number one at what I am going to do when I am released from prison?*" Then (1) Find someone in the prison population with whom you can speak regarding the refinement of your gift(s) or idea. And rest assured, if they are truly knowledgeable about your subject matter, they will challenge your logic, your legitimacy, and your ability to bring your idea to market, (2) search the Internet for your nearest competition, to determine the overall viability of your business model in general. Then, upon discovering that you have indeed uncovered a niche, (3) brand yourself by creating and securing Internet domain names that cleverly describe what you know (if your unique skill set is your niche) or what you are selling (if your unique discovery is your niche product), then . . .

Legally Protect Your Brand: Now it is time to sit down and begin the process of writing out a business plan, detailing your idea or your product from top to bottom. Then go to legalzoom.com (or consult an *intellectual property attorney*) to either copyright, patent, or trademark your business model, product, or trade-name and logo combination. Then . .

Establish A Blog: Write Articles As Industry Authority: Here, you can take your brand for a test drive out into the marketplace of ideas. The combined effort of creating and executing (provided you can write well) will quickly reveal if you are on the right track or not; or, in the alternative, this combined effort will stimulate public feedback that would improve upon your business model—valuating it closer to perfection as you move closer to being released from prison. Then ultimately.

Establish A Website Presence: Finally you can take your refined business model to the market; provided, of course, that you adhere to the method(s) as promulgated in Chapter Three regarding "Running A Business" from prison. You do not want to be, nor should you have to be, in violation of BOP policy in order to accomplish any of the tested "reinventing yourself" strategies stated above.

The Power Of Solitude: Henry Ford once said, "The hardest thing for a man to do is think." I'm not absolutely certain of what Mr. Ford meant by that remark, but gauging from the plain language of such a remark, he must have meant "clear, systematic thinking—through and through." Ford was a true visionary, a man who knew how to think clearly—through and through—in order to bring his dream, Ford Motor Company, to life. Who knows how much solitude Mr. Ford had to endure before bringing his dream to life? Well I can attest: as a former CEO and founder of my own industrial finance and investment firm, countless hours of solitude were necessary in order to think clearly—through and through—before something great would come together. There are two distinct types of solitude: one that blesses and one that curses, both are brutally painful. The solitude that blesses, however, is the kind from which you allow wisdom to bring both great ideas and the "new you" into existence. Solitude that blesses makes for a successful exit from prison. Solitude that curses, on the other hand, is the kind through which you allow anger and bitterness to consume you as a raging fire would consume dry brush in a desert wasteland. If you take away nothing else from this book, it is my hope that you remember this: Prison's desire to squeeze and hurt almost always overpowers most of its guests—including you. Those who are especially susceptible to prison's desire are the arrogant, rebellious ones who ultimately become prison's treasured prize. Me personally, I have chosen not to rebel, choosing instead to endure the pain, but with an attitude that has allowed solitude to eventually bless me. So I have undertaken every step laid out in this chapter, and then some, in the exact order as listed. Even if you choose not to explore such lengths, you could still emerge from prison with a powerful, well-thought out, well-documented plan for a new revitalized, newly reinvented you. The key determining factors are desire and belief—the streams from which all great comebacks flow.

Halfway House: Pros And Cons

When mentioning a halfway house to a prisoner, you might as well be mentioning the word "freedom" in the same breath, even though freedom is far from being the case. Despite the implications, halfway houses are not freedom, and they certainly are not your home.

Halfway houses are, in essence, "prison light", but still prison nonetheless. Halfway houses are an integral extension of the federal prison system, complete with guards, census counts, and, in most instances, controlled movement.

Even though halfway houses are privately owned by independent contractors[13], the BOP is always present in one form or another, making sure that every inmate is in strict compliance with that particular halfway house's charter. Experience teaches that halfway houses can be nothing more than a revolving trap door that catapults the ill-prepared, unskilled offender right back into prison time and again. Conversely, the prepared and highly-productive prisoners who are skilled (meaning you) are often in and out of the halfway house before the requisite term of halfway house expires. Then again, there are those prisoners who refuse halfway house upon discovering the truth about certain halfway houses. As such, some prisoners elect to simply stay put until their entire term expires, then go straight home. So how does one best navigate through the murky waters when making a decision regarding halfway house? Let's discuss the considerations:

First, Consider What You Are Entitled To Receive: That's nothing! You are entitled to absolutely nothing when it comes to early release to halfway house. Yes, we see and hear of what others have received. But that's them. Not you. Let me be clear, halfway house is a privilege extended to each inmate on an individual case-by-case basis, based solely on the discretion of the BOP's staff. So once you come to terms with this reality, your transition will be much easier for you when the time comes for you to be released from prison. With that

[13]As part of receiving halfway house privileges, you must first agree to pay 25% of your gross earnings from employment to the halfway house during your term of residency. This amount, however, may not exceed the subsistence care costs (at $80,00 per day, 7 days a week, or $560.00 per week, irrespective of weekly income being higher. (Source: BOP Minutes of Meeting with U.S, Probation, Residential Re-entry Administrators and select Inmates, Wednesday, March 10, 2010 at FPC Taft in California).

said, let's consider the Federal Code and Rules that govern the BOP's discretionary application of a prisoner's halfway house privileges.

Consider The Federal Criminal Code And Rules: Pursuant to Title 18 U.S.C., the Federal Code and Rules directs the BOP of its rights and powers when determining a prisoner's place of imprisonment. Specifically, the BOP is directed to "ensure that a prisoner . . . spends a portion of the final months . . . [in a] Community Correctional Facility," which is a halfway house. Pursuant to the Second Chance Act of 2007, the BOP has the discretion to grant a prisoner up to 12 months halfway house. But according to a March 3, 2010 meeting between a select group of prisoners (which included yours truly, Mr. CEO), and BOP officials, no prisoner is actually going to receive a full 12 months of halfway house/home detention—even if the prisoner has served 30 years in prison. According to the BOP speaker—Mr. Painter, BOP/CCM, Long Beach—"six months is sufficient per the Director of the BOP." Conversely, that same year, on July 2, 2010, a memo from the Senior Secure Institution Manager, Tony Strauses, directed the Warden to implement a strategy to maximize the use of the statutory 12-month RRC (Residential Reentry Center) placement for eligible inmates. Bottom line: Congress has given the BOP complete discretion to grant a prisoner up to 12-months halfway house/home detention. Although we are indeed witnessing prisoners' halfway-house/home- confinement time moderately increase, we are not witnessing many prisoners under a term of 15 years receive the full statutory 12 months as permitted by Congress. Why? Because as long as the BOP maintains discretion over this policy, it will always decide what is in its own best interest—and that is to keep as many citizens locked up behind bars as possible. If not, who else will hire them? When pushed though, there are some constants you can count on. When the BOP is considering your halfway house/home detention term.

The BOP Considers Your Education, Economic Status, And Employability: More means less, according to a BOP constant. In other words, the more you have—education, money, a place to stay—the less halfway house you need. How do they know what you have? Your PSR tells them. Remember? Every important matter that involves YOU begins with your PSR. And, in case you are wondering, as your financial and family conditions deteriorate while you are in prison, too bad. That's the cost of your going to prison, according to the BOP. Point being, if your PSR says you have a home, you have a 401(k), or other savings—and that you are reasonably educated, you will, no doubt, receive minimal halfway house/home detention time. Conversely, the worse off your PSR states you are (or were when your PSR was written), the more halfway house/home detention time you will likely receive.

The BOP Considers Your Term Of Imprisonment: All things being equal, you will likely receive 10% of your gross term of imprisonment, or up to six months maximum, regardless of your term of imprisonment. Usually about 17 to 19 months prior to your release date (or sooner if your sentence is, of course, less than 12 months), you will be summoned by your Case Manager to sign your halfway house documents. Although, keep in mind at this particular time of signing your documents, you may advance an argument for a bit more halfway house time, provided you have a compelling reason for doing so. Sometimes it works, most times not. Either way you have nothing to lose.

Consider Foregoing Halfway House Time Altogether: Sounds crazy? It happens more times than you would expect. Here's why. For starters, every city and county in the United States does not have a federal halfway house sitting there, eagerly waiting for prisoners to be released into their housing facility. Fact is, many halfway houses are over 100 miles from where some prisoners' release addresses are located. That means a prisoner faces the following obstacles: (1) The prisoner is released from prison with no financial resources, after which he or she must (2) purchase a vehicle that (3) must be insured, then (4) fueled and maintained weekly, and then (5) drive some 200 miles per day, round trip. Now here's the kicker. On top of obstacles 1 – 5 above, there is where the prisoner must agree to hand over 25% of their gross salary or wages while living in a halfway house, or 12½% of their gross salary or wages while on home detention. Considering these 6 obstacles, the thought of foregoing halfway house time does not sound so crazy after all, does it? Wouldn't it be easier, less expensive, and certainly less stressful to simply stay in prison, free of charge, until your final release date arrives—on which you would be released straight home? Although prison officials would frown on such a course of action by prisoners, there's nothing that they could do. Accepting halfway house time is not mandatory. You can simply say "thanks, but no thanks" and not suffer the burden of a halfway house. Again, every prisoner's case and set of circumstances differ. Whatever the case, you will know what is best when the time comes.

Relocating Might Help: Eighteen months prior to release, qualified inmates may apply for halfway house relocation, provided the inmate has (1) moderate to strong family ties in the jurisdiction (or city) where they wish to relocate, (2) an adequate living arrangement and a dwelling (or domicile) that is acceptable to the local probation officer who is required to visit the inmate's new address, and 3) A reasonable chance of securing gainful employment in the jurisdiction where the inmate seeks to transfer. Each circumstance and request for jurisdictional transfer varies, which means other conditions may apply. Nevertheless, perhaps a total change of friends and acquaintances is exactly what is needed to ensure a successful exit from prison. In any event, should you find relocation of interest, be advised that you should begin exploring the possibility of a jurisdictional change as early as possible, as in no later than 18 months prior to your release date (or consult your Unit Team for specifics). The key is, you should first solidify your relocation plans with your family or friends, then discuss your relocation desires with your Case Manager. Fittingly enough, I, for one, will be seeking a jurisdictional transfer from the Eastern District of California to the Central District of California for the following reasons: (1) although my birth home and my criminal offense jurisdiction are in the Eastern District of California, my business strengths and my principal business contacts are in the Central District of California, (2) the market potential, based on the consulting services I offer, is much stronger, which affords me a faster, more efficient comeback, and (3) there are no warm sandy beaches in the Eastern District of California—no, not one. So yes, jurisdictional transfers have their advantages.

Home Detention: Pros And Cons

All things considered, home detention is as good as it gets for a convicted federal offender. Who wouldn't want to be sentenced to serve a term of imprisonment in the comfort of their own home? In like manner, the Second Chance Act expands to pre-sentencing mitigation strategies for white-collar and other non-violent offenders. In like manner, the Second Chance Act extends to post-incarceration strategies. Here's how. Halfway houses across the country are encouraged and incentivized to get you out of the halfway house and onto home detention as quickly as possible, like as in about three weeks following your arrival. However, there are conditions for such an expedient release to home detention. They are: (1) you must have a solid, verifiable full-time job acceptable to the halfway house, (2) you must have stable, verifiable living arrangements acceptable to the halfway house, and, (3) that you comply with and adhere to the terms and conditions of your halfway house contract, even though you are on home detention. So you might want to consider reaching out to friends or family and attempt to secure employment and housing before you are released from prison. Many prisoners have done just that. Why not you?

In-Prison Certificates Matter

Unfortunately, most prisoners make the crucial mistake of failing to consider the long view where post-incarceration is concerned. However, as former executives and businesspersons, we dare not make such mistakes, right? Instead, our goal is to be made whole again in the shortest amount of time possible. To do so, it's imperative we free ourselves from post-prison probation in about half the court-ordered, supervised-release time. Is such a reduction even possible? Absolutely. Experience reveals that most federal probation officers usually will not object to a 50% reduction in supervised-release time, provided you have the following: (1) clear conduct during the first half of your supervised-release time on his or her caseload, (2) that you have complied with all the terms and conditions posed by the probation officer during the first half of your supervised-release term, (3) that your life style, work conditions, and your family and living conditions are favorable, (4) your fine and/or restitution obligations are satisfied, and (5) your past in-prison record of programming demonstrates your rehabilitative efforts. Point here is nothing champions the cause for supervised-release reduction better than having as many certificates of commendation from "meaningful" prison programs as possible, such as teaching life-skills classes or leading religious services. Now, as earlier stated, probation will usually support an application for a reduction. But the U.S. Attorney? That's a different story. He will definitely oppose it by pointing out any infraction you committed during supervised release. No problem though, for its probation who carries the weight with the court. Not the prosecutor. So maximize your time in prison should you desire to minimize your time on supervised release.

FREQUENTLY ASKED QUESTIONS

The Secrets To A Successful Exit From Federal Prison

Q. This question is more a philosophical inquiry than an implemental inquiry. How can you, Mr. CEO, have hope for a successful exit from prison when you are serving a sentence of 24½ years (or 293 months)?

A. Invariably, many people ask me that question—a very good question. Usually my answer is distilled down to just one word: faith. Listen carefully. It was once said that nothing focuses the mind like being shot at—literally. Borrowing from that saying, I coined my own saying: Nothing exposes ones faith (or lack thereof) like having to walk into a fiery inferno while at gunpoint. In other words, I never knew the depth of my faith in God—and in the finished work of Jesus Christ—until I was rendered totally helpless, penniless, and family-less, while standing in the midst of the fire. So my faith is the only answer I could offer. Now, to some, that may sound trite. To others, outright unbelievable. So be it. All I can do, however, is testify, in truth, of what facing, enduring, and completing a quarter century in the fiery crucible of federal prison reveals about the power of the God in whom a man of faith relies. For I can attribute nothing else to my survival but for the grace and mercy of God.

Q. In the chapter entitled "Networking From Within Prison", my question is this: will my probation officer allow me to stay in contact with one of the "elites" once I am released from prison?

A. Not without a compelling reason why continued contact is needed. In my personal experience, several of my highly successful business-class students from prison were granted permission to stay in touch with me by their probation officers, while others were denied permission. Those who were granted permission were either business owners or college students whom I relied on to aid with the writing of my business books and/or my business consulting and mentoring programs. So each request is on a case-by-case basis. But it is certainly possible given the right circumstances.

Reinvent Yourself

Q. Okay, but you are a former CEO. You have connections. You have resources. You have a college and law school education. It's easy to 'reinvent yourself' when you have such resources. What about those of us who lack what you have? What if we have nothing? How do we 'reinvent' ourselves while in prison?

A. Again, here's my point about your being a highly effective prisoner. Go to college and obtain your degree. It's virtually free. And as for college textbooks, you can borrow them from other inmates who are taking the same classes you are taking. This is, by and large, more times than not, the norm in prison. Next, you can write books, songs, poetry, screenplays, the list goes on. All you need is a pencil, paper, and discipline. Lots of discipline. You can start a blog for free through wordpress.com if you have something to write about in which readers are interested. There's no excuse.

Using The Internet As A Tool For Reinventing Yourself

Q. What is the BOP's official policy on prisoners having websites, Facebook accounts, YouTube accounts, etc.?

A. The BOP does not make the Internet available to its prison population whatsoever. Therefore, what your friends and family do for you or on your behalf is of no concern to the BOP. Therefore, no official policy statement exists, nor is one warranted.

Halfway House: Pros And Cons

Q. Are there certain circumstances that threaten a prisoner's halfway house privileges?

A. Most definitely. Here are three examples where one could be denied halfway house time: 1) Receiving an Incident Report (a.k.a. a shot) that results in the loss of good-time credits, 2) the designated halfway house does not have an available bed at the time of your projected release date, or, 3) for some reason, you fail to pass medical clearance during your pre-release preparations.

Home Detention: Pros And Cons

Q. Is it true that I would still have to pay the halfway house 25% of my gross income, even though I am on home detention?

A. No, that's not true. Even though home detention is nothing more than an extension of the halfway house and even though you must comply with all of the terms and conditions or the halfway house, only 12½% of your income is paid to the halfway house.

Q. What if I am retired, disabled, or I simply cannot find a job? Would I be disqualified for home detention?

A. If you are retired and on a fixed income, you will be allowed home detention. However, if you are medically disabled and unable to work: forget home detention, and more than likely, halfway house also. Why? If you are not medically cleared to work, most halfway houses will not accept you due to liability reasons. Thus, if you cannot secure employment in a reasonable amount of time, forget home detention. However, under the Second Chance Act of 2007, halfway houses are offering more services to inmates who have difficulty securing gainful employment. In other words, the days of automatically sending inmates back to prison for not securing employment are over, so long as efforts toward employment are in earnest.

Q: ***Do you have any other questions for Mr. CEO?***

A: Go to our website: http://frenchcuffsblog.com . Fill out the contact form with your question and we will get back to you as soon as possible.

frenchcuffsblog.com

"Separation"
Your absence has gone through me,
like thread through a needle.
Everything I do is stitched with its color

—W. S. Merwin

In this chapter . . .

Oh God, What Now?

Walking A Mile In His Handcuffs

The Top Ten Prison Policies A Family Should Know

Notifying Your Loved One When There's an Emergency

Post-Sentencing Legal Considerations

Other Family Survival Considerations

Frequently Asked Questions

CHAPTER SEVEN

FAMILY SURVIVAL AND SUPPORT GUIDE

Oh God, What Now?

Finally, the reality of prison hits home—hard. From inside your silent, oppressive and empty home, you sit still as a statue, numb as can be, staring blankly into space, wondering, "*oh god, what now?*" Sure, you and your husband, your fiancée, your boyfriend, your partner, or your father (whom I shall collectively refer to as your "loved one" throughout this chapter) discussed, planned, strategized, and perhaps even prayed over what you should do and how you should do it on that dreaded day when the prison doors slam shut, separating the two of you. Yet now that this dreaded day has come, it seems as though everything the two of you discussed and agreed on suddenly makes absolutely no sense at all. None! So what now? The answer: trust wisdom. Trust experience. My daughters and I know what you're going through, or subject to go through. So let's talk . . .

Get Out Of The "Now" State-Of-Mind: Yes. Get out now or you will never get out. For your immediate well-being, you have to do your level best to pull yourself out of the "now"—as in that "hopeless" state-of-mind. Instead, fix your mind on the broader picture. The picture that is more in line with the relative length of time your loved one will be away—much the same as a military family would do when a loved one gets deployed to the field of service. For instance, how many years will your loved one be away? One, three, five—or more? If so, I encourage you to consider certain projects or personal-growth goals you could undertake and accomplish in that time frame. Perhaps you could go back to college and acquire an advanced degree. Or take on a career with more challenging responsibilities. Or perhaps you could start a small in-home business as my wife and sister did when I had to go away to serve my term of imprisonment.

Point is, if you sit around in a "now" state-of-mind, you run the risk of imploding. The "now" state-of-mind is not only brutal, it's dangerous. It will only keep you trapped inside your home that quickly becomes a cave of darkness and despair. Yes, Even with the best laid, well-executed plans, days of darkness and despair will still come. Over time they will grow farther apart and fewer in between if you resist the now view and embrace the long view. The key is for you to act today. Not tomorrow. Today. Otherwise it will be too late.

Seek Positive Reinforcement: When I found myself suddenly mugged by reality during my first week in federal prison, I called my brother, Ken, to inform him of my whereabouts. To my utmost surprise, my brother, Ken, during a telephone conversation, did not waste any time bemoaning my circumstances. He did not succumb to the negativity of my plight. To the contrary. From the onset, he said the following: "*Hey, now that's it's all over, it's time to get busy. Time for you to focus your energy on the things you can do in there. We're your family. Let us worry about the things you can't do out here.*" I was shocked to hear my brother take the long view, the positive view, the productive view. Not once did he dwell on the "now" view, or succumb to the "now" state-of-mind. Similarly, my mother and my sister had also taken the long view. From day one, my family as a whole refused to wax in words of sorrow and despair because I was in prison serving a 24 ½ year sentence. My brother, mother, and sister *did not* mope over my circumstances. Instead, they encouraged me to take each day in stride, trust in God, and fix my eyes on the long view. Question is, where do your family and close friends stand? Likewise, if you are left alone because your loved one is now in prison, can you count on them for positive reinforcement? Or are they going to push you farther back into your cave of despair? If the latter, you and your loved one will surely implode beyond any chance of recovery. Instead, fight back. Stay positive. Stay strong. And stay connected to positive people for positive reinforcement at every turn.

Change Your Environment: Yes, I know. Easier said than done. However, if it's at all possible, move out of your existing dwelling if your loved one's prison sentence is, in your opinion, entirely too long—which, of course, is a relative term. One year could be too long, but maybe not to the extent of having to move out of your existing home. Or in the alternative, redecorate all or part of your home; or more practically, rearrange things. Point being is that new things give rise to new perspectives in the wake of trying circumstances that prison introduces to your life. With a new perspective, you reduce the chance of slipping into a rut, or as I alluded to earlier, slipping into a "dark cave" within your own home out of sorrow and despair.

Below are several other survival techniques that came with fifteen years of suffering through and enduring prison life.

Walking A Mile In His Handcuffs

Consider your mental stress and anguish right now, then multiply it by five. Consider your fear and uncertainty, then multiply that by five. Consider your feelings of confinement and depression, then multiply both by five. Life in prison is a constant "in-your-face" torment that pounds on your every nerve, and tests your every limit—times five. Your loved one is literally trapped inside a caged area with nowhere to escape, be it physically or mentally. He is surrounded by, and is forced to live with, hundreds of strange and twisted men from strange and twisted places, men who speak with strange and twisted tongues. Between the inmate population and the cabal of prison guards, your loved one is tense, tightly wound, as well as—continuously tormented. They are relying solely on instinct to survive. Above all, mind you, he or she is worried sick about you and the children and the remainder of the family. Of course, depending on your loved one's faith, their attitude, and their ability to deal with adversity, the length of time before they adjust will vary. Some men prisoners adjust as soon as one month, others not at all. Women prisoners longer. Again, it all depends on each individual's brawn, as well as the security level of the prison facility where your loved one is housed. Whether your loved one is housed at a high-security penitentiary or a minimum-security prison camp, they are told what to wear and when to wear it. They are told what to eat and when to eat it. They are told when and where to sleep, and when to get up. They are told when they can visit with you and when they can't visit with you. Why, even if they should die in prison, the body would not be released to you until the prison officials are good and ready to release it. Point being is that at no time during your loved one's term of incarceration are they in control of any significant aspect of their daily lives. This alone adds an altogether different layer of anxiety to your loved one's prison life. So unless you have been in prison and have experienced its constant dangers, including its day-to-day psychological grind, it is nearly impossible to relate. Frankly, it is what it is. And thus your loved one has to do his or her level best to survive. Below are the Top 5 things you can do from home that will greatly help your loved one quickly and safely adjust to—and ultimately survive through—federal prison:

1. *Schedule A Visit*: If you are your loved one's immediate family (wife, children, mother, brother, sister, etc.) and you are listed in their Presentence Investigation Report (PSR), you would be eligible to visit your loved one within the first week of their commitment to prison, so long as your loved one has submitted a written request to have immediate family members, (who are listed in his PSR and children of 16 years or younger), placed on their visiting list. However, extended family members (in-laws, aunts, uncles, etc.) would be required to receive, complete, and return the

prison's official visitor request form. The same, of course, would apply to friends. Again, all children sixteen years or younger are exempt and may visit with an approved adult. Nevertheless, a visit from family—especially from wives or husbands—are the single greatest emotional lift a prisoner could receive. Plus, a visit from wives and husbands allow families to revisit their combined strategy for survival, and, if need be, make the necessary adjustments. Make no mistake. Visiting is food for the soul of a prisoner, which will give that much-needed sustenance that will hold them together until the next visit. Plus, visiting is the sustenance for the soul of a prisoner's family as well. So get up, get out of the house, and visit your loved one.

2. *A Letter With Pictures*: Each weekday afternoon between 2 PM and 4 PM, prisoners gather around the lobby or office area of their living quarters and wait for the correctional officer to drag in his huge canvas bag and announce with a booming voice: "Mail Call!" Then, like children around the Christmas tree, prisoners gleefully gather about, waiting and hoping for their names to be called. Mail Call gives prisoners something to look forward to; plus, if his name is called constantly—even if it is for a newspaper subscription—it lets others know that someone (or some computer) out there is thinking about him.

Greater yet, perhaps somebody out there really loves him. Admittedly, for us male prisoners, Mail Call demonstrates to the fellas, if you will, that "she still loves me." When a man receives a letter in the mail from his wife, he actually sniffs it in hopes that the perfume residue from her fingers is trapped inside the envelope (a bit silly of course, but very true). Plus, letters and pictures bring immeasurable joy to your loved one for weeks and months on end. Your letters are read and re-read time and again before your loved one files them away. Oh, but the pictures of you and the children will adorn his cold, metal locker from which he is forced to live, and soften the hard metal slab on which he is forced to sleep. Yes, just as pictures are worth a thousand words, letters from home are worth a thousand hugs.

3. *Keeping Your Loved One Well Informed*: Be it by phone, by a visit, or by letter, nothing makes your loved one feel less significant than learning that something has gone awry with you, or the children, or the home, or the business, through a third party. And even though there might be little your loved one can do for you from the confines of prison, his being informed and staying informed are central to a stable heart and mind, even if it's bad news. Take it from one who knows. For a male prisoner, being informed keeps him in the family loop. In addition, it gives him an opportunity to contribute through whatever means are available to him. Yes, believe it or not, he still has means. For example, recently I learned that my sister was becoming increasingly discouraged with her business because her income became static. No upward increases at all. Upon further investigation into my sister's dilemma, I immediately consulted with a friend of mine (a fellow prisoner) who educated me on the power of "Search Engine Optimization" as it relates to the Internet. Upon informing my sister of my discovery, she hired an Internet consultant (who was actually an existing

client of my sister's business) and implemented search engine optimization techniques that improved my sister's website exposure. The net result is that my sister saw a substantial increase in her Internet sales revenue. Now, imagine how that made me—a prisoner—feel? Vindicated and validated! I was so greatly empowered and encouraged to be a part of, and to have made a difference in, my sister's life—from prison! Think about it. How did this all come to be? By my family's understanding of how important it was to my frame of mind—be it with good news or bad news—to be kept informed on important family matters.

4. *Reconnecting Through The Arts*: One of the toughest and most heart-wrenching realities about prison life is the loss and the breakup of families.

Unfortunately, your loved one will see or hear about how a fellow prisoner has lost his family to divorce or desertion. We hear the stories on a weekly basis. With so much pain and despair all around him, your loved one will often wonder if he will still have a wife and family when they are released. All too often families drift apart over time, and if there is little to no effort towards keeping each other's hope alive, prison will be the end of your family as you've known it to be. However, when combined with the other subsections in this chapter, something as simple as the simultaneous reading of books provide a unique and lasting method for reconnecting and rekindling your relationship, even from a distance. For instance, if you and your loved one find a book—be it a novel, a self-help, or a non-fiction book—and commit to read it at the same time, the two of you will have far more to laugh and talk about instead of the all-too-common arguing and whining over circumstances that neither you nor he can effectively control. As for me, my brother and I are writing a book together. My sister and I are building our websites together. My lady friend and I are writing and reading screenplays together. So when I call home or when I receive a visit, **there is always something new and exciting to build on, or to laugh and talk about.**

But wait: here is a story that's really worth mentioning. A fellow prisoner was determined to keep his relationship with his wife alive, in spite of his six-year prison sentence. So he decided to put his mind to work, from which he eventually formed an idea. Knowing that his wife found fulfillment in her work as a youth counselor for abused children, he decided to take up crocheting while in prison. Over time he learned how to crochet stuffed animals that complemented the short stories his wife wrote and read to the children who lived at a local shelter. Then once their inventory of animals began to grow, she began to donate the animals to the children of the shelter. Fast forwarding to today, the project has now been funded by a private grant and is a success. With this business model in hand, the couple has designs on their own single moms' shelter when prison life is over, with further plans to expand their stuffed-animal concept into an internet-based business. So reconnecting through the arts is a powerful tool through which families and their loved ones could consider as a means of keeping the family together.

5. *Where Faith Counts The Most*: It is said that "no one knows how strong the tea in a teabag is until the bag is dunked inside hot water." The same could be said of a person—or even a family—that's dunked into the scalding hot water of life's afflictions.

Well, for those of us who believe in something greater than ourselves, the heat from life's afflictions help us see life's dark and ugly circumstances in an entirely different light. Bottom line: we yield to God who enables us to embrace the affliction of being separated from family and locked away in prison. But a God-centered prisoner also understands the real pressures and difficulties imposed on his family, which is why during times such as these your family's faith in God is the key lifeline to family cohesiveness. Then, there are those who have a real deep-seated selfishness about themselves, which is all too obvious when trouble comes. But a married couple, a downright committed couple, who has a healthy fear of God—and yet has experienced great suffering—will seldom do this. They are very tender and gentle, and understand—by way of their faith—what suffering really means. A true believing couple, or a family as a whole, knows that all things work together for good, for those who love God, for those who are called according to God's purpose.

Therefore, your loved one will surely find strength when they are reminded of the Author and the Finisher of your faith, and that you—his wife and family—will walk this journey with him, by faith, and not by feelings nor by sight. For that is where faith in someone greater than you (or God) counts the most. The central point here is to continually tap into the strength of your faith, then constantly discuss and demonstrate that strength through faith to one another.

The Top Ten Prison Policies A Family Should Know

Are you aware that much of what you say or do could result in serious repercussions for your loved one? Did you know that one slip in judgement on your part could lengthen your loved one's prison sentence by causing him to lose good-time credit? Below are the top 10 prison policies that, if violated by you or other family members, your loved one will suffer the consequences. In fact, you could even find yourself arrested and thrown in federal prison. How? Let's examine some of these policies and pitfalls:

1. Telephone Policy: Prison policy prohibits inmates from engaging in any form of telephonic communication other than the garden-variety one-way (or person-to-person) phone calls. In other words:

a) No three-way calls. A three-way call, according to prison policy, is when there is more than one person at a time on the line, even if the other party is in the same house on the same phone line from inside a different bedroom of the house. So if, for instance, you are speaking to your loved one from your kitchen phone and your daughter picks up and chimes in from her bedroom phone, your loved one in prison would be in violation of engaging in a three-way call

b) No speaker phone calls. Again, policy dictates that only one person on the phone at the time. Passing the phone around from person to person is fine. But speaker-phone calls would be in violation. And,

c) No relay phone calls. Relay phone calls are when you are on the phone with your loved one with the phone's receiver to your left ear, while simultaneously relaying your loved one's message to another party from another phone in your right ear, hence the term "relay." Should your loved one violate any of the above policies, he could receive a telephone-restriction sanction for a period of up to six months, plus up to 60 days in solitary confinement (the Hole), or the loss in good time credit of up to 27 days—or possibly a disciplinary transfer—or any combination thereof. Granted, for a while, you and your loved one might get away with violating these policies, but both of you will pay in spades when he is caught.

2. Visiting Policy: Visiting privileges are essential to the health of your loved one's mind, body, and spirit. Nothing makes him walk taller. Nothing makes his smile broader. And nothing lightens his burdens better than a family visit. But know this: visiting is a privilege, not a right. And you'd best believe that each and every prison official is quick to warn prisoners that visiting is a privilege that could be taken at the bat of an eye. With that in mind, you would be well-served by knowing the five most common reasons why prisoners lose their visiting privileges:

a) Excessive or inappropriate touching: Prisoners fall prey to this infraction more than any other visiting-related infraction. Should your loved one get too touchy-feely with his or her spouse or other companion, and is spotted by a guard's watchful eye, the visit will be embarrassingly terminated. You, the visitor, would in turn be escorted out of the visiting room, while your loved one would be handcuffed and immediately escorted to the Hole. So here's how it works. Upon visiting your loved one, you may hug and kiss one another (much like your hug and kiss following your wedding ceremony) as permitted by prison policy. That's *one hug and kiss only,* although no hugs and kisses during the course of your visit. Upon terminating your visit, you are then permitted by prison policy to repeat the same. Naturally the strict adherence to this policy is more prevalent at higher-security prisons than the lower-security prisons. Please heed the advice of experience. Play it safe. Protect your visiting privileges. And remind your loved one what family visits mean to your state of healthiness also, thereby reinforcing the importance of protecting your visiting privileges.

b) Mingling with fellow inmates' families: It seems like a perfectly good and wholesome gesture of social behavior, right? Two inmates who are friends just happen to have family visits on the same day without realizing it. Then, all of a sudden the two inmates spot each other while sitting with their families. So one inmate and his family gets up and introduces his family to the other inmate and his family. Sounds reasonable, right? Well not according to the BOP's visiting policy. Your loved one is to enter the visiting room, locate his or her party, and proceed directly to that party's table. Your loved one is prohibited from stopping and shaking hands while being introduced to other inmates' families. Naturally, the strict adherence to this policy is more prevalent at higher-security prisons than lower-security prisons. Yet again, my advice is to play it safe and avoid drawing attention to yourselves.

c) Arguing, Fussing, And Fighting: More often than not, prisoner's and their visitors (usually of the opposite sex) will have a verbal or a physical altercation. Oftentimes the altercations stem from some sort of domestic dispute, a dispute that turns heated during a face-to-face visit. Surely no one in their right mind would plan on having a physical altercation inside the visiting room of a federal prison. Make no mistake, though. Tempers do flare up at times due to the unforgiving, unrelenting pressure that prison tends to level upon domestic relationships. However the question is: Is it worth losing your family visits for as much as a year? Because an altercation in the prison's visiting room could result in a one year to an indefinite suspension of your visitation privileges.

d) Introducing "soft" contraband into the prison: Soft contraband is considered any and every item that you, the visitor, bring into the prison (including legal and authorized items, i.e. vending machine money, babies' diapers, car keys, etc.) that leaves your possession and placed in the possession of your imprisoned loved one. In other words, what's permitted to be in your possession is *not* permitted to be in your loved one's possession at any time. Should your loved one get caught with your possessions, it would be construed by the guard that your loved one is attempting to smuggle drugs, weapons or other contraband into the prison. Incidentally, a guard's greatest fear (as it relates to visiting) is an inmate smuggling in drugs, cell phones, or a weapon into the prison during his or her watch, for that would be grounds for the guard's demotion or termination. Speaking of drugs, cellphones, and weapons, we now turn to our fifth and most severe reason why visitors lose their visiting privileges.

e) Introducing "hard" contraband into the prison: Hard contraband is any and every item that you bring into the prison that is deemed as drugs, a cellphone, or a weapon by prison officials. If discovered and confirmed as drugs, a cellphone, or a weapon, you could be arrested on the spot and taken to jail, then later charged with the serious federal offense of introducing contraband into a federal prison institution. Suffice it to say, your loved one would suffer the wrath of the BOP, which means you would not likely see your loved one again until they are released from prison. Why take that chance?

From one extreme to the other, we have covered the five most common reasons why prisoners lose their visiting privileges. So take heed and remain diligent toward keeping your family connected to your loved one throughout the entire term of their incarceration.

3. Prison Mail Policy: Prison policy prohibits inmates from receiving:

a) sexually-explicit and nudity-depicting publications and photographs,
b) criminal case file documents pertaining to your loved one's case, unless sent by an attorney. Not by family,
c) hard-cover books, unless the books are sent directly to your loved one by the publisher or a bookstore. Family may, however, send soft cover books and magazines,
d) mail from inmates from other state or federal prisons without prior approval from the warden where your loved one is incarcerated. For instance, if two brothers are in different federal facilities and wish to communicate, both wardens must grant simultaneous approval, and,
e) any form of care packages, i.e. food or clothing items, writing and art supplies (books and magazines are okay), and oversized posters and calendars. In each of these prohibited instances, mail will be returned to its sender without any sanctions being imposed on your loved one; that is, unless you attempt to mail in contraband or perhaps information that could be construed as

"aiding in an escape plan" (i.e. a drawing of the prison, or aerial photo of the prison, or a map of the prison's surrounding area).

4. Legal Documents-In-Possession Policy: By the time your loved one's case is settled and he is finally at his designated prison facility, a plethora of legal documents and court transcripts have likely amassed. Yet among them all, the most important legal documents you should keep safely tucked away at home are:

a) your loved one's trial and sentencing transcripts,
b) the Presentence Investigation Report (PSR or PSI), and,
c) the Judgement and Commitment order.

Fact is, the more legal documentation you have at home, the better. However, while in prison your loved one is not permitted to receive copies of his legal file directly from home. Instead, copies of his legal files must be mailed to, or taken directly to, the prison by an attorney, should your loved one decide to reopen his or her case due to newly discovered evidence or a change in the law that might lower the prison sentence. Therefore, it is important that you maintain an organized file copy of all of your loved one's legal documents should the need to reopen the case become necessary down the road.

5. Inmate Trust Account Policy: The Inmate Trust Account Policy was designed to govern all procedures pertaining to your loved one's in-prison money matters while in prison. This includes your loved one's commissary account, telephone account, prisoners' payroll matters, voluntary pay-outs by prisoners, and, of course, the full and accurate accounting of the money sent to your loved one by family and friends. Prison policy prohibits inmates from:

a) sending money from one inmate's account to another inmate or inmate's family,
b) receiving money from another inmate or an inmate's family, and,
c) having any currency on his person at any time, including while at visiting with friends and family when considering vending choices.
Items 1 and 2 above are all too often violated by inmates who instruct their friends or family to send money to another inmate. And all too often these violators are caught (from either speaking over the phone, writing about it in a letter, or by prison officials tracking and cross referencing names of payees), then hauled away to administrative segregation (The Hole) in which he or she could face steep sanctions, such as:

- 45 to 60 days in the Hole,
- face the loss of up to 14 days good-credit time, and
- possibly an administrative transfer.

So play it safe. Send money to your loved one, and *only* to your loved one. Knowing and following the rules will avoid this needless pain and suffering altogether.

6. Financial Responsibility Program (FRP) Policy: The Financial Responsibility Program's purpose is to collect monthly or quarterly payments from inmates—payment that are applied to his court-ordered fine or restitution. According to prison policy, FRP payments are voluntary, meaning your loved one does not have to enter into an FRP contract with the prison. However, there's a catch: if your loved one *refuses to* enter into an FRP contract, he will be punished—and punished indeed. For example, your loved one:

a) will be denied favorable living quarters until he agrees to enter the FRP program,
b) will be denied full access to his $320.00 monthly commissary spending limit and thus subjected to a $25.00 monthly spending limit until he volunteers,
c) will be denied favorable work assignment and given the worst possible work assignment,
d) will be denied halfway-house time. Yes, prison officials exert great pressure on inmates who refuse the FRP payments, even though the inmate has no means of earning any real money whatsoever. But prison officials well know that with enough

> applied pressure in all the right places, an obstinate prisoner will undoubtedly apply pressure on his family, insisting that his family send money in order to satisfy prison officials. Absent a court-ordered payment schedule in your loved one's Judgement and Commitment Order, there's no way to avoid FRP sanctions.

Therefore, the key here is for you to work with your loved one and find a balance between how much money the family should or should not send on a regular basis. The key to FRP is to keep the payments as low as possible until your loved one is released from prison; or until the fine or restitution is paid in full.

7. The "Family-Business" Policy: In this book much was discussed regarding federal prison policy pertaining to the prohibition of inmates "running a business" while in prison. If you are left with running part or all of a pre-existing family business, prison rules only permit your loved one to *counsel* you on matters pertaining to the business from over the phone, by email, or by regular mail. What your loved one is "not" permitted to do is *order* you—as in directing you—to do this or that with the business. He is "not" permitted to render business decisions on behalf of the business while in prison. To the contrary. You must render *all* final decisions. Otherwise your loved one runs the risk of being accused of violating BOP policy, resulting in up to 90 days in administrative confinement (The Hole), loss of telephone privileges, loss of commissary privileges, and possibly the loss of good-time credit.

8. Medical Services Policy: The medical services policy requires that all federal inmates who are in the physical custody of the Bureau of Prisons receive adequate medical, dental, and eye care. Some inmates, however, are totally dissatisfied with the term "adequate," simply because it means just that: adequate. In prison, there are no frills and thrills whatsoever with regard to our medical services. The care is subpar. Every medication is generic, unless there is no other medication available for a particular ailment other than the brand-name medication. The same principle applies to aid-based equipment and eyewear. No frills. With that being the case, your loved one's medical needs might suffer a bit, depending on the severity of his or her medical condition. And in case you were wondering, no, you cannot have your insurance or anyone else pay for special medical treatment or equipment for your loved one. That includes paying for medical care out of your own pocket, even if it is a life-or-death situation. Sorry, that's federal prison policy. So what can you and your loved one do in order to combat such a policy should your loved one fall into serious medical straits, yet the prison is doing nothing about it? Here are the steps you might consider:

a) Make sure your loved one initiates his Administrative Remedies process at once, otherwise, by law, all other efforts will fall on deaf ears,

b) Once you have confirmed that your loved one has begun the Administrative Remedy process, contact the prison warden's office regarding your loved one's complaint. Better yet, have a lawyer make the call; and, if that does not work,

c) contact your U.S. Senator, who, I know from first-hand experience, will surely get the prison warden's attention—provided your loved one has initiated (though not necessarily completed) the Administrative Remedy process. A quick warning, however, when considering the aid of your U.S. Senator. Make sure it is a matter regarding your loved one's life or limb. And be prepared with well-organized documentation pertaining to your issue. Otherwise you and your loved one lose credibility, as well as any future support from your Senator.

8. *Halfway House Policy*: As a general rule of thumb, your loved one will (or should be) permitted to serve the final 10% of his sentence in a halfway house in the jurisdiction where the offense was committed. However, if the jurisdiction where the offense was committed is not the home base of your loved one, policy permits your loved one to apply for a "Jurisdictional Transfer/Relocation" to an available halfway house nearest home. When your loved one's

case manager makes a recommendation on how much halfway-house credit should be granted, be advised that

a) your loved one will receive approximately 10% halfway house credit, not to exceed six months (yes, the Second Chance Act of 2007 allows up to 12 months of halfway house credit, but the BOP's official position is six months maximum, regardless of the number of years in prison your loved one has served),

b) while in the halfway house—or even on home detention—your loved one is, in essence, still in federal prison. In other words, if your loved one violates the halfway house rules, the U.S. Marshal's office is just a phone call away. And rest assured, they will not hesitate to return your loved one to "the real" prison for the duration of his or her sentence, and,

c) halfway house time and home detention are a privilege, not a right, notwithstanding the fact that any halfway house or home detention time granted or denied is subject to the full discretion of the Bureau of Prisons.

This begs the question: What can you do to assist your loved one as he or she prepares to transition from prison to halfway house? Answers:

d) make sure your loved one provides you with a copy of the halfway house's rule booklet, which is supposed to be provided to your loved one not less than 3 months before release. By reviewing the halfway house's rules ahead of time, both you and your loved one will know in advance what must be done (and not to be done) in order to expedite your loved one's full release from prison,

e) make sure that you are available to greet and meet with the federal probation officer when he or she calls you regarding a home inspection for your loved one's eventual halfway house-to-home transition, and,

f) make sure you are available to assist your loved one with securing stable easy-to-verify employment. For example, e-mailing your loved one's resumes and cover letters to potential employers would be an excellent first step. Equally important, make sure your loved one is up on the latest employment tools and websites associated with his or her skill set or trade—just to name a few. Bottom line here is for you to be as assertive and creative as possible.

10. Supervised Release Policy: Upon the completion of the halfway house cycle, your loved one's file will be handed off to the federal probation officer who visited you for the home inspection in preparation of your loved one's discharge from the halfway house.

As for the Supervised Release Policy, your loved one will be interviewed and informed of such policies, specifically in relation to what the court had ordered per your loved one's Judgement and Commitment documentation. The term "supervised release" means your loved one is now fully and officially released from the stronghold of the Bureau of Prisons, and is now considered a full functioning member of society. By law, however, your loved one must be supervised (or watched) for a predetermined period of time, usually one, three, or five years, depending on the committed offense. And, of course, it is the responsibility of the probation officer to supervise your loved one's principal social activities, i.e. work, legal, financial, travel, and business activities. It is the probation officer's job to ensure that your loved one does not fall back into criminal activities during the prescribed term of supervised release.

So what can you do to assist your loved one while they are on supervised release? Answers:

a) Do your level best to have your loved one change his or her circle of influence, specifically the people (whom they call friends and associates) who were likely the cause of your loved one losing their way in the first place. This is important, primarily because of those of us who fall into prison are usually influenced by someone or something that caused us to go astray. Ultimately, however, we are responsible for our own actions—specifically those actions that prompted us to violate the law. After all, we are adults who know right from wrong. Problem is, now that your loved one is on supervised release for a prescribed term, doing the "wrong" thing can get them violated and sent back to prison. For this reason, your loved one's associations—or "circle of influence"—must be your principal concern.

b) Rest assured that your loved one will, in some manner or another, remain in contact with someone from the prison(s) where your loved one once served time. Staying in direct contact with a former inmate or a known felon without the consent of your loved one's probation officer could get your loved one "federal expressed" back to prison should the probation officer discover that contact with a former prisoner is in fact the case. Listen, if your loved one has a lawful, compelling reason to stay in touch with a particular inmate or a known felon, believe it or not, the probation officer will indeed consider it. In many instances, the probation officer will approve the request so long as the reasoning has merit. I know from first-hand experience, in that several former inmates and I are permitted to stay in contact due to the many books and screenplays we have co-written. So I know it can be done the correct way, provided there is a good reason—a legitimate reason—to do so. As such, there is no reason for your loved one to take any unnecessary chances. To that end, make sure you communicate that to your loved one; and,

c) strive for as much stability in both your family and your work lives as possible.

Here's why. At some point—which is usually the halfway point of your loved ones term of supervised release—your loved one could be eligible for early supervised release consideration. Imagine that! Cut three years of supervised release in half! How? If your loved one has demonstrated that they are stable, both at home and at work, and that he has complied with each and every term and condition per the probation officer's request, the chances are great.

However, any setbacks along the way would only aid in the government prosecutor's quest to destroy any attempt your loved one makes toward securing early probation termination. So during the term of your loved one's supervised release, compliance and stability are essential. And you are the key toward making that happen.

Notifying Your Loved One When There's An Emergency

What does one do when there is a family emergency? How do you go about contacting your loved one when his child or a family member is admitted to the hospital? Or God forbid, should someone pass away all of a sudden? And what about an emergency furlough home for your loved one should a family member pass away? Let's take a look at how the BOP facilitates family emergencies.

The Prison Chaplain: The prison's chaplain's office is your principal point of contact when or if there is ever a family emergency; that is, should you not hear from your loved one in the interim. The prison chaplain is a non-denominational intermediary whose job is to provide pastoral care and counseling to the inmate population, regardless of an inmate's religious faith or lack of religious faith. Experience teaches that a prison chaplain, by and large, is the closest thing to being a "normal, caring person" who does not treat you or your incarcerated loved one as though the two of you are an enemy of the State (although some prisoners are indeed enemies of the State if the truth be told). Upon contacting the chaplain, you, the family member, set in motion the following:

1. a paper trail with a timeline indicating that you made an attempt to inform the prison, and thus the prisoner, that a family emergency exists,

2. such a notice prompts the prison to act—meaning the chaplain must, by policy, inform your loved one of the nature of your emergency, and,

3. this effort clears the way for the chaplain to approve unmonitored chaplain-office phone calls (at no cost to your loved one) until the emergency is under control. Also, keep in mind, your loved one's basic phone service is limited to 300 phone minutes per month, which means your loved one will need all the free and flexible phone time he can get. Therefore, following an emergency, your first call should be placed to the prison chaplain's office.

Your Loved One's Unit-Team Counselor: One would reason that anyone who held a position titled "counselor" would be slightly on par—empathically speaking—with the prison chaplain. This is especially when it comes to a helpless prisoner who has suffered a family emergency. Unfortunately that's not the case. Here's why: Most counselors are former correctional officers, which means, in truth, most could not care less about your emergency. Although much like the chaplain, your loved one's Unit Team counselor must undergo the same procedures when you contact the counselor with your emergency. Chances are, the counselor will attempt to pawn you off onto the chaplain's office. But if the counselor has a heart, he or she will attend to your request. Your best bet, however, is to make the prison chaplain your first point of contact.

The Duty Lieutenant: Sometimes an emergency will occur over the course of a weekend or during a holiday, which means the chaplain and the counselor might be off duty. Should that be the case, there is always a "lieutenant-in-charge" on duty 24/7. So when all else fails, call the prison and insist on speaking with the lieutenant who is in charge. Ultimately all roads pertaining to family emergencies lead back to the chaplain's office, but now you know the protocol if the chaplain is not available when a family emergency arises.

Post-Sentencing Legal Considerations

It's amazing what your loved one discovers about his or her case *after* the shock and awe of conviction and incarceration eventually subside. In the legal profession, it's called "Post-Conviction Law", which entails, in greater part, the challenge of later-discovered Constitutional errors that might have occurred during the "pre-conviction" proceedings, primarily defense attorney errors that rise to the level of a Constitutional breach. Problem is, your loved one is now in prison (or on probation) and his defense attorney has long been paid in full and is long gone. The question now is what can you do if and when your loved one calls you and says, "*I think I might be able to get back into court and challenge my sentence!*" What would you say? Or what could you do to help? Let's explore some ideas.

The Paper Trail: First and foremost, the journey down the road toward a successful post-conviction challenge begins with the paper trail that was established and left behind by the attorney who represented your loved one, and by the courts where the case was adjudicated. Between the two, critical post-conviction information may be lying dormant—information that may very well overturn your loved one's prison sentence. However, there is no way of knowing—unless these documents are retrieved and reviewed by an attorney who knows what they are looking for. But first things first. Let's begin with that single most important document from the federal clerk's office.

The Federal Court Docket Sheet: Ask your loved one if he or she has a copy of the court's docket sheet pertaining to their case. If not, you could go on *pacer.gov*, enter the name of the District Court that adjudicated the case, then enter your loved one's name and case number. Following the prompts on *pacer.gov* you should be able to download your loved one's docket sheet. So what's the significance of the docket sheet? Good question:

1. The docket sheet is the official journal of the court. It reveals the step-by-step proceedings and filings that involved your loved one's case from the very first day to the present,

2. The docket sheet reveals the official chronology of various documents filed—including who filed them—in case those documents are needed in later proceedings (as would be the case in a post-conviction matter), and,

3. the docket sheet reveals the official proceeding or filing dates, whether it was in open court or in the judge's private chamber, and who was present at the precise time of day. With the docket sheet in hand, there can be no mistake as to where your loved one's critical court documents are. There's no better way to begin.

The Defense Attorney: Armed with a copy of the official docket sheet, your loved one will know exactly what documents—by name and by date—to obtain from his former defense attorney. But be prepared. Most "former" attorneys in criminal cases drag their feet when it comes to releasing files to a former client. Understand though, when your loved one advises the attorney, in writing, that he is acting as a pro se litigant in his own post-conviction case, the former attorney is obligated, by law, to release the files to your loved one, so long as the defense attorney is no longer carrying an account balance owed to him by your loved one.

Moving Forward: If your loved one is fortunate, he or she already has all of the pertinent legal documents in their possession, while a copy of those same documents are at home in safe keeping with you. Be that as it may, you and your loved one must remain mindful (if you don't know already) that your loved one has only ONE YEAR from the date of the final judgement of his case to file for post-conviction relief. Otherwise it will, without exception, be too late. So speak with your loved one as early as possible about any post-conviction relief sought. And then begin assisting your loved one with the process of pulling together those much-needed court documents.

Other Family Survival Considerations

More often than not, when a family member encounters the criminal justice system that results in a prison sentence, naturally family members suffer. That's a given. Yet unbeknownst to everyone, there are other extenuating collateral damages that could plague the family left behind. With this in mind, let's take a look at the three most common "collateral damages" family members—principally wives—often face.

Property Seized By The Government: Depending on the nature of your loved one's offense, he or she may be headed for, or may have already had, a civil forfeiture proceeding where part or all of his assets were seized. Chances are, when your loved one was indicted and arrested, certain business assets and personal property were seized on the spot. But seizure alone does not mean the entire asset-seizure process is complete. That, of course, all depends on the extent from which the alleged "dirty money" (money from illegal activities) used to purchase assets—such as real estate, automobiles, art work, jewelry, and other assets—might have—derived. For instance, you may be living in a home; or, perhaps you are driving a vehicle that could very well be the subject of forfeiture proceedings. If so, what should you do in the event you find yourself trapped in such a predicament? I will answer that question. But in doing so, I will need to establish the situational backdrop.

Forfeiture Proceedings: At some point during the course of your loved one's legal proceedings, one of you—if not both of you—received a formal "Forfeiture Proceeding Notice" in the mail or in person by a process server. The purpose for serving the Notice on you or your loved one is to compel one of you to contest the seizure and forfeiture of your assets. Why? To afford you an opportunity, in open court, to prove that the seized assets *were not* acquired with the "proceeds from unlawful activities" (dirty money), thereby compelling the government to return your assets to you.

On the other hand, if you waive the forfeiture proceeding or inadequately prove that the assets were acquired with "lawful proceeds" (clean money), that would then clear the way for the government to liquidate your assets; provided, that is, the asset(s) such as real estate are not encumbered by a lender. In that instance the lien holder must likewise prove its position before the asset(s) is returned or released. To do so you must appear in court and(1) present a clear and convincing documentation trail proving that the asset-acquiring proceeds were in fact legal proceeds, and(2) prove that you had no knowledge that the asset(s) was used in the commission of a crime. Clearly this is a situation where the advice of an attorney should be sought prior to engaging the forfeiture proceedings.

Innocent Spouse Tax Relief: Did your loved one's criminal offense leave you with a steep income tax bill? In some instances, an innocent spouse of an incarcerated spouse may be relieved of the federal tax debt, its interest, and its penalties from a joint tax return.

According to the IRS, there are three (3) types of relief available to married persons who filed joint returns:

1. Innocent Spouse Relief,
2. Separation of Liability Relief, and,
3. Equitable Relief.

As for Innocent Spouse Relief, you must

1. prove you filed a joint return,

2. demonstrate there is an understated tax on the return that is due to erroneous items of your spouse,

3. demonstrate that when you signed the joint return, you did not know, and had no reason to know, that the understated tax existed, and,

4. convince the IRS that taking into account the totality of circumstances, it would be unjust to hold you responsible for the understated tax. Bottom line? It must be clear and convincing that you did not know, nor had a reason to know, about the understated tax.

As for Separation of Liability Relief, you must

1. have filed a joint return, but have been divorced at the time of the filing, or,

2. have been separated at the time of the filing. And just as with the Innocent Spouse Relief, it must be clear and convincing that you did not know, or have reason to know, about the understated taxes.

Finally, as for Equitable Relief, you must

1. not be eligible for Innocent Spouse Relief nor Separation of Liability nor relief from liability by community property law,

2. have understated or unpaid taxes,

3. not be entitled to any refund,

4. demonstrate that it would be unjust to hold you liable for the unpaid tax,

5. not have transferred assets to another to avoid or evade the tax,

6. not file your return with the intent to commit fraud, and,

7. prove you did not know, nor had reason to know, that funds intended for payment of taxes were misappropriated by your incarcerated spouse.

Even though the above information is a matter of public information, I advise you to seek the advice of a tax professional should you decide to engage the IRS in any of these relief provisions.

Good Ol' Fashioned Bankruptcy: Of course, bankruptcy proceedings will not eliminate or even slow down a civil forfeiture proceeding or outright eliminate tax liabilities as you would hope. But bankruptcy proceedings surely ought to be of strong consideration for a family who has lost its principal breadwinner to federal prison. Depending on the bankruptcy proceeding you choose, certain debts can be outright eliminated, others reorganized, others re-negotiated downward. And depending on the simplicity or complexity of your family's assets and liabilities, you could choose the self-help method of filing bankruptcy or you could contact a bankruptcy attorney, which, of course, is always the best course of action if you can afford to do so.

FREQUENTLY ASKED QUESTIONS

Oh God, What Now?

Q. In this subsection, you stated that a wife or family as a whole should "get out of the 'hopeless' state-of-mind." But how is that logically possible when my loved one, the breadwinner of the family, has gone to prison for one, three, or five years?

A. Yes, believe me. I know it stinks to high heaven. But as with all of life's tragedies (and this certainly qualifies as a tragedy), we must catch our breath in order to step away long enough to see the distant, clear-blue horizon that's beyond the "now"—beyond your present-day tragedy. Stepping away from the tragedy allows you to breathe, make rational short-term decisions. Any decision, for example, that is made in the midst of your tragedy will likely prove to be irrational, regrettable, and counter-productive. Besides prison—although tragic—is not the end of the world. I received a 25-year sentence. I lost everything, wife included. For 4 ½ years she held on. However, following the loss of my first three appeals, she made the decision to divorce me and move on with her life. My children, however, were from a previous marriage. Yet still it wasn't the end of the world. Both my former wife and I parted ways without being embroiled in anger, self-pity, and despair. And today we remain cordial. Keep in mind, however, I received a 25 year sentence during which my wife held strong for 4 ½ years. That said, I know how all things are relative to each family or individual. In other words, one year in prison for your loved one could be as 25 years in prison would be to me. It's all relative. Whatever the circumstance, you must find the strength to step away from the "now" in order that you may rise above the fog of your tragedy.

Walking A Mile In His Handcuffs

Q. In this subsection, you discussed the subject of 'keeping your loved one informed.' But how does a family keep a loved one informed if he is in solitary confinement (The Hole), or while he is in transfer mode?

A. First, go to the Inmate Locator on our website where you purchased this chapter and confirm that your loved one is actually where you understand them to be. For things have a way of changing quickly in the BOP. Second, phone the prison and ask to speak to your loved one's counselor. Inquire into why your loved one is in the Hole and whether they are restricted from receiving mail or visits. If not, visit with them.

Or in the alternative, postal-express (U.S. Mail only) a letter to them right away, due to their not having ready access to a telephone or even postage stamps. Remember, the Hole is hell!

The Top Ten Prison Policies A Family Should Know

Q. In the subsection titled "Telephone Policy", is there any way I can reduce the cost of our telephone expenses from my loved one's end or from my end? And if so, is there a method of increasing the number of phone minutes beyond the existing 300-minute limitation imposed by the prison?

A. This gets a bit tricky, but here's the deal. Let's say your loved one is in Florence Colorado's prison camp and you are in California. You could obtain a local Florence phone number from which you could receive forwarded calls to your cell phone telephone. With that, your loved one's calls are charged at the local Florence rate. You, however, will receive the call at the rate that is in your plan. That alone would provide a significant savings. And as for increasing your loved one's minutes beyond the 300-minute limit, here are some standard exceptions:

1. during the holiday months of November and December, phone minutes are increased to 400 minutes,

2. during a family emergency (verified through the prison chaplain or counselor), your loved one may receive up to 100 extra minutes—one-time only,

3. if your loved one becomes a "yard informant" for the prison officials—informing officials about the illicit activities going on throughout the prison. However, I would advise against siding with prison staff on such matters. It's not safe, and

4. rely on email, which is now available in most prisons.

Otherwise there are no other legitimate (and I emphasize "legitimate") methods for reducing costs or increasing your loved one's monthly phone minutes.

Q. In the subsection regarding 'Visiting Policy', how many visitors can our loved one have at one time?

A. Each prison institution's limit varies, which means you would need to contact the prison for the exact number, or go to our site aafpamerica.com and click the menu button for "Prison Reports" and purchase an updated report on where your loved one is incarcerated. However, the range between the four institutions where I served time permitted from 5 to 8 visitors, infants included. There are instances where family and extended family travel long distances—together—to visit an incarcerated loved one, sometimes 10, sometimes 12 people. Whatever the number, your loved one may request a one or two time "Special Visit" from the prison's Unit Manager or Associate Warden.

Q. In the subsection regarding 'Inmate Trust Account Policy', is there a maximum limit on the amount of money my loved one can have in his inmate account (aka "his books"?)

A. No. I have seen account balances in excess of $20,000.

Q. Do the prison officials, or for that matter, the federal government frown on inmates with large sums of money on their books?

A. Only if it is suspected that the funds are from ongoing criminal activity from outside prison, or from another inmate. Otherwise no problem.

Q. In the subsection regarding 'Pre-existing Business Ownership', will my loved one be permitted to receive business reports such as financial statements, copies of proposals, or letters from business sources?

A. Yes. He may receive those reports and then some. Me personally, I have been receiving them for 15 years—no problem. That said, however, I know that on occasion I am being closely monitored by prison officials just in case I slip up and "give orders" instead of just "giving advice" from which my sister may freely consider when *she* makes the final business decision. My sister, *not* me. And during my recorded telephone conversations, I make it clear that "I advise, you decide." Therefore, your loved one should adopt this principle.

Notifying Your Loved One When There Is An Emergency

Q. You mentioned the awful thought of the passing of a family member while my loved one is in prison. Well, should such a tragedy occur, what is the prison's policy regarding my loved one receiving an escorted and non-escorted furlough to the funeral?

A. Furloughs are as rare as hen's teeth, even at the federal prison camp level, even if there is a death in the family. Yes, I have seen furloughs at the medium-security level, low-security level, and at the minimum-security level. Problem is

1. furlough requests require weeks, if not months, of advanced planning—which means should the emergency furlough receive approval, it probably would be too late,
2. inmates have no legal right to a furlough,
3. which means furloughs are at the full discretion of the prison's warden; and,
4. four out of five requests for furlough are, sad to say, denied. So yes, furloughs do happen. But please, don't look for your loved one until he or she arrives.

Q: *Do you have any other questions for Mr. CEO?*

A: Go to our website: http://frenchcuffsblog.com/. Fill out the contact form with your question and we will get back to you as soon as possible.

frenchcuffsblog.com

DISCLAIMER AND DISCLOSURE NOTICE

APPENDIX A

FEDERAL PRISON LOCATIONS:

WA
MT
ND
MN
NB
OR
ID
SD
WY
MI
VT
ME
NS
NY
NH
NE
IA
MA
NV
OH
IN
CT
UT
MO
RI
AR
TN
DE
NJ
NM
MD
LA
FL
Gulf of California
Gulf of Mexico
Mexico
Cuba
Puerto Rico
Guatemala
Caribbean Sea

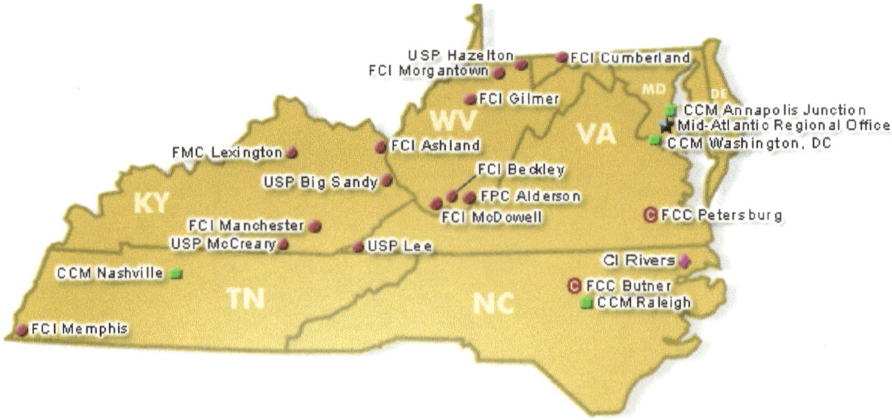

Mid-Atlantic Region (MXR) — Regional Office: Annapolis Junct, MD

FPC Alderson	USP Big Sandy	FCC Hazelton	USP McCreary	RRM Nashville	RRM Wash. DC
FCI Ashland	FCC Butner	USP Lee	FCI McDowell	FCC Petersburg	
RRM Baltimore	FCI Cumberlan d	FMC Lexington	FCI Memphis	RRM Raleigh	
FCI Beckley	FCI Gilmer	FCI Manchester	FCI Morgantown	CI Rivers	

KEY

Boxes shaded: Residential Drug Abuse Program (RDAP) location
FCI = Federal Correctional Institution | MCFP = Medical Center for Federal Prisoners
FMC = Federal Medical Center | USP = United States Penitentiary
FPC = Federal Prison Camp | RCI = Rivers Correctional Institution
FSL = Federal Satellite Low | RRM = Residential Reentry Management

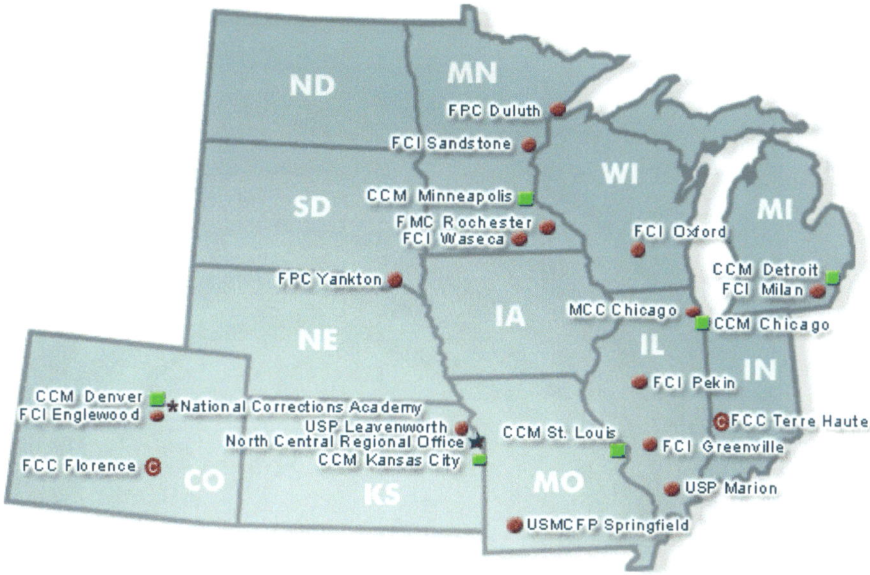

North Central Region (NCR) — Regional Office: Kansas City, KS

MCC Chicago	FPC Duluth	RRM Kansas City	RRM Minneapolis	FCI Sandstone	FCI Waseca
RRM Chicago	FCI Englewood	USP Leavenworth	FCI Oxford	MCFP Springfield	FPC Yankton
RRM Denver	FCC Florence	USP Marion	FCI Pekin	RRM St. Louis	
RRM Detroit	FCI Greenville	FCI Milan	FMC Rochester	FCC Terre Haute	

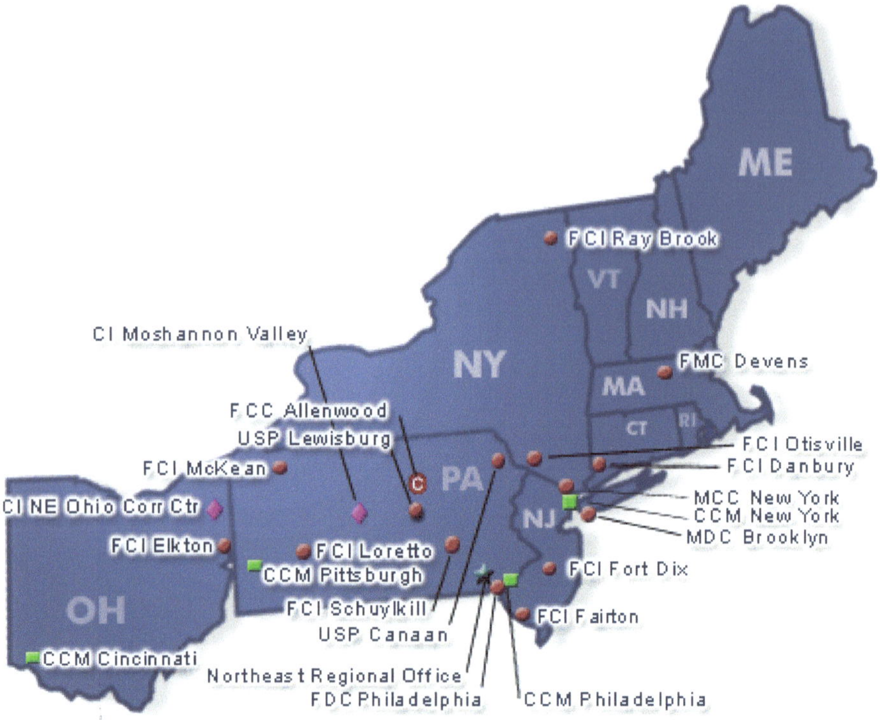

North East Region (NER) — Regional Office: Philadelphia, PA

FCC Allenwood	RRM Cincinnati	FCI Fairton	FCI McKean	FCI Otisville	FCI Ray Brook
FCI Berlin	FCI Danbury	FCI Fort Dix	CI Moshannon Valley	FDC Philadelphia	FCI Schuylkill
MDC Brooklyn	FMC Devens	USP Lewisburg	CI NE Ohio Corr Ctr	RRM Philadelphia	
USP Canaan	FCI Elkton	FCI Loretto	MCC New York	RRM Pittsburgh	

South East Region (SER) — Regional Office: Atlanta, GA

CI Adams County	FCC Coleman	FCI Jesup	RRM Miami	FCI Talladega
FCI Aliceville	CI D. Ray James	FCI Marianna	FPC Montgomery	FCI Tallahassee
RRM Atlanta	FCI Edgefield	CI McRae	RRM Montgomery	FCI Williamsburg
USP Atlanta	FCI Estill	FCI Miami	RRM Orlando	FCC Yazoo City
FCI Bennettsville	MDC Guaynabo	FDC Miami	FPC Pensacola	

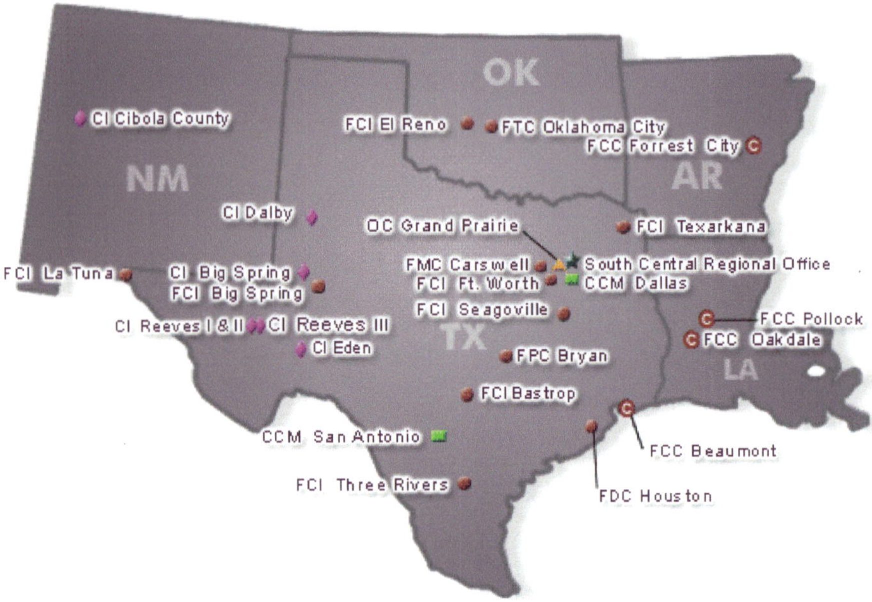

South Central Region (SCR) — Regional Office: Grand Prairie, TX

FCI Bastrop	FPC Bryan	FCI El Reno	FDC Houston	FTC Oklahoma City	RRM San Antonio
FCC Beaumont	CI Cibola County	FCC Forrest City	RRM Houston	FCI Pollock	FCI Seagoville
CI Big Spring	RRM Dallas	FCI Fort Worth	FCI La Tuna	CI Reeves I & II & III	FCI Texarkana
FCI Big Spring	CI Eden	CI Giles W. Dalby	FCC Oakdale	CI Willacy County	FCI Three Rivers

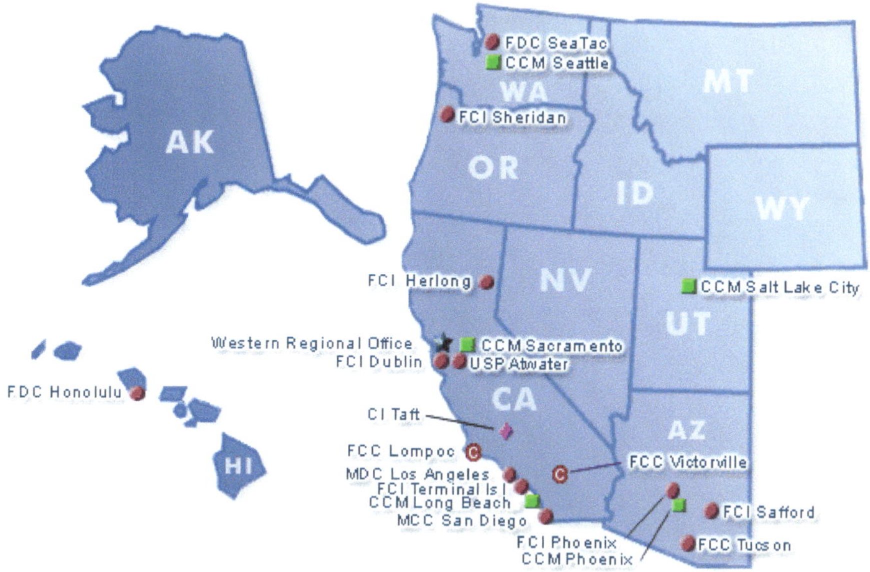

Western Region (WXR) — Regional Office: Stockton, CA

USP Atwater	FCC Lompoc	FCI Phoenix	RRM Salt Lake City	FCI Sheridan	FCC Victorville
FCI Dublin	RRM Long Beach	RRM Phoenix	MCC San Diego	CI Taft	
FCI Herlong	MDC Los Angeles	RRM Sacramento	FDC SeaTac	FCI Terminal Island	
FDC Honolulu	FCI Mendota	FCI Safford	RRM Seattle	FCC Tucson	

APPENDIX B

Federal Sentencing Guidelines

SENTENCING TABLE

(in months of imprisonment)

	Offense Level	Criminal History Category (Criminal History Points) I (0 or 1)	II (2 or 3)	III (4, 5, 6)	IV (7, 8, 9)	V (10, 11, 12)	VI (13 or more)
Zone A	1	0-6	0-6	0-6	0-6	0-6	0-6
	2	0-6	0-6	0-6	0-6	0-6	1-7
	3	0-6	0-6	0-6	0-6	2-8	3-9
	4	0-6	0-6	0-6	2-8	4-10	6-12
	5	0-6	0-6	1-7	4-10	6-12	9-15
	6	0-6	1-7	2-8	6-12	9-15	12-18
	7	0-6	2-8	4-10	8-14	12-18	15-21
	8	0-6	4-10	6-12	10-16	15-21	18-24
Zone B	9	4-10	6-12	8-14	12-18	18-24	21-27
	10	6-12	8-14	10-16	15-21	21-27	24-30
	11	8-14	10-16	12-18	18-24	24-30	27-33
Zone C	12	10-16	12-18	15-21	21-27	27-33	30-37
	13	12-18	15-21	18-24	24-30	30-37	33-41
Zone D	14	15-21	18-24	21-27	27-33	33-41	37-46
	15	18-24	21-27	24-30	30-37	37-46	41-51
	16	21-27	24-30	27-33	33-41	41-51	46-57
	17	24-30	27-33	30-37	37-46	46-57	51-63
	18	27-33	30-37	33-41	41-51	51-63	57-71
	19	30-37	33-41	37-46	46-57	57-71	63-78
	20	33-41	37-46	41-51	51-63	63-78	70-87
	21	37-46	41-51	46-57	57-71	70-87	77-96
	22	41-51	46-57	51-63	63-78	77-96	84-105
	23	46-57	51-63	57-71	70-87	84-105	92-115
	24	51-63	57-71	63-78	77-96	92-115	100-125
	25	57-71	63-78	70-87	84-105	100-125	110-137
	26	63-78	70-87	78-97	92-115	110-137	120-150
	27	70-87	78-97	87-108	100-125	120-150	130-162
	28	78-97	87-108	97-121	110-137	130-162	140-175
	29	87-108	97-121	108-135	121-151	140-175	151-188
	30	97-121	108-135	121-151	135-168	151-188	168-210
	31	108-135	121-151	135-168	151-188	168-210	188-235
	32	121-151	135-168	151-188	168-210	188-235	210-262
	33	135-168	151-188	168-210	188-235	210-262	235-293
	34	151-188	168-210	188-235	210-262	235-293	262-327
	35	168-210	188-235	210-262	235-293	262-327	292-365
	36	188-235	210-262	235-293	262-327	292-365	324-405
	37	210-262	235-293	262-327	292-365	324-405	360-life
	38	235-293	262-327	292-365	324-405	360-life	360-life
	39	262-327	292-365	324-405	360-life	360-life	360-life
	40	292-365	324-405	360-life	360-life	360-life	360-life
	41	324-405	360-life	360-life	360-life	360-life	360-life
	42	360-life	360-life	360-life	360-life	360-life	360-life
	43	life	life	life	life	life	life

APPENDIX C

Inmate Discipline Program

The following pages are what we call the "Pages of Hard-Knocks". Why the "Pages of Hard-Knocks"? Because when you break prison rules, prison will break you with slew of hard knocks. Given the opportunity, trouble, even while in prison, will seek you out—and find you if you are not wise, humble, and very careful. When trouble strikes, you pay a steep price, beginning with an Incident Report, which makes your time in prison that much more difficult. Receive an Incident Report, you lose privileges—even go to the SHU—the Special Housing Unit—aka the "Hole" for weeks, even months. For some, a significant amount of their time is spent in the Hole, whereas others can serve 25 years in prison without a single Incident Report.

In this section of the appendices, we list two tables of specific Incident Report sanctions. The first is identified as "Table 1", which details the Bureau of Prison's "Prohibited Acts and Available Sanctions". The second is identified as "Table 2", which details the Bureau of Prison's "Additional Available Sanctions for Repeated Acts of the Same Severity Level."

Following the issuance of a Formal Incident Report (aka a "Shot"), you suffer a major set-back. You could receive the lowest of sanctions (i.e. a 400- or 300-series shot), resulting in the loss of visiting, commissary, or preferred-living privileges, or a combination of these privileges.

The most severe sanctions (i.e. fighting, the possession of drugs, or possession of a weapon, etc.) can oftentimes lead to an altogether new indictment and a new prison sentence. So know the rules, and the consequences for breaking these rules, in advance:

Table 1. **PROHIBITED ACTS AND AVAILABLE SANCTIONS**

GREATEST SEVERITY LEVEL PROHIBITED ACTS

100 Killing.

101 Assaulting any person, or an armed assault on the institution's secure perimeter (a charge for assaulting any person at this level is to be used only when serious physical injury has been attempted or accomplished).

102 Escape from escort; escape from any secure or non-secure institution, including community confinement; escape from unescorted community program or activity; escape from outside a secure institution.

103 Setting a fire (charged with this act in this category only when found to pose a threat to life or a threat of serious bodily harm or in furtherance of a prohibited act of Greatest Severity, *e.g.*, in furtherance of a riot or escape; otherwise the charge is properly classified Code 218, or 329).

104 Possession, manufacture, or introduction of a gun, firearm, weapon, sharpened instrument, knife, dangerous chemical, explosive, ammunition, or any instrument used as a weapon.

105 Rioting.

106 Encouraging others to riot.

107 Taking hostage(s).

108 Possession, manufacture, introduction, or loss of a hazardous tool (tools most likely to be used in an escape or escape attempt or to serve as weapons capable of doing serious bodily harm to others; or those hazardous to institutional security or personal safety; *e.g.*, hacksaw blade, body armor, maps, handmade rope, or other escape paraphernalia, portable telephone, pager, or other electronic device).

109 (Not to be used).

110 Refusing to provide a urine sample; refusing to breathe into a Breathalyzer; refusing to take part in other drug-abuse testing.

111 Introduction or making of any narcotics, marijuana, drugs, alcohol, intoxicants, or related paraphernalia, not prescribed for the individual by the medical staff.

112 Use of any narcotics, marijuana, drugs, alcohol, intoxicants, or related paraphernalia, not prescribed for the individual by the medical staff.

113 Possession of any narcotics, marijuana, drugs, alcohol, intoxicants, or related paraphernalia, not prescribed for the individual by the medical staff.

114 Sexual assault of any person, involving non-consensual touching by force or threat of force.

115 Destroying and/or disposing of any item during a search or attempt to search.

196 Use of the mail for an illegal purpose or to commit or further a Greatest category prohibited act.

197 Use of the telephone for an illegal purpose or to commit or further a Greatest category prohibited act.

198 Interfering with a staff member in the performance of duties most like another Greatest severity prohibited act. This charge is to be used only when another charge of Greatest severity is not accurate. The offending conduct must be charged as "most like" one of the listed Greatest severity prohibited acts.

199 Conduct which disrupts or interferes with the security or orderly running of the institution or the Bureau of Prisons most like another Greatest severity prohibited act. This charge is to be used only when another charge of Greatest severity is not accurate. The offending conduct must be charged as "most like" one of the listed Greatest severity prohibited acts.

AVAILABLE SANCTIONS FOR GREATEST SEVERITY LEVEL PROHIBITED ACTS

A. Recommend parole date rescission or retardation.

B. Forfeit and/or withhold earned statutory good time or non-vested good conduct time (up to 100%) and/or terminate or disallow extra good time (an extra good time or good conduct time sanction may not be suspended).

B.1. Disallow ordinarily between 50% and 75% (27-41 days) of good conduct time credit available for year (a good conduct time sanction may not be suspended).

C. Disciplinary segregation (up to 12 months).

D. Make monetary restitution.

E. Monetary fine.

F. Loss of privileges (*e.g.*, visiting, telephone, commissary, movies, recreation).

G. Change housing (quarters).

H. Remove from program and/or group activity.

I. Loss of job.

J. Impound inmate's personal property.

K. Confiscate contraband.

L. Restrict to quarters.

M. Extra duty.

HIGH SEVERITY LEVEL PROHIBITED ACTS

200 Escape from a work detail, non-secure institution, or other non-secure confinement, including community confinement, with subsequent voluntary return to Bureau of Prisons custody within four hours.

201 Fighting with another person.

202 (Not to be used).

203 Threatening another with bodily harm or any other offense.

204 Extortion; blackmail; protection; demanding or receiving money or anything of value in return for protection against others, to avoid bodily harm, or under threat of informing.

205 Engaging in sexual acts.

206 Making sexual proposals or threats to another.

207 Wearing a disguise or a mask.

208 Possession of any unauthorized locking device, or lock pick, or tampering with or blocking any lock device (includes keys), or destroying, altering, interfering with, improperly using, or damaging any security device, mechanism, or procedure.

209 Adulteration of any food or drink.

210 (Not to be used).

211 Possessing any officer's or staff clothing.

212 Engaging in or encouraging a group demonstration.

213 Encouraging others to refuse to work, or to participate in a work stoppage.

214 (Not to be used).

215 (Not to be used).

216 Giving or offering an official or staff member a bribe, or anything of value.

217 Giving money to, or receiving money from, any person for the purpose of introducing contraband or any other illegal or prohibited purpose.

218 Destroying, altering, or damaging government property, or the property of another person, having a value in excess of $100.00, or destroying, altering, damaging life-safety devices (e.g., fire alarm) regardless of financial value.

219 Stealing; theft (including data obtained through the unauthorized use of a communications device, or through unauthorized access to disks, tapes, or computer printouts or other automated equipment on which data is stored).

220 Demonstrating, practicing, or using martial arts, boxing (except for use of a punching bag), wrestling, or other forms of physical encounter, or military exercises or drill (except for drill authorized by staff).

221 Being in an unauthorized area with a person of the opposite sex without staff permission.

222 (Not to be used).

223 (Not to be used).

224 Assaulting any person (a charge at this level is used when less serious physical injury or contact has been attempted or accomplished by an inmate).

225 Stalking another person through repeated behavior which harasses, alarms, or annoys the person, after having been previously warned to stop such conduct.

226 Possession of stolen property.

227 Refusing to participate in a required physical test or examination unrelated to testing for drug abuse (e.g., DNA, HIV, tuberculosis).

228 Tattooing or self-mutilation.

229 Sexual assault of any person, involving non-consensual touching without force or threat of force.

296 Use of the mail for abuses other than criminal activity which circumvent mail monitoring procedures (e.g., use of the mail to commit or further a High category prohibited act, special mail abuse; writing letters in code; directing others to send, sending, or receiving a letter or mail through unauthorized means; sending mail for other inmates without authorization; sending correspondence to a specific address with directions or intent to have the correspondence sent to an unauthorized person; and using a fictitious return address in an attempt to send or receive unauthorized correspondence).

297 Use of the telephone for abuses other than illegal activity which circumvent the ability of staff to monitor frequency of telephone use, content of the call, or the number called; or to commit or further a High category prohibited act.

298 Interfering with a staff member in the performance of duties most like another High severity prohibited act. This charge is to be used only when another charge of High severity is not accurate. The offending conduct must be charged as "most like" one of the listed High severity prohibited acts.

299 Conduct which disrupts or interferes with the security or orderly running of the institution or the Bureau of Prisons most like another High severity prohibited act. This charge is to be used only when another charge of High severity is not accurate. The offending conduct must be charged as "most like" one of the listed High severity prohibited acts.

AVAILABLE SANCTIONS FOR HIGH SEVERITY LEVEL PROHIBITED ACTS

A. Recommend parole date rescission or retardation.

B. Forfeit and/or withhold earned statutory good time or non-vested good conduct time up to 50% or up to 60 days, whichever is less, and/or terminate or disallow extra good time (an extra good time or good conduct time sanction may not be suspended).

B.1 Disallow ordinarily between 25% and 50% (14-27 days) of good conduct time credit available for year (a good conduct time sanction may not be suspended).

C. Disciplinary segregation (up to 6 months).

D. Make monetary restitution.

E. Monetary fine.

F. Loss of privileges (*e.g.*, visiting, telephone, commissary, movies, recreation).

G. Change housing (quarters).

H. Remove from program and/or group activity.

I. Loss of job.

J. Impound inmate's personal property.

K. Confiscate contraband.

L. Restrict to quarters.

M. Extra duty.

MODERATE SEVERITY LEVEL PROHIBITED ACTS

300 Indecent Exposure.

301 (Not to be used).

302 Misuse of authorized medication.

303 Possession of money or currency, unless specifically authorized, or in excess of the amount authorized.

304 Loaning of property or anything of value for profit or increased return.

305 Possession of anything not authorized for retention or receipt by the inmate, and not issued to him through regular channels.

306 Refusing to work or to accept a program assignment.

307 Refusing to obey an order of any staff member (may be categorized and charged in terms of greater severity, according to the nature of the order being disobeyed, *e.g.* failure to obey an order which furthers a riot would be charged as 105, Rioting; refusing to obey an order which furthers a fight would be charged as 201, Fighting; refusing to provide a urine sample when ordered as part of a drug-abuse test would be charged as 110).

308 Violating a condition of a furlough.

309 Violating a condition of a community program.

310 Unexcused absence from work or any program assignment.

311 Failing to perform work as instructed by the supervisor.

312 Insolence towards a staff member.

313 Lying or providing a false statement to a staff member.

314 Counterfeiting, forging, or unauthorized reproduction of any document, article of identification, money, security, or official paper (may be categorized in terms of greater severity according to the nature of the item being reproduced, *e.g.*, counterfeiting release papers to effect escape, Code 102).

315 Participating in an unauthorized meeting or gathering.

316 Being in an unauthorized area without staff authorization.

317 Failure to follow safety or sanitation regulations (including safety regulations, chemical instructions, tools, MSDS sheets, OSHA standards).

318 Using any equipment or machinery without staff authorization.

319 Using any equipment or machinery contrary to instructions or posted safety standards.

320 Failing to stand count.

321 Interfering with the taking of count.

322 (Not to be used).

323 (Not to be used).

324 Gambling.

325 Preparing or conducting a gambling pool.

326 Possession of gambling paraphernalia.

327 Unauthorized contacts with the public.

328 Giving money or anything of value to, or accepting money or anything of value from, another inmate or any other person without staff authorization.

329 Destroying, altering, or damaging government property, or the property of another person, having a value of $100.00 or less.

330 Being unsanitary or untidy; failing to keep one's person or quarters in accordance with posted standards.

331 Possession, manufacture, introduction, or loss of a non-hazardous tool, equipment, supplies, or other non-hazardous contraband (tools not likely to be used in an escape or escape attempt, or to serve as a weapon capable of doing serious bodily harm to others, or not hazardous to institutional security or personal safety) (other non-hazardous contraband includes such items as food, cosmetics, cleaning supplies, smoking apparatus and tobacco in any form where prohibited, and unauthorized nutritional/dietary supplements).

332 Smoking where prohibited.

333 Fraudulent or deceptive completion of a skills test (*e.g.*, cheating on a GED, or other educational or vocational skills test).

334 Conducting a business; conducting or directing an investment transaction without staff authorization.

335 Communicating gang affiliation; participating in gang related activities; possession of paraphernalia indicating gang affiliation.

336 Circulating a petition.

396 Use of the mail for abuses other than criminal activity which do not circumvent mail monitoring; or use of the mail to commit or further a Moderate category prohibited act.

397 Use of the telephone for abuses other than illegal activity which do not circumvent the ability of staff to monitor frequency of telephone use, content of the call, or the number called; or to commit or further a Moderate category prohibited act.

398 Interfering with a staff member in the performance of duties most like another Moderate severity prohibited act. This charge is to be used only when another charge of Moderate severity is not accurate. The offending conduct must be charged as "most like" one of the listed Moderate severity prohibited acts.

399 Conduct which disrupts or interferes with the security or orderly running of the institution or the Bureau of Prisons most like another Moderate severity prohibited act. This charge is to be used only when another charge of Moderate severity is not accurate. The offending conduct must be charged as "most like" one of the listed Moderate severity prohibited acts.

AVAILABLE SANCTIONS FOR MODERATE SEVERITY LEVEL PROHIBITED ACTS

A. Recommend parole date rescission or retardation.

B. Forfeit and/or withhold earned statutory good time or non-vested good conduct time up to 25% or up to 30 days, whichever is less, and/or terminate or disallow extra good time (an extra good time or good conduct time sanction may not be suspended).

B.1 Disallow ordinarily up to 25% (1-14 days) of good conduct time credit available for year (a good conduct time sanction may not be suspended).

C. Disciplinary segregation (up to 3 months).

D. Make monetary restitution.

E. Monetary fine.

F. Loss of privileges (*e.g.*, visiting, telephone, commissary, movies, recreation).

G. Change housing (quarters).

H. Remove from program and/or group activity.

I. Loss of job.

J. Impound inmate's personal property.

K. Confiscate contraband.

L. Restrict to quarters.

M. Extra duty.

LOW SEVERITY LEVEL PROHIBITED ACTS

400 (Not to be used).

401 (Not to be used).

402 Malingering, feigning illness.

403 (Not to be used).

404 Using abusive or obscene language.

405 (Not to be used).

406 (Not to be used).

407 Conduct with a visitor in violation of Bureau regulations.

408 (Not to be used).

409 Unauthorized physical contact (e.g., kissing, embracing).

498 Interfering with a staff member in the performance of duties most like another Low severity prohibited act. This charge is to be used only when another charge of Low severity is not accurate. The offending conduct must be charged as "most like" one of the listed Low severity prohibited acts.

499 Conduct which disrupts or interferes with the security or orderly running of the institution or the Bureau of Prisons most like another Low severity prohibited act. This charge is to be used only when another charge of Low severity is not accurate. The offending conduct must be charged as "most like" one of the listed Low severity prohibited acts.

AVAILABLE SANCTIONS FOR LOW SEVERITY LEVEL PROHIBITED ACTS

B.1 Disallow ordinarily up to 12.5% (1-7 days) of good conduct time credit available for year (to be used only where inmate found to have committed a second violation of the same prohibited act within 6 months); Disallow ordinarily up to 25% (1-14 days) of good conduct time credit available for year (to be used only where inmate found to have committed a third violation of the same prohibited act within 6 months) (a good conduct time sanction may not be suspended).

D. Make monetary restitution.

E. Monetary fine.

F. Loss of privileges (e.g., visiting, telephone, commissary, movies, recreation).

G. Change housing (quarters).

H. Remove from program and/or group activity.

I. Loss of job.

J. Impound inmate's personal property.

K. Confiscate contraband

L. Restrict to quarters.

M. Extra duty.

Table 2. **ADDITIONAL AVAILABLE SANCTIONS FOR REPEATED PROHIBITED ACTS WITHIN THE SAME SEVERITY LEVEL**

Prohibited Act Severity Level	Time Period for Prior Offense (same code)	Frequency of Repeated Offense	Additional Available Sanctions
Low Severity (400 level)	6 months	2nd offense	1. Disciplinary segregation (up to 1 month). 2. Forfeit earned SGT or non-vested GCT up to 10% or up to 15 days, whichever is less, and/or terminate or disallow extra good time (EGT) (an EGT sanction may not be suspended).
		3rd or more offense	Any available Moderate severity level sanction (300 series).
Moderate Severity (300 level)	12 months	2nd offense	1. Disciplinary segregation (up to 6 months). 2. Forfeit earned SGT or non-vested GCT up to 37 1/2% or up to 45 days, whichever is less, and/or terminate or disallow EGT (an EGT sanction may not be suspended).
		3rd or more offense	Any available High severity level sanction (200 series).
High Severity (200 level)	18 months	2nd offense	1. Disciplinary segregation (up to 12 months). 2. Forfeit earned SGT or non-vested GCT up to 75% or up to 90 days, whichever is less, and/or terminate or disallow EGT (an EGT sanction may not be suspended).
		3rd or more offense	Any available Greatest severity level sanction (100 series).
Greatest Severity (100 level)	24 months	2nd or more offense	Disciplinary Segregation (up to 18 months).

ABOUT THE AUTHOR

Although this work is the sole property of The Phoenix Trust, its authorship was the result of an extraordinary collaboration amongst scores of lawyers, Wall Street executives, real estate and oil field developers, engineers, and corporate CEO's—all of whom were (and some who still are) in federal prison for White Collar offenses—with terms of imprisonment that ranged from 18 months (or the lowest-security prison-camp level) to 25 years (or the high-security prison level). Along the way, we have developed a keen insight and a thorough working knowledge of the Bureau of Prisons (BOP) including its written and unwritten policies, procedures, and politics—at all four security levels. And because we are business executives (yes, some of us still have business, professional, and publishing interests) and former lawyers—and now former prisoners—we possess a uniquely objective perspective of how the system works both for and against its inmate population and society as a whole. Yes, we have something new to show and tell. With 1-in-100 Americans incarcerated*, the time has come for you to learn all about federal prisons.

*According to a 2008 study by The Pew Center on the States.

Index

A

B

C

D

E

F

G

H

I

J

R

S

T

V

W

Y